China's Blue Economy

The United States and China are each actively pursuing development of a Blue Economy to promote greater marine, maritime, and naval capabilities through more innovative, sustainable and environmentally friendly means. This book examines China's approach to developing a Blue Economy, compares China's efforts to developments in the United States, analyses prospects for cooperation and competition, and outlines strategic implications arising from China's linkage of the Blue Economy development concept to its Maritime Silk Road initiative. An understanding of the Blue Economy as it is being pursued in China and the Indo-Pacific region is extremely relevant for academics, industry professionals, and government officials.

Features

- Describes in detail the development of the Blue Economy concept in China over time
- Includes geostrategic analysis based on the author's extensive research and explains the implications of China's Blue Economy strategy for the Indo-Pacific region
- Discusses timely and important topics of interest to government, industry, and academic experts, both present and future
- Adds value to the studies, interdisciplinary collaborations, and expertise on a complex issue of strategic, technological, and economic concern
- Clarifies the linkages among Blue Economy, environmental and sustainable development and recognizes the importance of understanding the Blue Economy concept at a global scale

This book is written for everyone interested in Blue Economy studies, those who study and practice international relations, environmental policy and development, marine policy and governance, maritime and naval strategy, international and Asian affairs, as well as Indo-Pacific security matters.

China's Blue Economy

Evolution and Geostrategic Implications

Kathleen A. Walsh

CRC Press
Taylor & Francis Group
Boca Raton London New York

CRC Press is an imprint of the
Taylor & Francis Group, an **informa** business

Designed cover image: © iStock Photos

First edition published 2024
by CRC Press
2385 NW Executive Center Drive, Suite 320, Boca Raton FL 33431

and by CRC Press
4 Park Square, Milton Park, Abingdon, Oxon, OX14 4RN

CRC Press is an imprint of Taylor & Francis Group, LLC

ISBN: 978-1-032-49935-2 (hbk)
ISBN: 978-1-032-49937-6 (pbk)
ISBN: 978-1-003-39611-6 (ebk)

DOI: 10.1201/9781003396116

Typeset in Times New Roman
by Deanta Global Publishing, Services, India

Dedicated to my family and to those who endeavor to do good in this world.

Contents

Preface

So much has changed. In less than a decade, China has turned inward, the United States is dealing with insurrection and other anti-democratic disturbances, a global pandemic has shaken the entire world, and US–China relations are tracking continuously downward. This is not what earlier prognosticators had predicted. But here we are.

Around the same time that I first started working professionally in the China business, just before graduating from college, the world was also in a state of flux. That was January 1990, just a few short months after all that I had been learning in college about international affairs suddenly upended and the world we knew disintegrated as the Berlin Wall fell in November 1989, a historic event that we watched happen in real time on television. It had only been five months prior to that when the demonstrations and massacre at Tiananmen Square had captured the world's rapt attention. As I learned then, so much can change, and in a very short period of time.

What I also learned then is that no one knows what is going to happen next. The best we can do is to try to understand, identify, illuminate, and follow the tracks of the trends and dynamics that appear to be most powerful and lasting (whether in a good or malign way) and be prepared to be wrong in any forecasts for the future. With this approach in mind, this volume makes no predictions about the future: China's, the United States', or the future of US–China relations. So much can change and in a very short period of time. Under different leadership, whether in either or both countries, US–China relations could again veer toward more cooperation than competition, although this seems unlikely at the moment.

What this book does try to do is to understand, identify, illuminate, and track (to the extent possible under current circumstances) the concept of the Blue Economy and its evolution in China as well as its implications for US national security and (potentially) for US–China relations. China's development of the Blue Economy is a trend and dynamic that I have been watching for a decade. I did not think at first that this term, found in reviewing Chinese policy documents, would lead to anything tangible, much less a whole book. But over time, I have found the concept to be enduring and underappreciated, which is why I have taken the trouble to write down what I know.

I certainly do not claim to know it all when it comes to the Blue Economy. In fact, researching this topic has led me to an entirely new universe of experts in a wide range of expertise quite unlike my own. This interdisciplinary approach is essential to understanding complex, international, and cross-cutting issues, if difficult and time consuming. I am grateful to the many people to whom I have reached out over the years to squeeze them for information, insights, and further leads and for their generosity in doing so. My hope is that this volume will aid their respective efforts in terms of understanding where China fits in this puzzle.

I did not start out on this journey as an active environmentalist, a fan of oceanography, or knowledgeable in any way about underwater technologies, but I am more so today and better for having been exposed to all of these disciplines over the course of many years investigating the meaning of China's Blue Economy. So much has changed and, for me personally in this regard, in rewarding ways.

I have been fortunate, as well, in finding teaching as a vocation, something else I never planned to do. Those who teach know: they know how rewarding it is to watch students learn, in real time, and the look in a student's eyes when they have a realization. Every seminar I teach, I come away with new insights from my students, for which I am most grateful and smarter for them.

My hope is that the answer to the question I get asked repeatedly—what is the Blue Economy?—will become well-known across the country. This will relieve me of repeatedly having this awkward conversation! It will also, and more importantly, serve the interests of our country. The notion of the Blue Economy is no longer new. It is an idea that makes sense as the next step in the way we (humanity) develop that allows prosperity but does not continue to exploit in un-sustainable ways the water we drink, sail on, ship on, surf, and that provides the oxygen we breathe. Moreover, who does this best will have an advantage over others who do not. This advantage is likely to be in terms of the environment, community, economics, science, technology, and naval capability. From a national security perspective, for these reasons, pursuing development of a Blue Economy at home and abroad simply makes sense.

Change happens and is happening now, in both the United States and China in regard to realizing the Blue Economy's promise. Who will do it better? Only the future can say. But having a strategy certainly helps one's chances.

Change is disruptive, but also empowering, particularly for those outside previously established centers of power. With the end of the Cold War, many Cold War experts were at a loss. As a new entrant to the field at that time, the old barriers based on Cold War expertise had been lifted when it came to understanding contemporary international affairs. We are in, perhaps, a similar period now, when it is unclear what the state and shape of international politics will become following recovery from COVID-19, Russia's full-scale invasion of neighboring Ukraine, and the Sino-Russian alignment taking precedence over China's relations with the West once again. What role the Blue Economy ultimately plays in this context is to be determined. But it is evident that the Blue Economy is an enduring concept, which could find opportunity in the current international flux to upend the power balance in the Indo Pacific. This is why it is worth our attention, in addition to our shared concerns for our planet.

Acknowledgments and Disclaimer

There are numerous people, too many to list in entirety, who have advised, guided, and influenced the author's understanding on China, maritime power and security, and the Blue Economy. Some of those most consulted for this project are noted below.

In terms of initially inspiring me to write this volume, thanks are offered to Mr. Matt Merighi, formerly of the Fletcher School of Law and Diplomacy's Maritime Studies Program at Tufts University and currently Director of the Innovation Steering Group at the US Department of Defense, for his support as well as comments and conceptual contribution to an early draft of this study. He is to thank for the term adopted here of the "Great Blue Game." We had planned originally to co-author a monograph on this topic many years ago, but career opportunities interfered with this plan. Thanks go as well to Dr. Rockland (Rocky) Weitz, Director of Fletcher's Maritime Studies Program, for his support of these early, unpublished efforts, which provided the foundational premise of this book.

Most of all and essential to the author's understanding of China in the maritime realm are colleagues at the US Naval War College (NWC), particularly researchers past and present at the China Maritime Studies Institute (CMSI). Having been affiliated with CMSI from its start many years ago, my CMSI colleagues and others at the Center for Naval Warfare Studies (CNWS) have provided support and countless insights over many years on China's strategic, naval, and maritime objectives, including sponsored trips to China, support for events, shared research assistants, and Chinese-language translations that have provided deeper insights into PRC thinking. Particular thanks go to former CMSI Directors, Dr. Lyle Goldstein and Dr. Peter Dutton, as well as to CMSI researcher, Mr. Ryan Martinson, and others at CMSI. Their continued support of, and assistance on, this non-traditional area of research is most appreciated.

Appreciation is due in addition to the Naval War College Foundation for support of this work and to the Naval War College internship program for research and translations conducted over numerous years by Naval War College research assistant interns: Shazeda Ahmed, Claire Bilden, Lauren Dodillet, Sarah Estep, and Aileen Towner. Also, thanks go to the Naval War College, and specifically librarian Andrea Groce, for their assistance in developing a "South Pacific Islands" library research guide at the author's request.

Most importantly, the author is grateful for years of insights from pioneers on the Blue Economy, particularly the first person approached in an effort to understand the concept, Mr. Michael Jones, along with the many other US, Chinese, and other experts and practitioners the author has engaged over the past decade. Continuing support from the author's Naval War College colleagues, leadership, and supervisors in the National Security Affairs Department has been vital and immensely appreciated throughout the years as well.

Lastly, much appreciation goes to my family and friends and for their endless patience with me often ranting on about China and the importance of the Blue Economy over the past decade. And, though he passed away many years ago, if it were not for my mentor in China studies, Dr. Thomas W. Robinson, I would not have ventured into the China studies business in the first place, much less stumbled into China's Blue Economy as a research topic on which to write a book. What he taught me both professionally and personally has not been forgotten, nor has he. I remain grateful for his support in the early and formative part of my practitioner-scholar career, and I try still to pass along the lessons that I learned from him to other young professionals now.

All that said, the views expressed and any errors herein are solely those of this author and do not represent positions of the US Department of Defense, US Navy, US Naval War College, or any parts thereof.

Author Biography

Kathleen (Kate) A. Walsh is Associate Professor of National Security Affairs in the National Security Affairs Department at the US Naval War College (NWC) where she has taught policy analysis since 2006. Professor Walsh is Director of the NWC's Asia Pacific Studies Group (APSG), founder/director of the Oceanography and Maritime Security Group (OMSG), and was an inaugural member of the Naval War College's Faculty Advisory Council. Prior to teaching at the Naval War College, she was a senior consultant to Washington, DC-area think tanks, Senior Associate at the Stimson Center, and Senior Associate at a DC-area defense consulting firm, among other past positions in Washington, DC. Her research focuses on China and the Indo-Asia-Pacific region, particularly issues of security, technology, innovation, and ocean or Blue Economy issues. She is a graduate of Columbia University's School of International and Public Affairs (SIPA) with a master's degree in international affairs specializing in international security policy, and of the Elliott School of International Affairs at George Washington University, with a bachelor's degree in international affairs. She is also a member of the National Committee on US-China Relations.

List of Abbreviations

5G	Fifth Generation (telecommunications technology)
AOR	Area of Responsibility
APEC	Asia Pacific Economic Cooperation
BEA	Bureau of Economic Analysis (US Commerce Department)
BOEM	Bureau of Ocean Energy Management (US Interior Department)
BRI	Belt and Road Initiative
BTCA	BlueTech Cluster Alliance
CA	California
CAS	Chinese Academy of Sciences
CCG	Chinese Coast Guard
CCP	Chinese Communist Party
CCTV	China Central Television
CEQ	Council on Environmental Quality
CHOW	Capitol Hill Ocean Week
CMEE	China Marine Economy Expo
CMSI	China Maritime Studies Institute
CNKI	China National Knowledge Infrastructure
COSCO	China Ocean Shipping Company
COVID-19	Coronavirus Disease (number 19)
CPEC	China-Pakistan Economic Corridor
CRS	Congressional Research Service
CSBM	Confidence & Security Building Measures
DARPA	Defense Advanced Research Projects Agency
DC	District of Columbia
DIME	Diplomacy-Information-Military-Economic
DMZ	Demilitarized Zone
EEZ	Exclusive Economic Zone
ENMC	European Network of Maritime Clusters
EPA	Environmental Protection Agency
EU	European Union
FAO	Food & Agriculture Organization (United Nations)
FTZ	Free Trade Zone
FY	Fiscal Year
FYP	Five-Year Plan
GBG	Great Blue Game
GDI	Global Development Initiative (PRC)
GDP	Gross Domestic Product
GVA	Gross Value Added
HI	Hawaii

INDOPACOM	Indo-Pacific Command
IPEF	Indo-Pacific Economic Cooperation Framework for Prosperity
IWG	Interagency Working Group
MA	Massachusetts
MCI	Military-Civil Integration (PRC)
MFZ	Maritime Functional Zone
MIT	Massachusetts Institute of Technology
MOU	Memorandum of Understanding
MPA	Marine Protected Area
MSP	Marine Spatial Planning
MSR	Maritime Silk Road
NASA	National Aeronautics and Space Administration
NDAA	National Defense Authorization Act
NDS	National Defense Strategy
NEOC	New England Ocean Cluster
NOAA	National Oceanic and Atmospheric Administration
NOPP	National Oceanographic Partnership Program
NOPP-IWG	National Oceanographic Partnership Program Interagency Working Group
NORLC	National Ocean Research Leadership Council
NSS	National Security Strategy
NUWC	Naval Undersea Warfare Center
OBOR	One Belt, One Road (Belt & Road Initiative)
OCS	Office of Coast Survey (NOAA)
OECD	Organization for Economic Cooperation and Development
OES	Bureau of Oceans and International Environmental and Scientific Affairs (US State Department)
OMSG	Oceanography & Maritime Security Group
ONR	Office of Naval Research
OPC	Ocean Policy Committee (White House)
ORAP	Ocean Research Advisory Panel
ORM	Ocean Resource Management (White House)
OSD	Office of the Secretary of Defense (Pentagon)
OSTP	Office of Science and Technology Policy (White House)
PACOM	Pacific Command
PAP	People's Armed Police
PBP	Partners in the Blue Pacific
PIF	Pacific Island Forum
PLA	People's Liberation Army (PRC)
PLAN	People's Liberation Army Navy
PLANAF	People's Liberation Army Navy Air Force
PRC	People's Republic of China
PTWC	Pacific Tsunami Warning Center

QNLM	Qingdao National Laboratory for Marine Science & Technology
R&D	Research & Development
RAMSI	Regional Assistance Mission to the Solomon Islands
RDML	Rear Admiral
ROP	Regional Ocean Partnership (US)
S&ED	Strategic & Economic Dialogue
S&T	Science & Technology
SARS	Severe Acute Respiratory Syndrome
SCMP	*South China Morning Post*
SCS	South China Sea
SCSTAC	South China Sea Tsunami Warning Center
SDG	Sustainable Development Goals (UN)
SEZ	Special Economic Zone
SI	Solomon Islands
SIDS	Small Island Developing States
SOA	State Oceanic Administration (PRC)
SOE	State-Owned Enterprise (PRC)
SOS	Sustainable Oceans Summit
STA	US-China Science and Technology Agreement
STEM	Science, Technology, Education, and Math
TMA	The Maritime Alliance [renamed TMA BlueTech]
TPP	Transpacific Partnership
UCSD	University of Southern California-San Diego
UN	United Nations
UNCLOS	United Nations Convention on the Law of the Sea
UNCTAD	United Nations Conference on Trade and Development
UNEP	United Nations Environment Program
UNESCO	United Nations Educational, Scientific and Cultural Organization
US	United States
USNS	United States Naval Ship
WHOI	Woods Hole Oceanographic Institution

1

Introduction

The globe on which we reside is made up of mostly water. The water that we rely on for life, food, energy, industry, and commerce is increasingly being recognized as a vital yet endangered resource. The year 2021 marked the start of a new, worldwide, and decade-long (2021–30) endeavor focused on the world's oceans. As proclaimed by the United Nations General Assembly and first announced in 2017, the "Decade of Ocean Science for Sustainable Development" is meant to "fully support countries in the achievement of the 2030 Agenda for Sustainable Development ... [and] stimulate action over the next ten years in areas of critical importance for the planet, people, prosperity, peace and partnership."[1]

As this global effort suggests, the world has declared that the current decade represents an essential opportunity to learn about, collaborate on, explore, and more sustainably exploit the global ocean. According to the US Geological Survey, more than 70 percent of the Earth is water, with over 95 percent of that water being found in the world's oceans, the majority of it still as yet unexplored or unmapped. The growing consequences of climate change, among other global challenges as well as opportunities in terms of achieving more sustainable development, are a critical driver behind the world's renewed focus on the oceans. But it is not the only one.

The oceans also represent power—maritime (including naval) power—which is the aim in an escalating contest between the United States and the People's Republic of China (PRC), for regional as well as global predominance. As part of this contest, China and the United States each seek to develop a Blue Economy, a concept that fosters more sustainable development while also promoting innovation and more sustainable maritime industrial development across a myriad of commercial and military maritime-oriented endeavors. Who prevails in this contest is likely to hold sway over the maritime domain in the Indo-Pacific region throughout the remainder of this century.

In writing a book on the Blue Economy, one might expect that the term arose in the course of conducting marine environmental or sustainable development activities, through oceanographic research, or via employment in the maritime industry. But, for me, that is not the case. In fact, what environmental expertise, maritime industrial knowledge, and experience on the ocean I possess does not reach far beyond weekly consumer product recycling, my day job as a professor, and occasional whale watches, kayaking, and summer days spent on the beach. Instead, my area of study focuses on analyzing China's strategies, policies, plans, and practices related to science, technology, and innovation in an ongoing effort to understand what the

DOI: 10.1201/9781003396116-1

PRC's innovative efforts and advances (or not) mean for US–China relations and for US national security interests. It is through this strategic lens that I view China and its Blue Economy efforts, which is the focus of this volume.

Although having spent over 30 years focused on trying to understand the People's Republic of China and how its rise impacts and compares to the United States' own strengths, a term that was entirely new to me began to appear in the Chinese strategies, plans, and policies on innovation that I was reading just over a decade ago. That term was something called the Blue Economy. Chinese government documents do not typically freelance when it comes to employing policy terms, so I suspected that the phrase signified an important new initiative. Soon I was reading plans by Beijing to establish a "Blue Silicon Valley." This instantly piqued my interest, and I started to inquire further.

Out of curiosity and as an initial step, I began to ask academics and others around me if they knew what the term Blue Economy meant, as I had never heard it before. But much to my surprise, no one in my community that I asked a decade ago at first knew the term either, whether in English or in Chinese. Given my work as a civilian at a US naval institution, I found this collective lack of knowledge—then and, to an extent, still—both surprising and intriguing, driving me onward in an effort to unravel the mystery. If my learned colleagues had not heard of the term back then either, then we were clearly missing something, and potentially something important.

This volume is the result of ten years of investigation, research, analysis, and outreach to try to discern what the Blue Economy is, whether it is significant in terms of China's pursuits, and what it means for China's development and international relations with the United States as well as for US national security interests. The latter part of this ten-year period unfortunately includes years without the ability to travel domestically or abroad due to a global pandemic that began in China in 2019. Access to the internet and other communications, however, made continued investigation and research possible, but only from afar in the case of China. Due to COVID-19, the PRC remained closed to foreign visitors until March 2023, and the US State Department maintains as of the time of this writing a Level 3 Travel Advisory against visiting the PRC due to risks involving potential wrongful detention. Fortunately, I was able to visit China's capital in the summer of 2019, providing insights into Chinese foreign policy not long before the start of the pandemic. Virtual exchanges with Chinese and other experts have also proved invaluable. My hope is to travel to China again before long to explore the issue further.

As colleagues can attest, in my initial inquiries I was skeptical that China's pursuit of a Blue Economy would grow to be much more than rhetorical flourish. Having explored the issue in depth and across three continents over a substantial period of time, however, I have come away confident that the Blue Economy does represent an important aspect of US–China strategic competition (even if it fails), and that it will be a critical factor in the geostrategic contest unfolding in the strategically significant Indo-Pacific region. How China pursues its Blue Economy concept will also have important implications for its own development as well as for the environment, both the PRC's and the planet's.

The thesis of the volume is, as indicated, that China's adoption of the Blue Economy concept is an underappreciated element of its economic, technological, and military development, strategically significant, and key to the PRC becoming a modern maritime great power, both in terms of its advancing its domestic development and as part of China's overseas maritime power projection. China has developed comprehensive strategies to pursue and integrate both its domestic and overseas development of the Blue Economy; the United States, as yet, has not. This gap in US strategy constitutes a lost opportunity and potential hazard in what is characterized by the United States as a "strategic competition" with China.

Having written policy briefs, lectured and presented, moderated panels, and testified before a Congressional committee on matters concerning China and the Blue Economy over the years in attempting to illuminate these trends, it seemed time to put these findings on what is a still-underappreciated topic down on paper and in greater detail in hopes that the issue will be better understood and these findings will aid future research and analysis on the issue.[2] As such, this book is an attempt to document China's own approach to pursuing the Blue Economy over time and what this means for the PRC, for the United States, and for our ongoing geostrategic contest for power and influence in all things marine, maritime, and naval.

This book is *not* intended as the last word on China and the Blue Economy, much less what it means for US interests more broadly. It is a starting point to understand what is a still-evolving and not well-understood topic, from its early conception in China, how the concept has evolved in short order there and, for comparison, in the United States, as well as where these efforts might lead the PRC and US–China relations in the future. Many aspects of the Blue Economy issue remain unexplored in depth, particularly vis-à-vis China, and require additional academic study, data collection, and field research.

Among areas still to be explored in much finer detail are China's Blue Economy development activities at home and abroad, plus standardized quantitative as well as qualitative measures to determine how successful or not these efforts might prove and why. Such studies ought to be published by and accessible to both PRC and foreign scholars, researchers, and practitioner experts. While it is well established by now that measuring activities related to China's Belt and Road Initiative (BRI) has proven difficult, in part due to the opacity of China's political system, measuring what is occurring along the Maritime Silk Road component of the BRI and with regard to Blue Economy ventures there and elsewhere could prove even more difficult where some of this activity might take place offshore and in even more remote, politically or strategically sensitive areas. Also, determining the implications and impacts of Chinese (or other states') Blue Economy-themed agreements with states located in strategic locales is also difficult where these agreements are not made public.

In addition, issues related to China and offshore energy, undersea minerals, and deep seabed mining are also areas of study that merit a holistic and more strategically in-depth approach but are not fully explored here. Also, although China's role in distant water fishing and the reduction of fish stocks overall is getting media and scholarly attention, the broader issue of food security as part of the Blue Economy, and China's approach to it, has not as yet.[3]

Finally, study of the innovation, marine environmental, and climate change effects that Blue Economy development is having is needed but will lag to some degree given the still-early nature of many of these efforts and the time when their results will be felt. Time is in short supply, however, if humanity is to stem the hazardous effects of environmental damage and the cascading effects of climate change. For these and numerous other reasons, understanding China and its concept of the Blue Economy warrants substantial future scholarly, strategic, and policymaker attention.

The Blue Economy: What Is That?

It is rare, particularly in academia, to come across a concept, term, or phrase that others have not ever heard of before. Yet, that has been my experience, repeatedly, in studying the notion of the Blue Economy. Most of the people with whom I converse on a daily basis do not know what the Blue Economy is, although many are intrigued, as I was upon first encountering the term. When mentioning that I was writing a book on China and the Blue Economy, most people I encounter ask me: "What is that?" Given the repeated nature of this conversation, I've come up with a shorthand explanation, that most accept and easily understand. What I say is this: the Blue Economy is like the Green Economy but focused on water: marine, maritime, and naval development and as conducted in a more innovative and environmentally sustainable manner than in the past. That is the basic concept, anyway, as I've come to understand it over many years. While this shorthand definition suffices for purposes of moving on the conversation, there is much more to the concept and to the contest in developing Blue Economies, as this volume attempts to lay out.

Nevertheless, I am continuously struck by how readily such a simple definition is accepted. This is likely based on an understanding by anyone alive since about the 1960–70s of the more widely understood notion of environmental sustainability and subsequently of "green" measures, and how obvious a notion it seems to be. Anyone with basic comprehension of environmental conservation and sustainability can easily imagine how a more sustainable approach to the development of industry and resources on land could also apply to water. While the world long accepted environmental degradation as the price of industrial progress, that is no longer a bargain most advanced or even developing economies are willing to make, whether affecting land or bodies of water. Add to this the increasingly widespread acceptance of the growing hazards posed by climate change, and the appeal of developing a Blue Economy as a more sustainable means of marine, maritime, and naval development is evident. In fact, given the potentially existential threat that climate change poses to humanity, pursuit of a more "blue" economy seems essential for the planet.

A main challenge, therefore, in understanding the concept of the Blue Economy is why it is not a term as well-known across the United States or perhaps globally as its land-based counterpart, the Green Economy. As Chapter 2 lays out, a main reason why the Blue Economy is not a well-known term of art in the United States is likely in part because the term did not originate here. There is also no single, agreed-upon definition of the Blue Economy. Not surprisingly, where the term appears and is most well-known is in coastal regions around the world and in the United States. The reason is that these areas are highly dependent on ocean resources and maritime industries for their economies. Naturally, these regions seek to maintain their economic advantages over the long term by adopting more sustainable and innovative methods of development.

In the United States, coastal counties account for approximately 40 percent of the US population, according to the US Department of Commerce. The Blue Economy contributed over two million jobs to the US economy in 2018.[4] That's a lot of economic activity for an idea that is not widely known, much less understood. In fact, the extent of the United States' coastline reaches far beyond Maine and California coasts, stretching deep into the Pacific, for example, and representing extensive economic opportunity, strategic resources, and national interests. While the term Blue Economy might not yet be a household phrase, its value is coming to be understood, particularly as the ocean and maritime domains become more widely researched, viewed as a source of critical resources and as a competitive advantage, and likely also areas to be contested between states.

Another reason why the Blue Economy term in the United States is not widely used or understood is perhaps because, at least in coastal areas, all or many of the elements of a Blue Economy already exist. Most coastal areas are home to marine environmental groups, marine researchers and scientists, maritime industries such as shipbuilding and recreational boating, coastal tourist attractions, and the support services these businesses need (hotels, restaurants, banks, and more), as well as academic and often US government research facilities, with some areas also hosting US Navy facilities and bases. What has been missing is a more holistic approach to development and a term for joining these activities in a more strategic, coordinated, innovative, and sustainable approach to development. In short, whether adopting the term or not, some regions in the United States are already functioning as Blue Economies.

In looking at a map of Rhode Island, for instance, it quickly becomes apparent that all of the pieces needed to establish a Blue Economy exist already in the state or nearby region: a thriving tourist economy (from ferries heading to Block Island to tourist attractions in the sailing capital of Newport, RI, and beyond); maritime industries that include shipbuilding and repair; offshore windfarms (the first in the country); fishing and other maritime industries; academic institutions such as the University of Rhode Island, with its renowned oceanography programs and the nearby Woods Hole Oceanographic Institution (WHOI), plus my own Naval War College and the Naval Undersea Warfare Center, both of which are found on Naval Station Newport. The missing piece to help all of these actors and interests coordinate and enhance their individual activities in order to advance and prosper further—yet not at the others' or the environment's expense—was a strategic and collaborative approach to managing pursuit of these myriad interests in a way that would be more sustainable and innovation-oriented, so as to ensure that the rich marine and maritime resources of the region can be shared and persist for future generations to enjoy. This is the idea, generally, behind the Blue Economy, and why places like my hometown of Newport, Rhode Island are working to develop a local Blue Economy of their own. Having first learned of the term Blue Economy via research on China's concept, it was not entirely surprising to discover the notion had already taken hold in the United States, including in my own backyard.

Though many Americans still have not heard of the Blue Economy, there are already several other regions across the United States where Blue Economies are developing and some are thriving. These include states stretching from Maine to California, and Washington state to the Gulf Coast states of Alabama and Mississippi. Each state has distinct marine and maritime environments that drive how they invest in and pursue development of a Blue Economy. Some of these efforts even overlap, as is the case of Blue Economies being developed in both Massachusetts and nearby Rhode Island.

More Americans are likely to become familiar with the term Blue Economy as regional Blue Economies expand to also include more inland waterways, lakes, and rivers (beyond the existing Great Lakes' Blue Economy efforts) and as more "blue" jobs and opportunities become available to more job seekers. San Diego's main Blue Economy forum, an organization named TMA BlueTech, boasts more than 40,000 Blue Economy-oriented jobs in the San Diego region and links to these and more opportunities on its website. Job listings appearing in May 2023 ranged from interns to management positions in Blue Economy and maritime industry organizations, and from engineers of various sorts to marketing and sales positions, with job listings for positions located around the country.

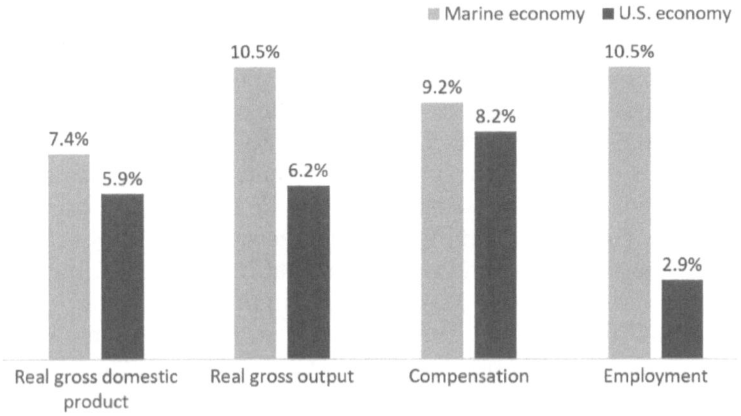

FIGURE 1.1
Growth in the US Blue Economy. *Source*: Bureau of Economic Analysis, 2023.

The US Department of Commerce calculates that in 2021, what it presently calls the "marine economy" contributed more than $432 billion to the US economy, accounting for nearly two percent of US gross domestic product (GDP) in 2023 dollars and representing an increase over previous years (as depicted in Figure 1.1).[5] Employment in the "marine economy" sector grew by over ten percent as compared to employment in sectors making up the rest of the US economy, which grew at only 2.9 percent.[6] According to the report, these numbers "reflected a rebound after the marine economy's 6.0 percent decrease in 2020, the first year of the COVID-19 pandemic."[7]

One of the challenges in both defining and calculating the impact of the Blue Economy, however, is determining what is "blue," what is not, as well as what is new in terms of being a result of Blue Economy dynamics, since many of the businesses and institutions involved pre-date the Blue Economy notion. What is new is a more *coordinated* and *strategic* effort to pursue more "blue" (as in sustainable and innovative) development methods in marine as well as maritime industry, which is expected to lead and already has led to new entrants into the traditional marine, maritime, and naval spaces. Similar to the public- and private-sector efforts to promote science, technology, education, and math (a sector known as STEM) as a means of enhancing US economic, innovative, and security interests, the Blue Economy represents an important new focus for potentially high-paying, rewarding, and community-enhancing jobs.

But while the Commerce Department's National Oceanic and Atmospheric Administration (NOAA) published in 2021 their own *Blue Economy Strategic Plan for 2021–2025*, and the White House an *Ocean Climate Action Plan* in 2023 that includes Blue Economy aspects, there does not exist a comprehensive national US strategy on developing the Blue Economy at home and abroad.

The US Navy's *Climate Action 2030* report also cites "blue tech" opportunities, but there is not a comprehensive Maritime Strategy that includes substantial Blue Economy elements, encompassing all stakeholders and elements of power (to include diplomatic, economic, technological, military, and ocean and climate sustainability dimensions). Nor does the United States have an international component of such a comprehensive strategy to ensure US global leadership on this important issue. While the initial efforts are commendable, they are partial and thus inadequate efforts to address the strategic maritime opportunities and challenges that the Blue Economy presents, particularly in terms of strategic competition in the Indo-Pacific region.

Meanwhile, China also is developing its own Blue Economy. In China's case, strategies, plans, and policies drive Blue Economy development in different regions across the country as well as in terms of exporting China's Blue Economy development concepts and plans to countries overseas. In these respects, the People's Republic of China is ahead of the United States in pursuing development of a Blue Economy, both at home and abroad, in a strategic fashion.

China's progress is due in part to the fact that, unlike in the United States, Chinese development efforts start with national strategies that are meant to trickle down to the regional, provincial, and local levels of government: a top-down approach to governing. This is in contrast to the typically highly disorganized, market-driven approach followed in the United States, where local governments follow market dynamics or what is often referred to as "bottom-up" development that evolves more organically based on local-market conditions. Consequently, China's Blue Economy efforts are likely more well-known to its population and appear to comprise a far more prominent aspect of PRC development and public diplomacy compared to the United States.

Given China's rising power and the very different approaches to developing a Blue Economy as practiced in China as compared to the United States, a contest between the United States and the PRC is already afoot, in terms of both domestic and international development of the Blue Economy concept. Domestic development of the Blue Economy in each country is expected to aid each state's maritime industrial and naval capabilities, making the Blue Economy a key element of national power and strategic advantage. On the international stage, the Blue Economy concept has become a new tool in diplomatic engagement and an unexpectedly central focus in US and PRC efforts at influencing key states in the Indo-Pacific region. The latter dynamic is illustrated in a case study on the Solomon Islands, a small but strategically located island nation-state in the South Pacific with an interest in the Blue Economy that both the United States and China seek to leverage for broader geostrategic gains.

Because this new, "blue" dimension of US–China competition is likely to come as a surprise to many Americans, this book seeks to lay out a basic understanding of the Blue Economy, focusing mainly on how the concept is developing in the PRC, how that development compares to the US approach, and how the ongoing US–China competition is playing out in what is arguably the most strategically important part of the globe, the Indo Pacific. Later chapters analyze prospects for US–China cooperation as well as competition in developing Blue Economies. This analysis builds on chapters outlining strategic implications arising from China's linkage of the Blue Economy development concept to its Maritime Silk Road and related initiatives, and the implications of all of this for what is conceived of here as an emerging "Great Blue Game." The study concludes with policy considerations essential to ensuring US interests are met in the face of new, "blue" opportunities and challenges, particularly those emerging from the PRC. How this contest unfolds will have long-standing economic, environmental, scientific, technological, and geostrategic implications for the United States, our allies, partners, and other relationships around the globe.

A Decade of Investigating the Blue Economy

In order to understand China's concept of the Blue Economy and its import for geostrategic concerns, and especially those related to US national security, the author interviewed or otherwise engaged with a wide range of governmental and non-governmental experts virtually and in person over the period of a decade (2013–23). This research and investigation spanned three continents: Asia, Europe, and North America. Over a period of five years, the author conducted research trips on the Blue Economy to the PRC, visiting Beijing, Shanghai, Dalian, and Qingdao (2014–19). In addition, the author conducted in-person interviews with experts in Asia (Malaysia, 2018) and in Europe (Belgium, 2019) on the Blue Economy and China's efforts in this regard.

Interviews and engagement with US experts spanned the entire ten-year period (2013–23). Exploring the meaning behind the Blue Economy involved visits to states from California and Hawaii to Maine, Massachusetts, New Hampshire, Rhode Island, and Washington, DC, to ask experts how they conceive of the Blue Economy and how they are planning for a more "blue" future and means of development, or to discuss what China's Blue Economy efforts mean for the United States. These efforts included visits to the Pentagon and repeat visits to what is today called Indo-Pacific Command in Hawaii.

Plans to visit more locations and return visits to China were shelved due mainly to the COVID-19 pandemic that put a stop to travel, both domestic and international, from spring 2020 to late 2022. During this period, as well as before and after, the author has had numerous virtual, electronic, or in-person exchanges with experts from around the United States as well as from Australia, Canada, China, Indonesia, Japan, and the United Kingdom in order to round out and update understanding of China's Blue Economy concept and related activities.

As a first effort to determine the broad outlines and import (or not) of China's Blue Economy concept, the author researched the topic in depth and traveled to China in April and September 2014 (visiting Beijing, Shanghai, Qingdao, and Dalian on these visits) to conduct additional research in preparation for organizing an international workshop in Newport, RI, in December 2014 on "US and Chinese Perspectives on the Blue Economy: Development Concepts, Innovations and Implications." Under the aegis of the US Naval War College's China Maritime Studies Institute (CMSI), this first-of-its-kind event, organized by the author, brought together leading government and non-governmental experts on the Blue Economy and elements thereof from China and the United States. This event spurred subsequent research in China and elsewhere, publications, events, and outreach efforts. These activities included establishing an Ocean and Maritime Security Group (OMSG) electronic listserv of community experts on the Blue Economy established and maintained by this author. The OMSG group has provided over the past decade a means of continuously engaging with ocean scientists and experts on the Blue Economy ranging from researchers at the Woods Hole Oceanographic Institution, the Scripps Institution of Oceanography, the Graduate School of Oceanography at the University of Rhode Island, and the University of New Hampshire's Coastal Marine Laboratory, as well as Newport's own Naval Undersea Warfare Center, among other centers of expertise and individual experts.

The author reached out also to those studying the Blue Economy, such as the Middlebury Institution's Center for the Blue Economy in Monterey, California, and those involved in developing Blue Economy clusters and investment startup ventures in that state and beyond. Over the years, I have learned much from pioneers in this field, such as Michael Jones, founder of The Maritime Alliance and TMA BlueTech in San Diego, California, and co-founders Mark Huang and Alyssa Peterson of SeaAhead, currently headquartered in Massachusetts.

The author has had the opportunity also to engage with a wide range of PRC, US, and international academics, policy experts, and government officials with knowledge and insights on the Blue Economy in China and beyond via hosting, moderating, attending, and presenting at events, conducting outreach efforts and visits to Blue Economy clusters and organizations in the United States and China, as well as participating in virtual and in-person think tank and Track II (unofficial, academic) dialogues with PRC and other international experts.

In particular, the author's involvement in the Center for American Progress' "Rising Scholars" series of US–China Track II dialogues (2014–20), directed by Dr. Melanie Hart and taking place in various locations around the globe, were of tremendous help in understanding China's, the US's, and others' views on the Blue Economy and related issues as well as the evolution of these views over time.[8] These dialogues provided unusually frank and open discussions on sometimes sensitive issues and across a myriad of perspectives (through economic, energy, environmental, and security lenses) informed by briefings from US and foreign officials involved in these various aspects of US–Chinese relations, including ocean, maritime, and naval affairs.

Finally, the author conducted an extensive review of the Blue Economy literature as published both in China (mainly via online research) and in the United States over the past decade and in co-authoring with an international set of experts a published study that included a review of PRC literature on the Blue Economy.[9]

It has been a decade since a new term first appeared on my computer screen: the Blue Economy. While not setting out back then to write a book on the topic of China and the Blue Economy, the issue has kept this author continuously and sufficiently intrigued so as to spend substantial time, attention, and travel to try to better understand this topic and its importance to China's development, to US–China relations, and to the geostrategic contest that is taking shape.

China, the Blue Economy, and 21st-Century Maritime Power

While the term Blue Economy is not widely known across the United States, it is not hyperbole to suggest that who prevails in the contest to develop robust Blue Economies could shape the rest of the 21st century, in geostrategic terms and particularly in the maritime as well as naval domains. In order to fully understand the import of China's pursuit of a Blue Economy and what it will mean for the United States—as well as for US allies, partners, and friends in the Indo-Pacific region—it is necessary to explore the issue both in terms of China's domestic development and in a broader, strategic context.

China's emphasis on developing a Blue Economy coincides with and supports Beijing's ambition to become a maritime power, a concept that incorporates both civilian and military capabilities (such as shipbuilding, fishing, and ocean exploration capabilities, as well as naval power) and the capacity for soft and hard powers (diplomacy and defense) along with economic and financial power projection.[10] To be a maritime power is, in turn, key to the PRC becoming a global Great Power and possible regional or even global hegemon. Though academic debates persist over whether, and the degree to which, becoming a Great Power is Beijing's intention, Chinese leader Xi Jinping's strategies and policies over the last decade make clear that under his rule, China's quest for "national rejuvenation" represents a return to what Beijing views as China's rightful and central place in world affairs. Xi's stated goal is for China, in fact, to become a maritime *Great* Power by 2050.

What is also now clear is that China's novel concept of developing a Blue Economy is intended to serve its domestic economic, industrial, technological, military, and environmental goals while also serving to integrate neighboring and regional economies, to extend Chinese influence overseas and along what Beijing has termed a Maritime Silk Road in order to advance China's geostrategic ambitions more broadly. If the United States and its allies, partners, and friends in the region and beyond are to compete effectively in this emerging geostrategic "Great Blue Game," understanding China's notion of a Blue Economy and how it differs in important ways from US and other Western conceptions is an essential first step.

Notes

1. Intergovernmental Oceanographic Commission, "The United Nations Decade of Ocean Science for Sustainable Development, 2021–2030" (Paris: United Nations Educational, Scientific and Cultural Organization, 2018), https://unesdoc.unesco.org/ark:/48223/pf0000261962.
2. In particular, this volume builds on testimony presented to Congress in 2019. See Kathleen Walsh, Testimony before the House Subcommittee on Coast Guard and Maritime Transportation Hearing on "China's Maritime Silk Road Initiative: Implications for the Global Maritime Supply Chain" (October 2019), https://transportation.house.gov/committee-activity/hearings/chinas-maritime-silk-road-initiative-implications-for-the-global-maritime-supply-chain.
3. Anna Farmery et al., "Blind Spots in Visions of a 'Blue Economy' Could Undermine the Ocean's Contribution to Eliminating Hunger and Malnutrition." *One Earth* 4, no. 1 (2021): 28–38.
4. NOAA, "NOAA Blue Strategic Plan 2021–2025" (Washington, DC: US Department of Commerce, 2021).
5. Bureau of Economic Analysis, "Marine Economy" (Washington, DC: US Department of Commerce, updated June 8, 2023), https://www.bea.gov/data/special-topics/marine-economy.
6. Bureau of Economic Analysis, "Marine Satellite Account, 2021," Press Release (June 8, 2023), https://www.bea.gov/news/2023/marine-economy-satellite-account-2021.
7. Bureau of Economic Analysis, "Marine Satellite Account, 2021."
8. Meetings in which the author took part included Washington, DC; Honolulu, HI; Tokyo, Japan; and Brussels, Belgium. The 2020 event had been planned to be convened in Seattle, Washington, but was held virtually due to the COVID-19 pandemic.
9. Michael Fabinyi et al., "China's Blue Economy: A State Project of Modernisation." *The Journal of Environment & Development* 30, no. 2 (2021): 127–48.
10. McDevitt, Michael, *Becoming a Great "Maritime Power": A Chinese Dream* (Washington, DC: Center for Naval Analyses, 2016).

References

Bureau of Economic Analysis. 2023. "Chart 1: Growth in the US Marine Economy Compared to the US Economy (2021)." in *Marine Economy Satellite Account,* June 8. https://www.bea.gov/news/blog/2023-06-08/marine-economy-satellite-account-2021.

———. 2023. "Marine Satellite Account." *2021. The BEA Wire,* June 8. https://www.bea.gov/news/blog/2023-06-08/marine-economy-satellite-account-2021.

Fabinyi, Michael, Annie Wu, Sallie Lau, Tabitha Mallory, Kate Barclay, Kathleen Walsh, and Wolfram Dressler. 2021. "China's Blue Economy: A State Project of Modernisation." *The Journal of Environment & Development* (Sage) 30 (2): 127–148. https://journals.sagepub.com/doi/10.1177/1070496521995872.

Farmery, Anna K., Edward H. Allison, Neil L. Andrew, Max Troell, Michelle Voyer, Brooke Campbell, Hampus Eriksson, Michael Fabinyi, Andrew M. Song, and Dirk Steenbergen. 2021. "Blind Spots in Visions of a 'Blue Economy' Could Undermine the Ocean's Contribution to Eliminating Hunger and Malnutrition." *One Earth* 4. https://doi.org/10.1016/j.oneear.2020.12.002.

Intergovernmental Oceanographic Commission of UNESCO. 2018. *The United Nations Decade of Ocean Science for Sustainable Development, 2021–2030.* Paris: United Nations Educational, Scientific and Cultural Organization. https://unesdoc.unesco.org/ark:/48223/pf0000261962.

McDevitt, Michael. 2016. "Introduction." *By Becoming a Great "Maritime Power": A Chinese Dream,* edited by Michael McDevitt, 1–7. Washington, DC: Center for Naval Analyses.

National Oceanic and Atmospheric Administration. 2021. *NOAA Blue Strategic Plan 2021–2025.* Washington, DC: US Department of Commerce, 18. https://aambpublicoceanservice.blob.core.windows.net/oceanserviceprod/economy/Blue-Economy%20Strategic-Plan.pdf.

Ocean Policy Committee. 2023. *Ocean Climate Action Plan: A Report by the Ocean Policy Committee.* Washington, DC: The White House. https://www.whitehouse.gov/wp-content/uploads/2023/03/Ocean-Climate-Action-Plan_Final.pdf.

Office of the Assistant Secretary of the Navy for Energy, Installations, and Environment. May 2022. *Department of the Navy Climate Action 2030.* Washington, DC: Department of the Navy.

Walsh, Kathleen A. 2019. "Testimony." *House Subcommittee on Coast Guard and Maritime Transportation Hearing on "China's Maritime Silk Road Initiative: Implications for the Global Maritime Supply Chain".* Washington, DC, October 19.

2

Origins and Expansion of the Blue Economy Concept

The notion of a Blue Economy is a relatively recent, roughly turn-of-the-century concept and one on which the United States, China, and others are competing on and cooperating to define, develop, and institute effectively. The evolving conception of what constitutes the Blue Economy and how it is being developed will impact the contest for maritime power among China, the United States, and other maritime states. The road to understanding the Blue Economy begins with its predecessor: the Green Economy.

The Green Economy Expands into the Blue Economy

Due to an environmental movement that began in the West in the late 19th century but became more widely activist in the 1970s, most people on the planet are aware by now of the notion of a "Green Economy." "Green" signifies a method or product that is more environmentally attentive. It means sustainable development, recycling, and other more environmentally conscious approaches to industrial production, consumer purchasing, economic development, and even more environmentally friendly means of developing military capabilities. The US Navy, for instance, at one time pursued development of a "Green Fleet" of warships that could run on biofuel. This was an effort aimed at helping the environment through reduced emissions while reducing fuel costs and limiting US dependence on foreign oil supplies. Sustainability, renewable energy, and reducing carbon emissions to limit climate change are continuing concerns for maintaining a technologically and operationally superior US military.

As societal norms have advanced and the hazards associated with climate change have become more apparent and more widely understood, the notion of what is "Green" has expanded further. The United Nations Environment Program (UNEP) defines the Green Economy today as follows:

> A green economy is defined as low carbon, resource efficient and socially inclusive. In a green economy, growth in employment and income are driven by public and private investment into such economic activities, infrastructure and assets that allow reduced carbon emissions and

DOI: 10.1201/9781003396116-2

> pollution, enhanced energy and resource efficiency, and prevention of the loss of biodiversity and ecosystem services.[1]

In other words, the notion of the Green Economy is to find ways to develop economically while also being conscious of the environmental consequences of this growth so as to ensure that such development is sustainable and more equitable over the long term. This approach invokes the idea of a natural ecosystem, which is apt given the focus of the Green (and Blue) Economy is on conserving nature at the same time as pursuing economic, industrial, and technological development.

Environmental consciousness in the United States oftentimes is linked with the publication of Rachel Carson's groundbreaking book, *Silent Spring*, published in 1962. Environmental activism followed, and the Nixon administration established the Environmental Protection Agency (EPA) in 1970. The concept of the Green Economy came along only years later. The term "Green Economy" was first proposed in a report written for the Government of the United Kingdom in 1989 by a joint academic and private-sector venture focused on environmental and economic matters.[2] Importantly, this report emphasized the notion of a two-way relationship between the environment and economics, in particular indicating the importance of an interaction between the two fields (environmentalism and economics). This interaction is what promotes more *sustainable* development, as opposed to economic development alone, which often depletes or harms the environment, as had occurred for centuries since the Industrial Revolution.

Following a similarly dynamic approach, the Blue Economy builds on the foundations laid by the Green Economy but with a specific focus on water and marine areas. Today, the People's Republic of China (PRC), the United States, and others are actively pursuing development of what is sometimes called an "Ocean Economy" or "Sustainable Ocean Economy" but is more commonly called the "Blue Economy" or "Sustainable Blue Economy." The Blue Economy is a concept designed to promote innovative development of greater marine, maritime, and naval capabilities while endeavoring to do so through more sustainable, conservation- and environmentally friendly means.

The notions of a "Green" and "Blue" Economy can overlap (such as in coastal regions, where land meets the sea). Being more popular, what is termed "green" can include what could be considered more "blue" (water-based) programs and projects. For instance, a 2020 report on Green Development in China's Belt and Road Initiative includes "Green" Economy projects in Ghana on container port development and a hydroelectric power project in Pakistan.[3] These same projects could be counted also as "blue" in other contexts, making accurate measurement of such activity more difficult.

Nonetheless, the Blue Economy is typically focused on assets and activities that are found out to sea or on and under the water rather than on land, per se, which is where the Green Economy concept focuses primarily.

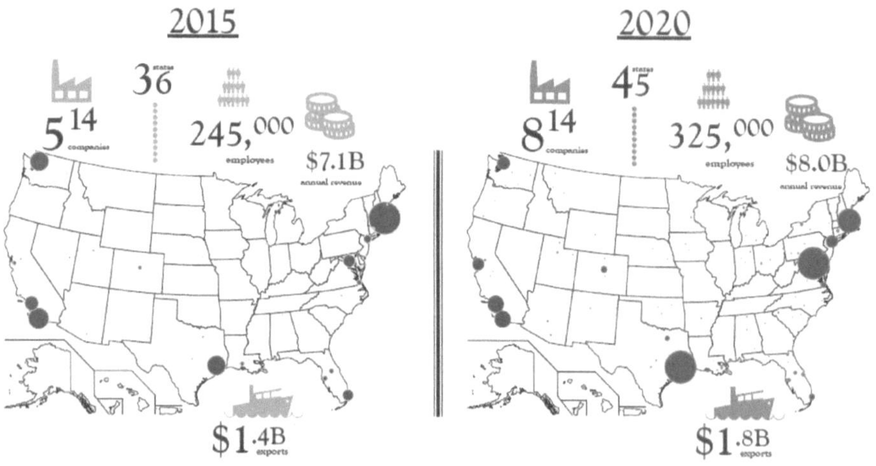

FIGURE 2.1
Growth in the US Blue Economy (2015–20). *Source*: National Oceanic and Atmospheric Administration, 2021.

Yet, the two concepts cannot be entirely separated. As the United Nations Environmental Program (UNEP) points out, "A worldwide transition to a low-carbon, resource-efficient Green Economy will not be possible unless the seas and oceans are a key part of these urgently needed transformations."[4] The opposite also holds true: a vibrant Blue Economy cannot prosper without a sustainable approach to preserving and developing the land.

Although there is not yet a consensus on how to define the Blue Economy, nor a standard method of accounting for it, the economic importance of Blue Economy-related activities is already apparent. As previously noted, the United States Commerce Department calculated that what it variably terms the "Ocean" or "Marine" Economy contributed over $432 billion to US gross domestic product (GDP) in 2021, representing 1.9 percent of US GDP.[5] This amount represents an increase over prior years, as shown in Figure 2.1, and faster growth than in the US economy overall.[6]

The US valuation is on par with what the European Union calculates as gross value added (GVA) by the Blue Economy, estimated to be around one percent (ranging from 1.1 to 1.6 percent) of total EU GVA over time (2009–20).[7]

In contrast, China's annual *Ocean Development Report* claimed that the PRC's "marine economy" contributed nearly 10 percent of China's GDP in 2016, which would equate to roughly US$1 trillion. China's goal is reportedly to have the Blue Economy reach 15 percent of GDP by 2035.[8] By 2019, Chinese state media was reporting that the PRC's "Gross Ocean Product" had increased to a total of the equivalent of $1.4 trillion (2021 dollars).[9]

While the above numbers are not readily comparable and should be viewed with skepticism until more standard and universal accounting methods are available, it is already clear that the ocean, marine, maritime, and generally "blue" space today is receiving greater industry, academic, and government attention, representing an important new area of opportunity and study.[10] As with the public's general acceptance of more "green" measures to promote sustainable development on land, the benefits promised by a "blue" economy are likely to lead many to adopt more innovative and sustainable development efforts in the marine, maritime, and naval space. In fact, the United States and China are already in competition for how to pursue a Blue Economy as well as how to define it.

As is discussed in Chapters 3 and 4 in greater detail, the United States and the PRC have been pursuing development of a Blue Economy in distinct ways and emphasizing different priorities in developing new, blue economic, industrial, innovative, and strategic capabilities. At the same time, both countries continue to look to and learn from one another in this regard, at times seeking opportunities for cooperation as well as competing in the Blue Economy arena.

Yet, leaders of both countries also have emphasized economic nationalist-themed policies and recently engaged in a serious US–China trade war that continues today in some respects. There are questions also about the seriousness with which either country is prioritizing environmental concerns and sustainable development activities as part of respective Blue Economy efforts, particularly when environmental interests compete with economic, technological, maritime, and naval interests. What the United States and China decide to do (and to not do) in these regards will not only impact respective domestic development efforts but also our shared marine environment and global climate efforts. As the world's top carbon dioxide emitters, what the world's two largest economies decide with regard to advancing the Blue Economy will impact the planet, future geopolitics, and generations to come.

Where cooperation and competition related to the Blue Economy are arguably likely to matter most in strategic terms is in the Indo-Pacific region. The Indo-Pacific region—spanning the Indian Ocean and all of the Pacific Ocean—is where the United States and China are engaged already in a contest for influence, access, presence, and leverage in the maritime domain—a strategic contest dubbed in Chapter 6 of this volume the "Great Blue Game."[11]

The Blue Economy development concept has emerged as an important but often overlooked part of the ongoing strategic contest between the United States and PRC, especially given its role in Xi Jinping's Maritime Silk Road (MSR) component of his ambitious Belt and Road Initiative (BRI).[12] Development of the Blue Economy will impact how the Great Blue Game is played, who will come out on top, and what environmental and security picture emerges in the Indo-Pacific region. If, as has happened in the past, this "game" is played at the expense of the other or third parties, it is ironically the marine environment that is most likely to suffer.

Defining the Blue Economy: It Depends on Whom One Asks

The Organisation for Economic Co-operation and Development (OECD) projects that by 2030 the Blue Economy will "have the potential to outperform the growth of the global economy as a whole, both in terms of value added and employment."[13] If so, or even coming close to these projections, the Blue Economy will be an important strategic concern for all countries. But what exactly is this new, "blue" economy? The answer depends on whom one asks.

One of the most challenging aspects of understanding the Blue Economy and its potential significance is in trying to determine just what it is and from whence it came. There is as yet no definitive global consensus on what the term Blue Economy means; experts have agreed that an effort to define the term is needed for scholars, officials, businesses, and interest groups to advance progress in this field of study and to enhance domestic and international collaboration as well as competition.[14]

In fact, the very origin of the term "Blue Economy" is in dispute.[15] The entrepreneur Gunther Pauli's work initially popularized the term dating back to the turn of the century.[16] But others have made claims to the term's origin as well, including government officials from Canada, Australia, and China.[17] Importantly, the term is native to neither China nor the United States.[18]

Many date the term's origins to the Rio+20 United Nations Conference on Sustainable Development in 2012, which coined the term "green growth," defined there as "fostering economic growth and development while ensuring that natural assets continue to provide the resources and environmental services on which our well-being relies." This general concept soon thereafter was adapted by the Small Island Developing States (SIDS) group to apply to ocean, coastal, and inland areas and hence was dubbed "the Blue Economy."[19] In other words, the Blue Economy can be understood generally in terms similar to the more widely known concept of the "Green Economy" (an idea promoting more environmentally aware and sustainable means of production, consumption, and disposal on land) but distinct in terms of centering on oceans, lakes, rivers, and other marine, maritime, and naval domains.

As noted, the term "Blue Economy" today is often used interchangeably with other terms such as "Ocean Economy," although distinctions are occasionally made, as in varied US and Chinese definitions discussed in Chapter 5. In addition to the terms "Ocean Economy" and "Blue Economy," officials and scholars at times employ terms such as "Maritime Economy" or "Marine Economy," sometimes interchangeably with the "Ocean" or "Blue" Economy but other times in distinct ways.

In Western application, at least, there appears to be little dispute in distinguishing between the terms marine or maritime: "maritime" being connected more broadly to industry, both commercial and military (whether "blue" or also sustainable in nature or not), while "marine" refers more specifically to elements "of, found in, or produced by the sea," often referring to marine species, habitats, and environmental or oceanographic studies.[20] China's definitions of these same terms, all of which are used in various contexts, are discussed in detail in Chapter 3, and are harder to disentangle from each other. The term, Blue Economy, however, is the one used more often in contemporary Chinese domestic and foreign policy documents and when conveying the notion of an innovative and more environmentally sustainable marine, maritime, and naval development ecosystem. In fact, adoption of the term Blue Economy (or not) is part of a contest over influence between the US and PRC governments, as discussed in Chapter 5 addressing US–China relations.

In Europe, the academic literature more often applies the term "Blue Growth" in accordance with European Union policies.[21] Yet the term "Blue Growth" is also used interchangeably with, and typically means the same thing as, the "Blue Economy." This situation has led some European scholars to recommend adopting the more commonly used Blue Economy term and defining it as "synonymous to a *sustainable* ocean economy."[22] In a recent document, the White House acknowledges also that the term "Sustainable Ocean Economy," which it notes that the World Bank applies, is synonymous with the term Blue Economy.[23]

Throughout the rest of this volume, the term "Blue Economy" is applied as it is the term that China uses today in official documents, is generally equivalent to other terms being used, and given the fact that the term appears to have become more popularly applied internationally and across the United States. The term Blue Economy also conveys a more holistic, comprehensive, and dynamic approach and, thus, more strategic connotation, than do the other terms that are used.

Defining the Blue Economy: It's Complicated

What constitutes the "Blue Economy" also remains a subject of continuing debate. In fact, definitions differ even in terms of what the "blue" and the "economy" parts of the term refer to, as well as what the overall term connotes. What the definitions have in common is that all conceptions include *economic* factors and actors as important components of a Blue Economy. A contemporary and common understanding of the Blue Economy includes the following components.

Blue Is Green, but Marine

As noted above, to some, the "Blue Economy" is akin to the more widely recognized notion of a "Green Economy," which similarly emphasizes environmental conservation, sustainable development, and recycling efforts, but usually on land; the Blue Economy, by contrast, is focused specifically on areas of water—whether in, on, over, by, or of the water; whether related to fish, oil and gas, and other resources—and usually applied in geographical terms to all water or marine sources, whether in the form of rivers, lakes, streams, ponds, coastal areas, seas, or oceans.[24]

Blue Is Maritime

Some proponents of the Blue Economy emphasize the "blue" aspect of the term Blue Economy, meaning anything marine- or maritime industry-related or even simply water-based, whether present physically in the water or, as in industry, applied to or in water.[25] This notion of the Blue Economy emphasizes economic and industrial aspects, including maritime industries such as fishing, aquaculture, and oil and gas exploration, as well as shipbuilding, or generally any industry using water as a resource (e.g., hydropower). Note, however, that this definition does not necessarily focus on or value sustainable development and conservation as highly, notions that are typically conveyed by those applying the term Blue Economy today, particularly when used in the West.

The Blue Economy sector in the United States is already sizeable, enough for the US Department of Commerce to track in a separate account what it calls the "Marine Economy," which is comprised today of ten industry sectors. These ten sectors are: (1) marine living resources; (2) coastal and marine construction; (3) marine research and education; (4) marine transportation and warehousing; (5) marine professional and technical services; (6) offshore minerals; (7) coastal utilities; (8) nonrecreational ship and boat building; (9) coastal and offshore tourism and recreation; and (10) national defense and public administration.[26] In order to keep up with this fast-changing sector, the Commerce Department has had to expand and update continually how it accounts for and characterizes the Marine Economy.[27]

Blue Is Innovation

The idea that the "blue" in Blue Economy is focused on ocean or water-based issues, sectors, and areas has gained acceptance since Gunther Pauli first popularized the term Blue Economy around 2010.[28] Yet, Pauli's own Blue Economy work, then and now, focuses primarily on developing simply *innovative technological* approaches to achieving sustainable development, regardless of whether the activities are maritime (blue) or terrestrial in nature. An emphasis on innovation (whether related to "blue" waters or not) continues to predominate in Pauli's works but also other parts of the literature that do not necessarily focus on the marine or maritime components of the broader Blue Economy concept .[29] In Asia and elsewhere, for instance, when someone cites the term

Blue Economy, listeners might think this refers only to how to reform business practices so as to make them more innovative and sustainable, having nothing at all to do with marine, maritime, or naval concerns. Yet, as use of the term Blue Economy has evolved and expanded over time, innovation remains a core element of the concept, though now often focused on innovation of more *sustainable* marine, maritime, and naval capabilities. In fact, the innovation component of the Blue Economy concept today is a particularly important aspect of how the term is employed in both China and the United States.

The Blue Economy as All of the Above: Marine, Maritime, and Focused on Innovation

Although variously defined and applied, as outlined above, the Blue Economy concept today is increasingly understood as incorporating *all of the above ideas combined*: green, but blue, in the sense of promoting *marine*-based environmental conservation, sustainability, and innovative solutions; maritime in the sense of promoting a broad range of marine and maritime industries; and innovative in terms of promoting technological innovation in both commercial and military (primarily naval) spheres in more sustainable ways (see Figure 2.2). The World Bank, for example, defines the Blue Economy "as comprising the range of economic sectors and related policies that together

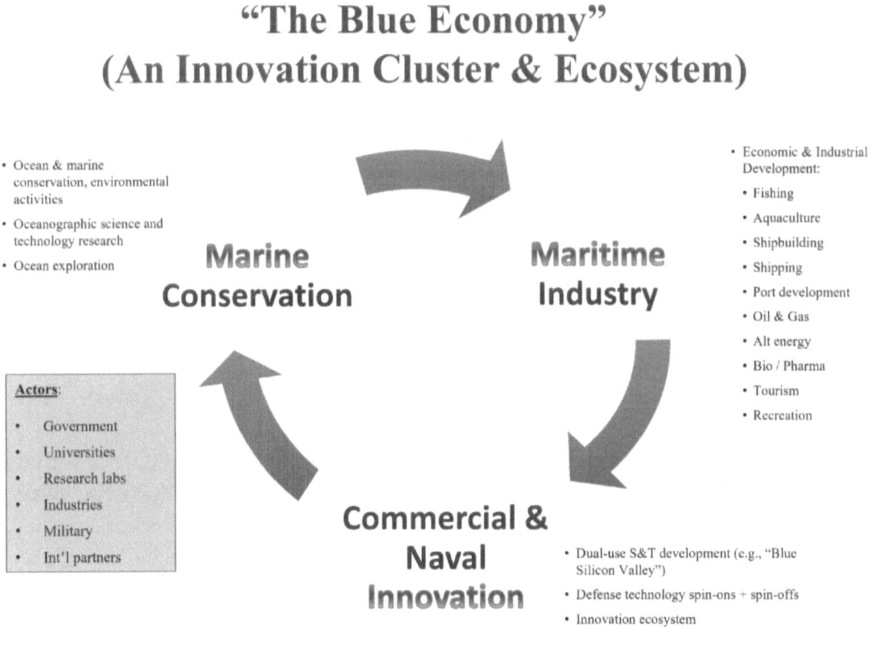

FIGURE 2.2
The Blue Economy concept. *Source*: Walsh, 2016.

determine whether the use of *oceanic resources* is sustainable" [emphasis added].[30] Innovation is inherent in this notion as a means of achieving more sustainable ways and means of development.

The Blue Economy as Industry Cluster and Innovation Ecosystem

A final, but critically important aspect to the term Blue Economy's evolution and contemporary use is what is meant by the second word: economy. This term is not meant to be static but should be understood as a *dynamic*, as the magazine *The Economist* defined the concept in 2015:

> a sustainable ocean economy emerges when economic activity is in balance with the long-term capacity of ocean ecosystems to support this activity and remain resilient and healthy.[31]

The notion of an *ecosystem* is particularly important to understanding the Blue Economy concept, as both a component and an outcome. The term Blue Economy as most commonly understood today is, in fact, as an ecosystem-oriented approach to development that is innovative and sustainable over time due to dynamic interactions occurring between and among the three core elements that most agree comprise a Blue Economy: (1) *marine* environmental conservation and sustainability efforts; (2) *maritime* economic activity, industry, and investment; and (3) marine, maritime, and naval (i.e., dual-use) scientific and technological *innovation*.

In fact, the idea of a dynamic ecosystem effect applies overall to a Blue Economy as well as to each of the three individual elements: marine conservation, maritime industry, and commercial and military innovation, each of which can have internal ecosystems that include distinct industry or technology clusters (as discussed below). In other words, a robust Blue Economy would include a vibrant, multi-sector maritime industry interacting with marine scientists, conservationists, shipbuilders, environmental activists, fishing and lobster crews, ocean explorers, naval engineers, and others, all working in their own spheres to find more innovative and sustainable methods of development such that the overall ecosystem benefits from these dynamic interactions. This ecosystem dynamic also includes the general public, who provide feedback in the form of population growth, tourism, job growth, etc.

Yet, as with any ecosystem, the results will be benign only if each element *positively* engages with and impacts (or takes into consideration) the other elements. A well-functioning Blue Economy requires a means for lobstermen to communicate their needs to oil and gas industry representatives, and vice versa, as well as for each to deconflict their interests with those of boaters, others in the tourist industry, as well as with any government or naval uses for the same waters, for example. As a matter of policy, ensuring an overall beneficial outcome requires considerable cross-disciplinary effort and resisting temptations toward adopting zero-sum, short-term approaches. Again, it's complicated.

Understanding conceptually what the Blue Economy is intended to be is not terribly easy; establishing a well-functioning Blue Economy as a reality on the ground is far harder. To coordinate and deconflict the many distinct stakeholders in, and uses of, the same marine area, policymakers around the world are using tools like marine spatial planning (MSP). For developing a Blue Economy-focused ecosystem, there also exists a basic model for developing an industry-focused innovative ecosystem: the industry cluster.

The most famous industry cluster and innovation ecosystem is, of course, the information technology-focused industry cluster known as Silicon Valley in California. China hopes to catch up to the United States technologically by developing its own versions of Silicon Valley, including a novel idea of developing a "Blue Silicon Valley" that focuses on development of a Blue Economy innovation ecosystem.

The Contemporary Blue Economy: A Sustainable Marine and Maritime Industry Ecosystem and Innovation Cluster

The arid air and brown landscape of Northern California are not how one imagines the world's most innovative patch of land. When traveling around Silicon Valley, it is hard to see how innovation happens here. The buildings are average, the landscape uninspiring, and the visible infrastructure pretty much the same as across the rest of the United States. What makes this part of the country the globe's leading innovation cluster is a mix of its people: entrepreneurs, venture capitalists, industry leaders, government researchers and officials, smart and ambitious, often young, people (university students, graduates, and dropouts alike), and those who bring all of these people together into a networked community where it is possible to pursue bold new ideas, innovative technologies, and scientific breakthroughs.

Since the emergence in the late 20th century of Silicon Valley, which is an idea rather than an actual place, many have tried to replicate its success. The challenge in doing so goes far beyond acquiring real estate, recruiting talent, and fostering a creative and attractive environment in which to work. It is a challenge that China continues to wrestle with in its efforts to become more innovative in its development.

In establishing an effective innovation cluster, there seems to be a degree of something intangible that brings all of the collective potential to fruition. That intangible something—having to do with interactions among a community of talent gathered in a single geographical area—and the difficulty in capturing this bit of magic, is what can hamper other clusters around the country and around the globe from establishing lasting and continuously prosperous centers of innovation. It is not simply a matter of establishing an area for innovation but fostering the potential for innovation to happen. In short, it takes the collective effort of many different actors to make a welcoming environment for innovative advances to be possible, for new ideas to flourish and seed even more new ideas, and for talented people to produce something innovative and potentially game changing. That community-based dynamic acts like an ecosystem, where one element in a certain area impacts another, with all of this activity creating an environment, one that can be benign or malign, depending on the nature of those interactions. Where the environment is welcoming and the ecosystem strong, innovation prospers.

The idea of an industry *cluster* was popularized in the business world by Harvard Business School Professor Michael Porter's work and is key to understanding how a Blue Economy is intended to function.[32] Clusters today are generally defined as "a regional concentration of related industries connected through various types of linkages and spillovers and supporting institutions."[33] Industry clusters also tend to develop a focus on particular advanced technology sectors, such as aerospace, information technology, biotechnology, and so forth.

Beyond Silicon Valley, other high-tech industry clusters exist across the United States, including Boston's Route 128 region and North Carolina's Research Triangle area. Each of these areas is home to one or more industry clusters (e.g., information technology, financial services, biotechnology, and education). These other industries were drawn to the same respective regions for similar reasons that originally drew the first high-tech firms or organizations to these locations. Taking San Diego as an example, what draws industry, researchers, and others to this location is the region's several industries—maritime, aerospace, defense, cleantech, advanced manufacturing, recreation, and more—that form separate industry clusters, each of which interacts separately and collectively with other parts of the larger San Diego-area ecosystem as a whole.[34]

Studies into regional industry clusters around the United States find that the interaction of such industry clusters promotes growth, investment, and innovation, that serves, in turn, to further expand these regions' economic prospects.[35] The growth of these industry and innovation clusters benefits the national economy overall as well, although not through market forces alone; some government involvement is necessary to ensure a strong and sustainable innovation cluster and that the rise and concentration of industry in innovation clusters serve the national economy and not only those regions that are host to these clusters.[36] Small startup firms benefit from early investors willing to take risks with capital, but government support is often needed to overcome challenges related to scaling up production and ensuring high-risk research and development is feasible to start as well as to pursue over time, among other challenges posed by innovation.

Efforts to develop a Blue Economy follow a similar approach and logic: developing strategies, policies, and practices to attract and keep businesses, researchers, students, entrepreneurs, investors, and other talented individuals in what is seen as a vibrant and attractive area to live, work and prosper, but centered around marine conservation, maritime industry, and commercial and naval innovation. California, once again, is home to what is arguably the most advanced Blue Economy to form thus far in the United States, this time located in the Southern California area around San Diego.

In San Diego and its environs, all the elements of an innovative Blue Economy industry cluster are evident in a single geographical area: a vibrant academic community, including ocean and marine scientists at the University of California at San Diego (UCSD) and its renowned Scripps Institution of Oceanography, as well as at public- and private-sector research institutions, innovative startup ventures and capital investors, a strong and diverse maritime industry, a large harbor, a deep water port, US Government research and US Navy presence, local and state governments supportive of marine conservation and Blue Economy development efforts, and located in a region known for its welcoming climate and high standard of living. This dynamic ecosystem is what makes the area an attractive place for people to live and work, students and faculty to attend college, and tourists to visit. Importantly, the region also boasts an independent, non-governmental organization that promotes the Blue Economy concept as a way of enhancing the regional economy through development of "blue tech" and "blue jobs." The result overall is a dynamic maritime sector with a diverse, mutually interdependent community of businesses, researchers, and marine environmentalists focused on developing more sustainable and innovative means of economic and maritime industrial development in a given geographic area that also serves to bolster US naval research. In other words, the main idea driving the Blue Economy concept is that of a thriving and environmentally conscious cluster of industries joined in an innovation ecosystem.

California, in fact, presents an interesting test case for how the concept of the Blue Economy might evolve further. While San Diego leads the nation in efforts to develop an industry cluster focused on the Blue Economy, Monterey, California's efforts to advance its Blue Economy focus more on marine conservation as well as conducting academic research about Blue Economy activities in the United States and abroad. Silicon Valley, situated further inland, is interested in the concept mainly in the innovative and venture capital opportunities that the Blue Economy promises. Understandably, each approach to the development of a Blue Economy suits the resources, geography, assets, talent pool, and industries found in each region. But this is also what makes defining the Blue Economy so difficult.

China, like many other countries, has long been trying to capture Silicon Valley's same innovative dynamic. Today, much like San Diego, China also seeks to develop its own Blue Economy innovation clusters by creating specific Blue Economy-oriented industrial and innovation zones built around particular industries, located near leading universities and research centers, supplied by government and private investments, and by providing incentives to produce new ideas, products, and innovative technologies. The PRC has had some notable innovation successes, generally, such as in the information technology sector with companies such as Huawei. In pursuit of its Blue Economy efforts, China's pilot effort is attempting to build what it terms a "Blue Silicon Valley" in the northeastern city of Qingdao, in order to aid China's innovative maritime and naval development capabilities. Whether the PRC can succeed in its efforts will impact its own development as well as the world's economic, industrial, environmental, technological, and security interests.

The Emergence of Blue Economy Clusters in the United States and around the World

Beyond San Diego, California, other Blue Economies (sometimes called ocean or maritime clusters) are sprouting up around the United States, as the concept catches on as a means of promoting new business opportunities and fostering innovation in ways that also preserve the environment. For instance, Blue Economy clusters are emerging in coastal regions in locations already mentioned, such as Monterey, California, and elsewhere, such as in Washington State, Alaska, Maine, and even competing Southern New England areas of Massachusetts, Rhode Island, and Connecticut. In-land areas, such as the Great Lakes region, also are developing new, Blue Economies.

These emerging Blue Economy clusters (whether formally adopting the term "Blue Economy" or not) are often sprouting organically as local entrepreneurs, business leaders, startups, and environmental activists seek new ways to spur local-area market opportunities in ways that also conserve the marine environment. This is a recent phenomenon. A 2018 study notes that "Over the last four years 20 incubators, accelerators and clusters focused on the Blue Economy and blue technology have formed in North America, bringing the current total to 26."[37] US legislators are interested in and have put forward bills in the 118th Congress (2023-24) to establish more "Ocean Innovation Clusters" across much of the United States.

While COVID-19 has affected some of the growth and momentum in development of Blue Economy clusters in the United States and elsewhere, earlier efforts to create and sustain new Blue Economies are likely to have resumed by late 2022, although there is as yet limited data in this regard. In my hometown of Newport, RI, where blue economy development efforts pre-date the pandemic, these efforts have since resumed as, it appears, have others.

The growing number of maritime or Blue Economy clusters and related initiatives in the United States means that each cluster is in various stages of development and being developed around each region's strengths. This number includes several California-based efforts: TMA BlueTech headquartered in San Diego, Alta Sea's efforts in Los Angeles, and ongoing efforts in Monterey, CA, where the Center for the Blue Economy research institution is located.

In New England, there have been several competing clusters: Newport, Rhode Island's own Blue Economy initiative; a Southeastern New England Blue Economy initiative; a Rhode Island Blue Economy Technology Cluster; a New Bedford, Massachusetts, Blue Economy cluster; a Cape Cod, Massachusetts, Blue Economy initiative; a North Shore, Massachusetts, Blue Economy Initiative; as well as a New England Ocean Cluster headquartered in Portland, Maine. All of these Blue Economy efforts across New England's generally small geographic area indicate a high degree of local interest in pursuing Blue Economy opportunities. Some of these likely will merge or be eclipsed by other efforts, as has already happened in the case of one effort, the Southeastern New England initiative.

Other Blue Economy clusters are found elsewhere around the country, such as Washington State's Blue Economy initiative; Alaska's Ocean Cluster Initiative; a Great Lakes initiative; an initiative in Alabama; and Mississippi's emerging Blue Economy cluster.[38] As time goes by, some of these competing Blue Economy clusters are likely to merge or, if not, at least coordinate more formally rather than compete in ways that might prove redundant. For instance, a recently announced initiative funded by the Office of Naval Research (ONR) joins Blue Economy programs at the University of Rhode Island, the University of Alaska-Fairbanks, and the University of Hawaii.[39]

Congress recently mandated in law, in fact, the establishment of several Regional Ocean Partnerships (ROP) "to coordinate the management of ocean, coastal, and Great Lakes resources among the members of the partnership."[40] The ROPs designated in this 2022 law are as follows:

- **Gulf of Mexico Alliance** [Alabama, Florida, Louisiana, Mississippi, and Texas]
- **Northeast Regional Ocean Council** [Maine, Vermont, New Hampshire, Massachusetts, Connecticut, and Rhode Island]
- **Mid-Atlantic Regional Council** [New York, New Jersey, Delaware, Maryland, and Virginia]
- **West Coast Ocean Alliance** [California, Oregon, Washington, and coastal Indian Tribes therein]
- **Regional Great Lakes Partnership** [to be determined]

Some of these groupings already exist, such as the Northeast Regional Ocean Council, which dates its origins back to 2005 but has competitors across New England. Being designated as federally recognized ROPs will grant each regional group with potentially greater resources, funding, and other support from the federal government, however, including $10 million in support of regional ocean partnership activities for each fiscal year starting in 2023 through 2027.[41]

Local interest in the Blue Economy is growing likely because it is potentially big business. A 2017 study on the "ocean enterprise" in the United States found that there were over 400 companies or others involved in business activities related to the ocean.[42] These enterprises are found along the eastern, southern, and western coastal areas of the United States with several inland locations or clusters appearing in the mid-west and western states, encompassing a total of 36 of 50 states. According to the study's survey, half expected ocean enterprise-related business to grow, yet most—58 percent of the 100-plus firms out of 400 responding— reported no overseas presence. Of the remainder, nearly half (44 percent) reported that the Asia Pacific and Europe make up at least five percent of their business. Yet, of those ocean enterprises with overseas business, a majority (63 percent) focused on businesses tied to or conducted in some way in relation to the Atlantic Ocean, with only 29 percent tied to activities related to the Pacific Ocean.

As suggested by the above and by China's pursuit of a Blue Economy as well, the emergence of ocean, maritime, or Blue Economy clusters is a global, yet relatively recent, phenomenon and a new area of competition and cooperation as more regions, countries, states, and municipalities seek to explore expanding "blue" opportunities. Areas seeking to develop Blue Economies are finding new research, businesses, and investment opportunities related to water (whether on, under, or above the water), along coastal areas, and in the oceans, as well as in ways that are more sustainable. For instance, some startup companies are innovating ways in which kelp and seaweed are farmed both at sea and in aquaculture fisheries. These innovative methods and technologies can be used in potentially new ways to produce more sustainable or bio-degradable products. Other startup ventures focus on undersea robotics that will better serve marine conservation, ocean science, and perhaps also naval undersea needs. Not surprisingly, Blue Economy-related clusters have emerged in areas where high-tech industry, talent, and services already exist, both in the United States and overseas.

There have been as yet only initial attempts to capture in detail the nature and extent of emerging Blue Economy or ocean-themed industry clusters being developed around the world; there is much more to learn about the burgeoning Blue Economy or ocean enterprise industry clusters in the United States and beyond.[43] Surveys conducted by the US Commerce Department's National Oceanographic and Atmospheric Administration (NOAA) indicate a near-doubling of ocean enterprises from 2015 (with 410) to 2020 (with 815 identified). Not all of these enterprises are new in the sense of being newly established, however; some are existing businesses newly counted in the ocean enterprise surveys.[44]

Congress is interested in fostering the growth of Ocean or Blue Economy clusters around the country, with bipartisan legislation introduced in both the Senate and House in June 2023. The Ocean Regional Opportunity and

Innovation Act (Ocean ROI Act) seeks to ensure that "at least one ocean cluster [is] in each NOAA Fisheries region – including the Great Lakes."[45]

What is clear is that new Blue Economies are developing across the United States and elsewhere in ways that are likely to impact US and other countries' economic growth and competitiveness in ways that could spill over into other sectors, both commercial and military. If Blue Economy and ocean industry clusters form into vibrant and industry-leading centers of innovation (or not), this also fundamentally could affect the ongoing strategic competition between the United States and China in both maritime and naval domains. The promise of the Blue Economy to enhance such strategic endeavors is exactly what is driving China to invest in its concept of a "Blue Silicon Valley."

Blue Economy Clusters Are Fostering International Cooperation

In an age of economic globalization, it is perhaps not surprising that advocates involved in developing regional Blue Economies are engaging with domestic and international counterparts to share insights, lessons learned, and to identify opportunities for further cooperation as well as competition. The Maritime Alliance (TMA) BlueTech organization in San Diego, for instance, has been involved in numerous collaborative efforts with other US as well as international counterparts. Similarly, Iceland's Ocean Cluster, established in 2012, has provided useful insights and advice in the formation of the Portland, Maine-based New England Ocean Cluster (NEOC) given their similar, northern latitude climates.[46]

Beyond these useful, but essentially ad hoc, forms of cooperation, more formal and strategic relationships and networks also are emerging. The San Diego-based TMA BlueTech, for instance, is a charter member of a BlueTech Cluster Alliance (BTCA), which connects institutions promoting Blue Economy cluster development in the United States and Europe.[47] A European Network of Maritime Clusters (ENMC) also connects 18 states across Europe. Another US-based organization, the World Ocean Council, helps US and international businesses to network with other maritime clusters around the globe.[48]

Blue Economy advocates and others interested or involved in Blue Economy matters also meet regularly at national and international, often ocean-themed, events, where there is opportunity to share more information and experience from different regions. More of this cross-regional and international collaboration is likely to occur given the rapid appearance of national and cross-regional Blue Economies, as well as individuals, organizations, and governments interested in developing them.

Efforts to establish what are sometimes termed "maritime" or "ocean" clusters, which share similar goals and dynamics as a Blue Economy cluster, have proliferated globally and rapidly. As reported in a February 2018 World Ocean Council White Paper, several dozen (40) ocean and maritime clusters already existed around the world, including in China.

The World Ocean Council White Paper described ocean or maritime clusters and their value added as follows:

> geographic concentrations of similar or related maritime firms—such as shipping, seafood, marine technology, and/or port operations—that share common markets, technologies, worker skill needs, and are often linked by buyer-supplier relationships and operate in close interactions with another directly and through multiple networks ... Competitive advantages are generated in the interplay between companies, further increasing the quality of related and supporting sectors—creating favorable conditions to mutually reinforce the Ocean/Maritime Cluster ecosystem. Promoting Ocean/Maritime Clusters can deliver added value including higher income and employment level, sustainable consumption and production, and the effective functioning of many industries in support of overall sustainable development.[49]

As indicated by the above, what are termed "maritime" or "ocean" clusters here closely approximate a "Blue Economy cluster," if not entirely or formally adopting the term. Subsequent reports and additional research on maritime, ocean, or Blue Economy clusters reflect a doubling and more of known clusters (including Blue Economy clustersupporting organizations) worldwide, from 40 such clusters identified by the World Ocean Council in 2018 to at least 89 in subsequent reports and research conducted by the author (see Figure 2.3). While the United States accounts for 18 of this total due to numerous local-area development efforts in pursuit of Blue Economies, Europe taken as a whole constitutes 58 of the 89 clusters identified, comprising the majority. China's sole named cluster represents its pilot development zone in Qingdao, which is currently functioning, while at least nine others are listed in government plans and are reportedly in development.

The pace of the growth in global Blue Economy clusters is not entirely clear as yet, however, since the doubling of known clusters identified since 2018 could reflect countries, clusters, and activists more able to conduct international outreach than an actual rise in the number of existing clusters. Since most of the reported clusters are located in North America and Western Europe, there are also potentially many more clusters that exist beyond these regions that have not yet been engaged by US or European Blue Economy experts. It is also not yet clear how many, if any, Blue Economy clusters have failed since having been established. Nevertheless, the ability to identify double the number of known Blue Economy-oriented clusters is impressive over a relatively short period of time (2018–23) and indicates substantial global interest in this concept.

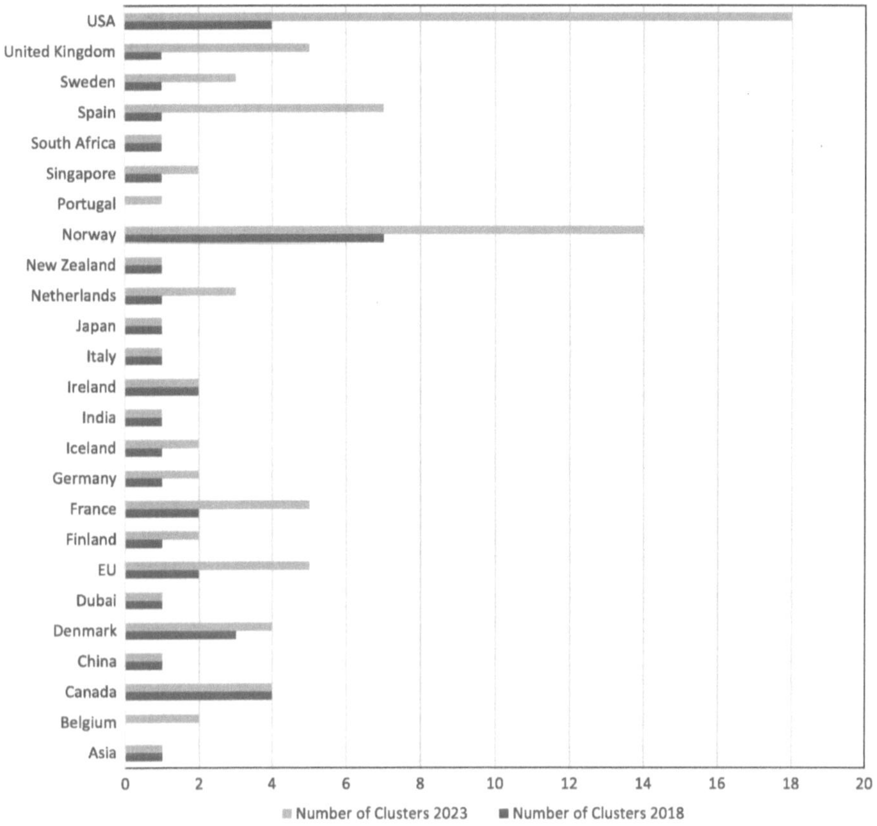

FIGURE 2.3
Growth in Global Blue Economy clusters (2018 and 2023). *Source*: Hansen et al., 2018; TMA BlueTech and Ocean Foundation, 2021; Ocean Foundation et al., 2023; Ocean Foundation et al., 2022; Author research, 2023.

Differing Models of Blue Economy Cluster Development

Interest in, and activism by, local communities and governments have generated most of the Blue Economy cluster development efforts in the United States to date. This bottom-up approach to generating economic and innovative opportunity via developing clusters of industry and technology innovation is typical of the United States' free market-based economy and approach to innovation. Some federal and state government support for developing offshore, coastal, and ocean areas exists, but until recent years has been limited and tends not to advance far without buy-in from local businesses, activists, and officials.

China, by contrast, follows a primarily top-down model of development in which national strategies, five-year plans, and policies drafted in Beijing dictate and guide development efforts at the regional, provincial and local levels. There might or might not be local officials, entrepreneurs, academics, and others interested and able to effectively implement these plans, much less in a dynamic, innovative, and sustainable manner. Alternatively, where there is local enthusiasm but national-level support is lacking, market-based opportunities might arise but are likely to remain geographically and politically constrained.

European states are pursuing what is called "Blue Growth" and in ways that share elements of each of the above models. The European Commission provides substantial funding, policies, principles, standards, and guidelines supporting Blue Growth initiatives that countries in the European Union are charged with implementing. Each government also supplements EU funding through local and regional efforts. As in both the US and PRC cases, local-area officials, entrepreneurs, and businesses in Europe will determine whether these efforts succeed over the long term or not.

Which cluster development model succeeds most effectively in terms of developing well-functioning, innovative, and sustainable Blue Economy cluster(s) is yet to be determined but reflects an ongoing economic and strategic competition. The successful model, however, is likely to be some combination of top-down, sustained government support mixed with vibrant local and private-sector, market-driven dynamism that provides national and regional return on investments while conserving the marine environment in the process. Moreover, whichever state(s) are best able to leverage their Blue Economy clusters is likely to enjoy a competitive strategic advantage in economic as well as potentially technological and defense terms, making this competition an important element of US and PRC strategy and policy.

The Blue Economy as a 21st-Century Strategic Maritime Advantage

Developing environmentally sustainable and marine resource-conscious, tourism-attracting regions, with advanced research and academic institutions situated within a maritime industry and innovation cluster (such as exists in San Diego) provides the United States with economic, technological, and strategic advantages given the commercial and naval capabilities that spill over within this dynamic innovation ecosystem. Other regions around the United States are attempting to do the same. These efforts are essential to ensuring an innovative and more sustainable approach to economic development, to maintaining a robust US maritime industry, and to continued naval scientific and technological advances. Such efforts in the United States, however, are hampered by the lack of a comprehensive national and international strategy for developing Blue Economy innovation clusters.

China, too, would like to develop its own San Diego-like Blue Economy clusters up and down its own coastline, as well as to network these clusters domestically and overseas, particularly via the Maritime Silk Road component of Xi Jinping's Belt and Road Initiative. Doing so effectively is seen as a way of sustaining China's shipbuilding and other critical maritime industries, to expand China's maritime and naval power, and to export China's own Blue Economy development model as a means of integrating China's economic development with other countries' in the region. As such, the Blue Economy represents a major, new opportunity for Chinese domestic development as well as its overseas diplomacy.

It is not yet clear whether China's plans to develop Blue Economy Development Zones or clusters domestically are realizing success or not, nor how quickly (or not) these plans are progressing. There is very limited data overall, few published articles available outside of China, and few on-the-ground testimonies as to whether and how China is making progress in this regard. The global pandemic also constitutes a serious hurdle for nearly every endeavor undertaken in recent years in China and elsewhere. At the same time, however, and based on past development achievements, it would be unwise to underestimate the potential for China to realize its Blue Economy plans and development efforts given they are founded on the economic development zone model that has spurred China's rise over the past four decades. Development of the Blue Economy is also an area of global maritime competition, a sector in which China has become rapidly adept in both commercial and military terms already. Xi Jinping's plans to incorporate the Blue Economy into Chinese foreign policy (as discussed in detail in Chapter 4) make it even more important to pay attention to this issue as it affects both domestic and international developments in the critically strategic Indo-Pacific region.

In addition, whether the United States' bottom-up model, China's more top-down development model, or something in between (perhaps Europe's combined Blue Growth model of mixed top-down and bottom-up drivers) serves to better and more quickly develop Blue Economies that foster innovative, sustainable, marine and maritime as well as naval development is not yet clear. What is evident is that the contest between the United States and China is already at hand, and that whichever model proves more successful domestically will also likely prove more attractive to third parties seeking to institute the same. This is why development of the Blue Economy—as an end in itself but also as a means to economic, technological, maritime, and diplomatic advantage—also represents a geostrategic contest for influence.

As discussed in Chapters 5 and 6, the United States and China are engaged already in just such a contest for influence in the Indo Pacific. The Solomon Islands serves as a case study where both the United States and China are offering this small South Pacific nation a multitude of Blue Economy-themed assistance while seeking myriad strategic trade and other types of agreements. It is this geostrategic contest—of developing innovative and sustainable Blue Economy clusters at home, developing Blue Economy models that can be exported to other countries, and promising Blue Economy investment and assistance to third parties in ways that form strong strategic relationships—that underlies what can be considered the 21st century's Great Game, or in this case, a "Great Blue Game."

At the time of this writing (summer 2023), China's more assertive and aggressive approach to conducting international affairs in the era of Xi Jinping has shifted the balance in Washington and elsewhere between cooperation and competition toward a strategy of mutual strategic competition. While there remain areas of cooperation and the potential for more between the United States and China (e.g., on climate change and ocean science), in other domains, particularly industry and military modernization, US–China relations are in decline and focused openly on seeking strategic, economic, and technological advantage vis-à-vis the other. US Government concerns over China's rapid naval modernization also make any sort of maritime cooperation difficult and naval cooperation highly unlikely but for select implementation of possible confidence and security building measures (CSBMs).

US–China diplomatic relations have become even more fraught as Xi's China has openly aligned with Russia in the context of Russian President Putin's invasion of Ukraine in 2022. This downward trajectory in US–China relations bodes ill for further cooperative efforts on developing the Blue Economy concept in the near term and likely heightens the competition for developing national and international maritime clusters where the Blue Economy is put into practice.

The decline in US–China relations means that each country today is pursuing development of the Blue Economy largely separately and in competition with the other. The Blue Economy concept's emphasis on fostering greater marine, maritime, and naval development and innovation while doing so in a more environmentally sustainable manner is likely to attract higher levels—both domestic and foreign—of investment, research, tourism, and other benefits. The country or region that is best able to leverage this concept for such purposes will have an advantage over the other.

Much like the cluster of information technology firms, researchers, and academic institutions that make up Silicon Valley and provide US industry and the military with continuous technological advantages through high-tech innovation and inventions, the Blue Economy concept also promises to provide technological and dual-use (civil and military) technological innovations for the marine, maritime, and naval sectors, if developing these capabilities in areas that remain attractive places to live and work, thereby making such efforts sustainable over the long term. For the United States and China, who are already enmeshed in strategic competition more broadly, the competition to develop the Blue Economy adds a new dimension to the Great Power contest and one that has domestic economic implications as well as geostrategic repercussions.

As mankind looks anew to the ocean and Earth's waters as a still-under-explored research frontier, as an important source for food and energy, as an increasingly critical factor in regional and global climate change, and as a source of maritime and naval power, the Blue Economy development concept and how it is developed by the United States and China is likely to become central to all of these efforts and prone to expand and evolve to meet these challenges and opportunities.

In order to better understand the nature of this strategic competition and its implications for the Indo-Pacific region and beyond, Chapter 3 details how China conceives of the Blue Economy, how the PRC has sought to implement its conception, and how Beijing's strategies, plans, and policies on the Blue Economy have evolved over time.

Notes

1. "Green Economy," United Nations Environment Program (2023), https://www.unep.org/regions/asia-and-pacific/regional-initiatives/supporting-resource-efficiency/green-economy.
2. David W. Pearce, Markandya Anil, and Edward B. Barbier. *Blueprint for a Green Economy* (London: Earthscan Publications, 1989).
3. BRI International Green Development Coalition, *BRI Green Development Case Study Report* (November 2020), http://en.brigc.net/Reports/research_subject/202011/P020201129780236943177.pdf.
4. United Nations Environment Program, *Green Economy in a Blue World*, 14th Global Meeting of the Regional Seas Convention and Action Plans (Nairobi: United Nations Environment Program, 2012), https://wedocs.unep.org/bitstream/handle/20.500.11822/12499/RS.14_INF.1.RS.pdf.
5. "Marine Economy," Bureau of Economic Analysis, US Department of Commerce (June 8, 2023), https://www.bea.gov/data/special-topics/marine-economy.
6. Bureau of Economic Analysis, "Marine Satellite Account, 2021," Press Release (June 8, 2023), https://www.bea.gov/news/2023/marine-economy-satellite-account-2021.
7. European Commission, *The EU Blue Economy Report* (Luxembourg: Publications Office of the European Commission, 2023), 8, https://op.europa.eu/en/publication-detail/-/publication/9a345396-f9e9-11ed-a05c-01aa75ed71a1.
8. Zhihai Xie, "Government Policy, Industrial Clusters, and the Blue Economy in the People's Republic of China: A Case Study on the Shandong Peninsula Blue Economic Zone," ADBI Working Paper no. 1296 (Tokyo: Asian Development Bank Institute, 2021), http://www.adb.org/sites/default/files/publication/762206/adbi-wp1296.pdf.
9. Xinhua, "Xi Focus: Building a Maritime Community with Shared Future for the Blue Planet" (June 7, 2021), http://www.xinhuanet.com/english/2021-06/07/c_139994197.htm.

10. On the difficulties with and diverse ways countries account for ocean and "blue" economic activities, see Charles S. Cogan, "Ocean Accounts from National Income to Blue Economy." *Journal of Ocean and Coastal Economics: Special Issue: Oceans and National Income* (Monterey, CA: Center for the Blue Economy, Middlebury Institute of International Studies) 2, no. 2 (2016), https://cbe.miis.edu/joce/vol2/iss2/12.
11. The author is grateful to Mr. Matt Merighi for coming up with this term in conjunction with an earlier conception of this study that we had planned initially to co-author.
12. The "Silk Road Economic Belt and 21st Century Maritime Silk Road," announced in 2013 as the "One Belt, One Road" (OBOR), is commonly known abroad as the "Belt and Road Initiative" since being renamed in 2016.
13. OECD, *The Ocean Economy in 2030* (Paris: OECD Publishing, 2016).
14. Michael Conathan et al., *Blue Future: Mapping Opportunities for U.S.-China Ocean Cooperation* (Washington, DC: Center for American Progress, 2018), https://www.americanprogress.org/issues/green/reports/2018/05/21/451064/blue-future/.
15. A Chinese interlocutor dates the origin of the term Blue Economy to a 1999 Canadian forum on "The 'Blue Economy' as a Key to Sustainable Development of the St. Lawrence"; bolstering the claim is the subsequent development of "Blue" clusters in St. Johns, Quebec, Halifax, NS, BC. Interviewed by author (2015).
16. Gunther Pauli, *The Blue Economy: 10 Years, 100 Innovations, 100 Million Jobs*, Report of the Club of Rome (Taos, NM: Paradigm Publications, 2010).
17. Personal communications with the author. See also Kathleen A. Walsh, "Understanding China's Blue Economy," *The Bridge* (Newport, RI: US Naval War College Foundation, 2014), 25.
18. Kathleen A. Walsh, "China's Blue Economy: Ambitions and Responsibilities" in Conference Report (Washington, DC: Center for American Progress, 2014), 19–25, https://cdn.americanprogress.org/wp-content/uploads/2014/11/ChinaReport-Global-FINAL.pdf
19. Anna Maria Eikeset et al., "What Is Blue Growth? The Semantics of 'Sustainable Development' of Marine Environments." *Marine Policy*, 87 (2018): 177–9.
20. OECD, *The Ocean Economy in 2030* (2016).
21. Kevin Charles, "Marine Science and Blue Growth: Assessing the Marine Academic Production of 123 Cities and Territories Worldwide." *Marine Policy*, 84 (2017): 119–29.
22. Luca Mulazzani and Giulio Malorgio, "Blue Growth and Ecosystem Services." *Marine Policy*, 85 (2017): 17–24.
23. Ocean Policy Committee, *Ocean Climate Action Plan* (Washington, DC: The White House, 2023).
24. Matt Merighi, "The Ocean Economy: Entrepreneurship and Maritime Security," Lecture of Opportunity at US Naval War College, Newport, RI (May 8, 2018).
25. Michael Conathan et al., *Blue Future: Mapping Opportunities for U.S.-China Ocean Cooperation* (Washington, DC: Center for American Progress, 2018), https://www.americanprogress.org/issues/green/reports/2018/05/21/451064/blue-future/.
26. Bureau of Economic Analysis, "Marine Satellite Account, 2021," Press Release (June 8, 2023), https://www.bea.gov/news/2023/marine-economy-satellite-account-2021.

27. In 2018, Commerce used the term "US Ocean and Great Lakes Economy," which calculated the contributions made by six economic sectors in the national economy as well as part of state and regional economies. These six sectors were: (1) living resources; (2) marine construction; (3) marine transportation; (4) offshore mineral extraction; (5) ship and boat building; and (6) tourism and recreation. NOAA Office for Coastal Management, *NOAA Report on the U.S. Ocean and Great Lakes Economy: Regional and State Profiles* (Charleston, SC: NOAA, 2018), 1–4.
28. Kathleen A. Walsh, "China's Blue Economy: Ambitions and Responsibilities" in Conference Report (Washington, DC: Center for American Progress, 2014), 19–25, https://cdn.americanprogress.org/wp-content/uploads/2014/11/ChinaReport-Global-FINAL.pdf.
29. For instance, see W. Chan Kim and Renee Mauborne's *Blue Ocean Strategy: How to Create Uncontested Market Space and Make the Competition Irrelevant* (Boston: Harvard Business School Publishing Corporation, 2015) and its follow-on, *Blue Ocean Shift: Beyond Competing – Proven Steps to Inspire Confidence and Seize New Growth* (New York: Hachette Books, 2017), both of which focus on identifying and adopting innovative business strategies not tied necessarily to marine or maritime concerns; as such, these "blue" initiatives should not be confused with broader Blue Economy efforts.
30. The World Bank and United Nations Department of Economic and Social Affairs, *The Potential of the Blue Economy: Increasing Long-Term Benefits of the Sustainable Use of Marine Resources for Small Island Developing States and Coastal Least Developed Countries* (Washington, DC: The World Bank, 2017), iv.
31. The Economist Intelligence Unit, "The Blue Economy: Growth, Opportunity and a Sustainable Ocean Economy," Briefing Paper for the World Ocean Summit, 2015 (London: EIU, 2015), 7.
32. Michael Porter, "Clusters and the New Economics of Competition." *Harvard Business Review*, 76, 6 (1998): 77–90.
33. Mercedes Delgado and Scott Stern, "The US Cluster Mapping Project: A New Tool for Regional Economic Development," US Cluster Mapping Launch Event at University of Minnesota in Minneapolis, MN: Institute for Strategy and Competitiveness, Harvard Business School (2014), 3, https://clustermapping.us/sites/default/files/files/resource/SS%20MD%20USCMP%20Launch%20Minneapolis%2009%2029%2014_FINAL_V3.pdf.
34. Michael B. Jones, "The Maritime Alliance & International BlueTech Collaboration," Presentation to the US-European Union Cluster Collaboration Seminar (May 16, 2017), 3, https://clustercollaboration.eu/sites/default/files/event_calendar/the_maritime_alliance.pdf.
35. Delgado and Stern, "US Cluster Mapping Project."
36. Robert D. Atkinson, Mark Muro, and Jacob Whiton, *The Case for Growth Centers: How to Spread Tech Innovation across America, Report* (Washington, DC: Metropolitan Policy Program, The Brookings Institution, 2019), 93, https://www.brookings.edu/wp-content/uploads/2019/12/Full-Report-Growth-Centers_PDF_BrookingsMetro-BassCenter-ITIF.pdf.
37. David Hume, A Growing Blue Economy in North America," *The Maritime Executive* (May 27, 2018).
38. David Hume, A Growing Blue Economy in North America."

39. This initiative is called RISE-UP, which stands for resilient, innovative, sustainable economies vis university partnerships. Its purpose is to "bring 'dual-use' products and technology to the commercial market, as well as launching new business ventures to have positive impacts on Rhode Island's, Alaska's and Hawaii's economies." James Bassette, "URI Research Foundation Received $2.4M Federal Grant to Launch RISE-UP Blue Economy Initiative," *Providence Business News* (June 15, 2023), https://pbn.com/uri-research-foundation-receives-2-4m-federal-grant-to-launch-rise-up-blue-economy-initiative/.
40. US Congress, *James M. Inhofe National Defense Authorization Act for Fiscal Year 2023*, Sec. 10202: Regional Ocean Partnerships (December 23, 2022).
41. NDAA FY2023.
42. ERISS Corporation and The Maritime Alliance, *The Ocean Enterprise: A Study of US Business Activity in Ocean Measurement, Observation and Forecasting*, Commissioned Study for the US Department of Commerce (Washington, DC: NOAA Integrated Ocean Observing System, 2017), https://cdn.ioos.noaa.gov/media/2017/12/oceanenterprise_Feb2017_secure.pdf.
43. ERISS and The Maritime Alliance, *The Ocean Enterprise*.
44. NOAA, The Ocean Enterprise Study 2015–2020: A Study of New Blue Economic Business Activity (Washington, DC: US Department of Commerce, 2021), https://cdn.ioos.noaa.gov/media/2021/12/OE-REPORT-2015_2020-FINAL_120721_web.pdf.
45. Nathan Strout, "US Lawmakers Want to Fund Creation of More Ocean Innovation Clusters," *SeafoodSource* (June 9, 2023), www.seafood.com.
46. New England Ocean Cluster representative interviewed by author, Portland, ME (2017).
47. Jones, "The Maritime Alliance & International BlueTech Collaboration," 8.
48. Hansen et al., *Ocean/Maritime Clusters: Leadership and Collaboration for Ocean Sustainable Development and Implementing the Sustainable Development Goals*, World Ocean Council White Paper 1, 808 (Economic Transformations and World Ocean Council, February 2018), 1–33, https://www.oceancouncil.org/wp-content/uploads/2018/03/EXEC-SUM-Ocean-Maritime-Clusters-and-Sustainable-Development-.pdf.
49. Hansen et al., 4–5.

References

Kathleen Walsh, interviews of US Blue Economy experts and advocates. 2012–19.

Atkinson, Robert D., Mark Muro, and Jacob Whiton. 2019. *The Case for Growth Centers: How to Spread Tech Innovation Across America*. Report, Metropolitan Policy Program, The Brookings Institution and Information Technology & Innovation Foundation. Washington, DC: The Brookings Institution, 93. https://www.brookings.edu/wp-content/uploads/2019/12/Full-Report-Growth-Centers_PDF_BrookingsMetro-BassCenter-ITIF.pdf.

BRI International Green Development Coalition. 2020. *BRI Green Development Case Study Report (2020)*. BRI International Green Development Coalition. http://en.brigc.net/Reports/research_subject/202011/P020201129780236943177.pdf.

Bureau of Economic Analysis. 2023. *Marine Economy Satellite Account, 2021*, June 8. https://www.bea.gov/news/2023/marine-economy-satellite-account-2021.

———. 2023. *Marine Satellite Account, 2021*. The BEA Wire, June 8. https://www.bea.gov/news/blog/2023-06-08/marine-economy-satellite-account-2021.

Charles, Kevin. 2017. "Marine Science and Blue Growth: Assessing the Marine Academic Production of 123 Cities and Territories Worldwide." *Marine Policy* (Elsvier) 84: 119–129.

Cogan, Charles S. 2016. "Ocean Accounts from National Income to Blue Economy." *Journal of Ocean and Coastal Economics: Special Issue: Oceans and National Income* (Center for the Blue Economy, Middlebury Institute of International Studies) 2 (2). https://cbe.miis.edu/joce/vol2/iss2/12.

Conathan, Michael, Melanie Hart, Blaine Johnson, and Shiva Polefka. 2018. *Blue Future: Mapping Opportunities for US-China Ocean Cooperation*. Conference Report, Center for American Progress, Washington, DC: Center for American Progress. https://www.americanprogress.org/issues/green/reports/2018/05/21/451064/blue-future/.

Delgado, Mercedes, and Scott Stern. 2014. "The US Cluster Mapping Project: A New Tool for Regional Economic Development." *US Cluster Mapping Launch Event at University of Minnesota in Minneapolis, MN*. Minneapolis, MN: Institute for Strategy and Competitiveness, Harvard Business School. Accessed 2018.

Economist Intelligence Unit. 2015. *The Blue Economy: Growth, Opportunity and a Sustainable Ocean Economy*. Briefing Paper for the World Ocean Summit 2015, The Economist Intelligence Unit, London: The Economist, 20.

Eikeset, Anne Maria, Anna B. Mazzarella, Simon A. Levin, Brynhildur Daviosdottir, Dane H. Klinger, Elena Rovenskaya, and Nils Chr Stenseth. 2018. "What is Blue Growth? The Semantics of "Sustainable Development" of Marine Environments." *Marine Policy* (Elsevier Ltd.) 87: 177–179.

ERISS Corporation and The Maritime Alliance. 2017. *The Ocean Enterprise: A Study of US Business Activity in Ocean Measurement, Observation and Forecasting*. Commissioned Study, US Department of Commerce, Washington, DC: NOAA Integrated Ocean Observing System. https://cdn.ioos.noaa.gov/media/2017/12/oceanenterprise_Feb2017_secure.pdf.

European Commission. 2023. *The EU Blue Economy Report 2023*. Luxembourg: Publications Office of the European Union. https://op.europa.eu/en/publication-detail/-/publication/9a345396-f9e9-11ed-a05c-01aa75ed71a1.

Hansen, Eric Rolf, Paul Holthus, Christopher L. Allen, Jeeho Bae, Judy Goh, Cristina Mihailescu, and Claire Pedregon. 2018. *Ocean/Maritime Clusters: Leadership and Collabortion for Ocean Sustainable Development and Implementing the Sustainable Development Goals*. World Ocean Council White Paper 1, 808, Economic Transformations Group & World Ocean Council. https://www.oceancouncil.org/wp-content/uploads/2018/03/EXEC-SUM-Ocean-Maritime-Clusters-and-Sustainable-Development-.pdf.

Hume, David. 2018. "A Growing Blue Economy in North America." *The Maritime Executive*, May 27.

Jones, Michael B. 2017. "The Maritime Alliance & International BlueTech Collaboration." *Presentation to the US-European Union Cluster Collaboration Seminar,* May 16. https://clustercollaboration.eu/sites/default/files/event_calendar/the_maritime_alliance.pdf.

Kim, W. Chan, and Renee Mauborne. 2017. *Blue Ocean Shift: Beyond Competing -- Proven Steps to Inspire Confidence and Seize New Growth.* New York: Hachette Books.

———. 2015. *Blue Ocean Strategy: How to Create Uncontested Market Space and Make the Competition Irrelevant.* Boston, MA: Harvard Business School Publishing Corporation.

Merighi, Matt. 2018. "The Ocean Economy: Entrepreneurship and Maritime Security." *Newport, RI,* May 8.

Mulazzani, Luca, and Giulio Malorgio. 2017. "Blue Growth and Ecosystem Services." *Marine Policy* (Elsevier Ltd.) 85: 17–24.

National Oceanic and Atmospheric Administration. 2021. *The Ocean Enterprise Study 2015–2020: A Study of New Blue Economic Business Activity.* Washington, DC: US Department of Commerce. https://cdn.ioos.noaa.gov/media/2021/12/OE-REPORT-2015_2020-FINAL_120721_web.pdf.

———. 2018. *NOAA Report on the U.S. Ocean and Great Lakes Economy: Regional and State Profiles.* Charleston, SC: NOAA Office for Coastal Management, 1–4. http:/coast.noaa.gov/data/digitalcoast/pdf/econ-report.pdf.

New England Ocean Cluster, Representative, interview by Kathleen A. Walsh. 2017. Portland, ME.

Ocean Foundation, et al. 2022. "Blue Tech Clusters in the Northern Arc of the Atlantic," June 16. https://storymaps.arcgis.com/stories/da20701b27734791a5a3809ade24adc2.

Ocean Foundation, et al. 2023. "Blue Tech Clusters of America," April 5. http://storymaps.argix.com/stories/3c3e46acf92f4f39bc42ca2b8307ae99.

Ocean Policy Committee. 2023. *Ocean Climate Action Plan: A Report by the Ocean Policy Committee.* Washington, DC: The White House. https://www.whitehouse.gov/wp-content/uploads/2023/03/Ocean-Climate-Action-Plan_Final.pdf.

OECD. 2016. *The Ocean Economy in 2030.* Paris: OECD Publishing.

Pauli, Gunther. 2010. *The Blue Economy: 10 Years, 100 Innovations, 100 Million Jobs.* Report to the Club of Rome, Taos, NM: Paradigm Publications.

Pearce, David, Anil Markandya, and Edward Barbier. 1989. *Blueprint for a Green Economy.* E-book - Routledge, Taylor & Francis (Reprint Series, Blueprint 1) 2013, London: Earthscan Publications. Accessed March 13, 2023. https://doi.org/10.4324/9780203097298.

Porter, Michael E. 1998. "Clusters and the New Economics of Competition." *Harvard Business Review,* 6: 77–90.

PRC, official, interview by Author. 2015. Beijing.

Providence Business News. 2023. "URI Research Foundation Received $2.4M Federal Grant to Launch RISE-UP Blue Economy Initiative." June 15. https://pbn.com/uri-research-foundation-receives-2-4m-federal-grant-to-launch-rise-up-blue-economy-initiative/.

Strout, Nathan. 2023. "US Lawmakers Want to Fund Creation of More Ocean Innovation Clusters." *SeafoodSource,* June 9.

The World Bank and United Nations Department of Economic and Social Affairs. 2017. *The Potential of the Blue Economy: Increasing Long-term Benefits of the Sustainable Use of Marine Resources for Small Islad Developing States and Coastal Least Developed Countries*. Washington, DC: The World Bank, vi. www.worldbank.org.

TMA BlueTech and Ocean Foundation. 2021. "The Blue Wave: Investing in BlueTech Clusters to Maintain Leadership and Promote Economic Growth and Job Creation." http://oceanfdn.org/wp-content/uploads/2021/04/The-Blue-Wave.pdf.

United Nations Environment Program (UNEP). 2023. *Green Economy*. Accessed March 13, 2023. https://www.unep.org/regions/asia-and-pacific/regional-initiatives/supporting-resource-efficiency/green-economy.

United Nations Environmental Program (UNEP). 2012. *Green Economy in a Blue World*. 14th Global Meeting of the Regional Seas Convention and Action Plans, Nairobi: United Nations Environment Program. https://wedocs.unep.org/bitstream/handle/20.500.11822/12499/RS.14_INF.1.RS.pdf?sequence=1&amp%3BisAllowed=.

US Congress. 2022. "James M. Inhofe National Defense Authorization Act for Fiscal Year 2023, Sec. 10202: Regional Ocean Partnerships." December 23.

Walsh, Kathleen A. 2014. *China's Blue Economy: Ambitions and Responsibilities*. Conference Report, Center for American Progress. Washington, DC: CAP, 19–25. https://cdn.americanprogress.org/wp-content/uploads/2014/11/ChinaReport-Global-FINAL.pdf.

Walsh, Kathleen A. 2016. "The Blue Economy & Environmental Security: Implications for the South China Sea," Presentation at the Walker Institute, University of South Carolina (September).

———. 2014. "Understanding China's Blue Economy." *The Bridge*.

Xie, Zhihai. 2021. *Government Policy, Industrial Clusters, and the Blue Economy in the People's Republic of China: A Case Study on the Shandong Peninsula Blue Econmic Zone*. ADBI Working Paper No. 1296. Tokyo: Asian Development Bank Institute, 20. http://www.adb.org/sites/default/files/publication/762206/adbi-wp1296.pdf.

Xinhua News Agency. 2021. *Xi Focus: Building a Maritime Community with Shared Future for the Blue Planet*, June 7. http://www.xinhuanet.com/english/2021-06/07/c_139994197.htm.

3

China's Blue Economy Concept and Evolution

China's meteoric rise is historically unprecedented. This rapid change has led to fast-paced developments in PRC society as well as its industrial, technological, and military capabilities. Following over four decades of economic reforms, China's economy is currently number one or two in the world, depending on how one calculates gross domestic product (GDP). Consequently, many millions once suffering severe poverty now live more comfortable and perhaps also more rewarding lives than they might have otherwise. Others in China have become entrepreneurs, industry titans, and high-technology industry leaders. According to a *Forbes* list, there were over 100 billionaires in China in 2022. China's military has been advancing rapidly as well, today boasting the world's largest naval fleet as well as advanced fighter jets, aircraft carriers, hypersonic missiles, and more of the world's most sophisticated military capabilities.

But the PRC's industrial revolution, like those in earlier eras elsewhere, has come at a cost, particularly to China's natural environment. Among Beijing's most pressing policy conundrums is how to continue industrial, technological, and military modernization while also pursuing more environmentally sustainable approaches to development. Such policy challenges and tradeoffs are not unique to China. But if Chinese Communist Party leaders wish to continue China's rise in a way that will lead to lasting power, particularly in maritime and naval terms, dealing with the long-term damage done to the environment already, and that which continues as a result of industrial development, will be essential. To date, however, it appears that Beijing's quest for economic and industrial development remains a top priority, even if at times at the expense of marine conservation. China's approach to the marine environment—at home and abroad—is also an important consideration for leaders in Beijing seeking to export China's model of development and, thereby, expand PRC influence to other countries seeking to replicate China's advances.

China's Blue Economy concept represents a potential solution (or at least partial response) to its industrial, innovation, and environmental challenges at home and is being promoted abroad as beneficial to other states dealing with similar issues. How China's concept of the Blue Economy develops and is implemented will be an indicator of what type of power China becomes and how the PRC is viewed by its neighbors in the Indo-Pacific region and

DOI: 10.1201/9781003396116-3

beyond. Chinese leader Xi Jinping has adopted the Blue Economy as a key feature of contemporary Chinese development and diplomacy and as a means of gaining strategic influence and promoting international investment and trade agreements, as well as being an aspect of China's efforts to project its military power and presence.

China's Environmental Crisis amid Quest for Growth

It is not news that China has a problem with pollution, both in its air and its water. Visitors to China often return with congested lungs and nasal passages, possibly due to breathing polluted air. Visitors are advised not to drink the water unless boiled. Beijing, in particular, is facing air pollution that is so bad on a regular basis that enormously large television screens set up in Tiananmen Square and showing a sunset were rumored to be for Beijing residents who rarely see the sun set due to the level of air pollution in the sky, regularly made worse by the dust blowing in from the nearby Gobi Desert. The image, projected in January 2014, actually was reported later as being part of a tourism ad campaign.[1] But the initial story ran worldwide and resonated anyway given its potential to be true.

China's air pollution problem was made starkly vivid when riding on a train starting in coastal Qingdao, where blue sky slowly transformed into smoggy gray skies as we traveled toward Beijing. Upon disembarking the train in China's capital, there were visible particles in the air on what was a particularly bad air-quality day. The cost of China's air pollution is alarming. Over a million people in China are estimated to have died prematurely due to air pollution.[2]

China's waterways are also polluted due to neglect, decades of industrial development, and dumping or seeping of toxic residues and sewage into nearby waters. This is not a problem unique to China. Where I grew up in industrial New England, one could not drink the water from the Merrimack River without getting sick (my grandmother did once and was hospitalized as a result). A proud theme song of nearby Boston is a beloved tune called "Dirty Water" by The Standells about the nasty, brackish, and sewage-laden water that used to be the Charles River. It is only through extensive efforts over decades by the community and with years of assistance from the federal government that the river has been cleaned up substantially. Although one still might not want to drink directly from it, boating, sailing, kayaking, and other marine activities—even swimming—are popular now along the Charles River. The Charles is today a main tourist attraction running by Harvard University, Massachusetts Institute of Technology (MIT), the Esplanade, and concert venue Hatch Shell, among other attractions, rather than an area to be avoided. A Chinese colleague, inspired by this example of marine conservation, once remarked that if Boston can clean up its notorious "dirty water" Charles, then Beijing can do the same. No doubt this is true. But China has an added obstacle in its way, which is its cultural attitude toward water and particularly coastal areas, which are traditionally viewed more as extensions of land to be exploited than as natural habitats to be preserved and enjoyed by the public, as is more apparent in the Western mindset.

China's coastline from its northern border with North Korea to the southern border with Vietnam (not counting disputed or other offshore islands) spans over 11,000 miles (18,000 kilometers) long.[3] Most tourists or other visitors to China, however, are unlikely to have sunbathed at the beach, gone boating recreationally, or surfed the waves of the East or South China Seas. This is because China's coastline is generally not oriented toward the ocean and toward tourism, at least not in the way or to the degree that beaches and coastal tourism are viewed in the West. Even in Qingdao, China, a region known for having a degree of environmental awareness, for having popular, relatively well-kept beaches, sea-side resorts, and as home to the infamous "tankini" spandex-based ultraviolet protection face mask, the number of beachgoers is not what one might expect in another coastal community elsewhere in the world where the beach, itself, represents a central destination for leisure and relaxation and is a popular holiday get away.

China's leaders are regularly pictured taking to the waters of the Bohai Sea each August in the resort town of *Beidaihe* where they go to escape the sweltering summer heat of Beijing and to make future Chinese Communist Party plans. Yet, even this high-powered beachgoing is viewed as an oddity more than something regular Chinese people often do (or can do), much less tourists.[4] As indicated by Qingdao's facekini masks, nor do Chinese people typically go to the beach for a tan, in part because more natural or pearly skin color is considered ideal. Nor is swimming a widely known skill in China (probably for the same reasons it was not in my own ancestors' homeland of Ireland), making beach going and boating potentially more hazardous. This perspective toward China's coastline and beach areas is important to understand when considering China's Blue Economy—the concept does not stem from the West's own, contemporary conservation-minded (or at least preservation-oriented) approach to the beach and our coastlines as having inherent value to the community, to the economy, and to the marine environment. As has been pointed out to me by Chinese colleagues, the different outlooks mark an important distinction and starting point when developing the Blue Economy.

While the attitude in China might be changing as the economy lifts people out of poverty, life styles change, and government policies incentivize more environmentally conscious policies in coastal regions and beyond, such a cultural shift will take time. China's government is actively trying to invoke in the Chinese population a sense of what the Party terms "ecological civilization" and an "ocean consciousness." Nevertheless, though marine conservation is a part of China's plans, and challenges such as coastal erosion and other issues do arise as concerns, interest in protecting the marine and beach environment typically observed in California or the Mediterranean is not the primary driver behind China's pursuit of a Blue Economy.

In fact, there was a good reason why someone like myself researching Chinese strategies, plans, and policies on science, technology, and innovation early on ran across the term Blue Economy. That is because China values the Blue Economy concept mainly as a means to realizing more innovative technological development in its marine, maritime, and naval sectors. The latter is what will help return China to its maritime heritage and to be not just a continental Great Power but also a global maritime Great Power. Chinese citizens, however, according to their government, lack an "ocean consciousness," leading central authorities to implement an extensive campaign on educating the Chinese public on ocean and marine matters as part of a larger effort to foster thinking on China as a maritime Great Power.[5] Sustainability is important to the concept, as is promoting a degree of marine conservation, but not as important as the technology and industrial innovation that a Blue Economy promises for Beijing's global maritime and naval ambitions.

This prioritization of the elements of China's Blue Economy concept, heavily favoring technological innovation aspects over others like conservation and sustainability, is not only this author's own interpretation but also that of PRC researchers, officials, and environmentalists. A non-profit environmental activist in northern China, for instance, shared the same conclusion, as have other environmentally conscious interlocutors from China engaged with over the years. These encounters occurred prior to the Chinese government's more recent clampdowns on speech and on any sort of criticism of Xi Jinping's Chinese Communist Party governance, when dialogue was somewhat more fruitful and conversations on matters of policy a little less risky to discuss. That Chinese citizens concerned about environmental matters were brave enough to share their insights and at some risk to themselves even then is something to admire and to take seriously.

To fully understand China's Blue Economy concept and how it differs from the United States or other Western approaches, however, it is essential to understand the concept's evolution in China. The innovation element of China's Blue Economy concept, while always important, was not the primary driver *initially* in pursuing this approach. In fact, the environmental and marine conservation elements took priority in the early days of developing China's Blue Economy. Over time, however, the emphasis has shifted toward innovation and also more toward the Blue Economy as a foreign policy tool in addition to a domestic development strategy. This evolution of China's concept holds important implications for how the concept is wielded in US–China strategic competition in the Indo Pacific and beyond as well as for issues like climate change that rely on China's and other states' approach to the environment.

China's Blue Economy Concept

As already indicated, China's Blue Economy development plans are similar to those in the United States and elsewhere but also have distinct differences. Most importantly, while all three main components of a Blue Economy—maritime industry, marine conservation, and commercial maritime and naval innovation—are evident in China's conception, the last (innovation) is the primary driver in the PRC's contemporary approach and, thus, most important to understanding China's own conception of a Blue Economy. At the same time, China has attempted for decades to foster increased awareness and conservation of its marine environment, with mixed results to date. It remains to be seen how much China's Blue Economy concept will enhance marine conservation and sustainable development efforts, or whether these will continue to advance slowly as a last priority behind the industrial and innovative elements of China's Blue Economy concept.

The term "Blue Economy" in Chinese is translated literally as *lánsè jīngjì*. This is, indeed, the term used most often to convey the concept of developing a Blue Economy in contemporary Chinese literature. For instance, China's 13th Five-Year Plan for National Marine Economic Development uses the term *lánsè jīngjì* throughout the document.

Other terms are also used, however, and at times are used interchangeably or to narrow or broaden the scope (for example, to focus more specifically on *maritime* or *marine* aspects of developing a Blue Economy).[6] Chinese authors commonly use the terms "Ocean Economy" or "Marine Economy" to designate maritime and marine industry activities, respectively, or to address China's broader maritime strategic interests (as discussed below); the concept of the Blue Economy is conceptually broader than a focus on industry in that it also includes the notion of sustainable development and marine conservation as part of an industry and innovation ecosystem.

When discussing the "Maritime," "Marine," or "Ocean" Economy, the Chinese translation typically used is *hǎiyáng jīngjì*, which translates literally as ocean economy. The latter term appears to have been favored over the term Blue Economy (*lánsè jīngjì*), at least around the years 2014–16. As a senior Chinese interlocutor at the time explained, the term *hǎiyáng jīngjì* (which he translated as Marine Economy) had been the preferred term in Beijing, as it included China's deep-sea interests and not only offshore or littoral interests, which is how the term Blue Economy was conceived at the time in Chinese documents, he said.

Another top scholar indicated, however, that the term Blue Economy (*lánsè jīngjì*) had been reconceived as part of the 13th Five-Year Plan (2016–20) to be focused more on deep sea, far seas concerns and as tied to the Maritime Silk Road. Hence, with the redefinition of the Blue Economy to reflect more of China's deep-sea and foreign policy interests, the coastal, shallow waters were designated as the "yellow economy" at this time. Since then, however, the term *lánsè jīngjì* translated as Blue Economy appears to have become used more widely in China for both coastal and far seas endeavors, likely also due to the term's use in China's foreign policy agenda. When discussing the Blue Economy, another term sometimes used is a combination: the "blue ocean economy" or *lánsè hǎiyáng jīngjì*.

Such delineations, shifts, and complications in meaning can be confounding to outside observers. The European Union's annual Blue Economy report noted in its 2021 version simply that China uses the terms "maritime economy" and "ocean economy" interchangeably with Blue Economy. Nonetheless, it is important when analyzing PRC documents to take note of the different terms being used to determine what aspect(s) of a Blue Economy are included in their assessments (or not), as well as how China's use of these different terms has changed over time.

A review of existing keywords referenced in the Chinese National Knowledge Infrastructure (CNKI) database of Chinese-language periodicals conducted in June 2022 also indicates that the term "blue economy" is more popularly used relative to the terms "marine economy" or "ocean economy." The CNKI database includes peer-reviewed PRC journals, some official documents, dissertations, and other scholarly information. Notably, though run by an ostensibly private information technology firm founded by Tsinghua University, the Chinese government has closed or limited access to CNKI and other online databases to some foreign institutions (including my own), making further inquiries difficult if not impossible. This is terribly unfortunate and shortsighted given the West's interest in better understanding modern China and during the post-COVID era when in-person access to Chinese libraries and other resources is more difficult as well. Without online access to PRC ideas and public, published analyses contained in such databases, our comprehension of what China thinks and what is happening will be sharply reduced (which is likely the idea behind restricting access).

Prior to being shut out, for the period 2007–22, periodicals citing the keyword "Blue Economy" (as translated from the Chinese term, *lánsè jīngjì*) appeared in the CNKI database in a maximum of 132 articles in the year 2013, with a total of 990 articles overall during this time period (comprising primarily dissertations and journal articles).[7] The top number declined through 2019 down to 25 articles and, following a brief uptick in 2020–21 to over 50 articles each year, landed at only 11 articles referenced as of mid-2022. Most articles (33 percent) focused on what the database termed "Reform of the economic system" followed by "Oceanography" (18 percent) and "Macroeconomic Management" (8.3 percent), a term that appears mainly related to transportation development programs. The majority of articles (143) over this period were authored by the Ocean University of China, with Shandong Normal University following with only 50 articles and Shandong University with 33 articles.

Not surprisingly, the term "Blue Economy" is referenced more often in CNKI-listed periodicals than is the term "Ocean Economy." The term "Ocean

Economy" appears in the database even earlier, from 1994 through 2021, but topped out at 14 references in 2012. References to the keyword "Ocean Economy" increased from 2008 to 2012, but then declined, with only two articles listed for 2021. Most references came from periodicals and newspaper articles. Ocean University of China again topped the list with 14 articles overall, followed by Guangdong Ocean University (8) and Ningbo University (7). Most of these articles focus on "Oceanography" (31.3 percent), "Reform of the economic system" (26.4 percent), and "Macroeconomic management" (9.8 percent). The decline in use of the term "Ocean Economy" fits with the shift toward using the term "Blue Economy."

A keyword search for "Blue Economy" also resulted in more references in CNKI's database than for the term "Marine Economy." From 1994 to 2022, "Marine Economy" tops out at 116 articles (2013) with an increase beginning in 2006 and declining after 2013 only marginally until a sharp drop off in 2021–22 to 27 references, a decline that could be related to COVID effects but also supports the shift toward employing the term "Blue Economy" under Xi Jinping-era strategies and plans. Most articles keyed to the term "Marine Economy" focus on "Oceanography" (43.8 percent), followed by "Reform of the economic system" (30 percent) and "Macroeconomic management" (1.3 percent). Dissertations and journal articles again dominate the total of 1,268 articles published with this keyword reference. Ocean University of China again tops the list of contributors at 143 references but was followed by Liaoning University at 121 and the State Information Center of the State Oceanic Administration (SOA) at 81.

This cursory review of CNKI database literature shows the relatively recent focus on and adoption of the term "Blue Economy," with a high of 132 articles in 2013, possibly related to planning for the 13th Five-Year Plan that spanned 2016–20. At the same time, the term "Blue Economy," though more popular than the other two keyword terms referenced, is far less popular a topic than, for instance, the Belt and Road Initiative (BRI). For comparison, a contemporaneous keyword search for the Belt and Road Initiative (translated as "One Belt, One Road" or *yīdài yīlù*) from 2015 to 2022 showed a high of 755 articles cited in 2018, with a low of 163 references to the keyword in 2022 (comparing favorably to the Blue Economy term's *high* of 132 references in one year).

The term "Blue Economy," when compared to the other two terms reviewed in the Chinese database, is also used in a more strategic manner and is focused on macro-economic development concerns, both domestic and overseas. The term "Marine Economy" is a more technically and economic policy-oriented phrasing. "Ocean Economy" is not as popular a term of art but is used at times in lieu of both of the other terms, particularly in cross-country comparisons.

While the term Blue Economy is relatively new in Chinese literature, the concept isn't wholly so. In fact, China has long acknowledged the need for, and sought to develop, a marine economy (encompassing, in the Chinese context, marine and maritime industries) and to institute more environmentally friendly policies and sustainable development strategies.

In 1998, for instance, the year of the United Nations-designated "International Ocean Year," the Chinese government published a White Paper on "The Development of China's Marine Programs." The paper noted that, "As a major developing country with a long coastline, China attaches great importance to marine development and protection, and takes it as the state's development strategy."[8] The White Paper also cites an earlier 1996 initiative (China Ocean Agenda 21) that "put forward a sustainable development strategy for China's marine programs," and that appears to be a precursor to later Blue Economy plans given the 1998 White Paper's emphasis on sustainable development of the marine sector and of "coastal economic belts and marine economic zones" as well as "reinforcing oceanographic technology research and development," among other objectives. The 1998 White Paper even notes that "in the early 1990s China built up a basic network jointly run by government departments, concerned enterprises, research institutes and coastal zones to promote oceanographic information exchanges," an apt description of what contemporary experts would want for and would call an ocean, maritime, or Blue Economy cluster.

Yet, in adopting the term Blue Economy, more contemporary PRC plans appear to give only cursory attention to marine environmental and conservation concerns. For example, in describing plans for developing Qingdao's Blue Economy Zone in 2014, the periodical *China Ocean News* outlines the plan's singular mission according to Qingdao's then-deputy mayor as being to establish a "Maritime Economy" that focuses mainly on economic and industrial aims as well as "building China into a great maritime power."[9] While marine environmental protection and conservation objectives are listed, they are clearly not the priority in this plan, which emphasizes scientific, technological, and civil-military integration aspects of maritime industrial development.[10] This same sentiment, that marine environmental protection and conservation objectives were part of China's Blue Economy conception but not the priority, has been echoed over many years by a variety of experts the author has engaged with in China and beyond.

China's marine environmental efforts pre-date adoption of the Blue Economy concept in PRC plans and continue to be implemented but, in practice, in ways that appear largely separate from contemporary Blue Economy development efforts. This dual-track approach holds important implications for how effective and sustainable (in every sense) China's domestic and foreign Blue Economy investments will turn out. Before exploring China's Blue Economy concept in greater detail, the following section provides a brief overview of China's marine environmental efforts and how they tie into China Blue Economy plans.

China's Marine Environmental Efforts and Ties to the Blue Economy

China's marine environmental conservation efforts lag more traditional, land-based environmental activities, which similarly struggle for attention and support in China given the Chinese Communist Party's long-time prioritization of economic development, often at the expense of environmental and conservation considerations. For marine environmental concerns, an added challenge is the contemporary Chinese public's low interest in, or limited connection to, marine, maritime, or ocean concerns unless directly involved in them.

As explained by a Chinese scholar in 2014, the marine environment and oceans in China have been viewed largely as areas to further exploit for economic development, particularly as land-based resources across Mainland China have been depleted and toxified, that is, used up.[11] Xi Jinping has emphasized the need to establish among the Chinese people the idea of establishing an "ecological civilization." The term, while not original to China, has been adopted and the concept made part of China's Constitution in 2018. The term as applied in China means generally achieving a harmony between man and nature and is intended to be the means by which the PRC can attain its commitment to the United Nation's Sustainable Development Goals (SDGs), among other goals.[12]

China's marine environment continues to struggle, however, due to widespread pollution, over-fishing, and the effects of land reclamation, climate change, and more. A recent review of Chinese marine environmental governance assesses part of the reason for the country's limited marine conservation success to date to be due to a delayed understanding of its importance to sustained economic development. "Different from Japan, the EU, the US and other major marine economies, marine environmental governance of China started in the 1980s, much later than them, and faces a more serious situation."[13]

China's specifically marine environmental protection efforts actually date back to 1982 with the promulgation of the national "Marine Environment Protection Law." This law was substantially revised in 1999 and included for the first time a concept to be implemented along China's coastal regions: marine functional zones (MFZ). The concept behind an MFZ is what the United States and other countries call marine spatial planning (MSP). The idea behind these zones or plans is to promote sustainability by controlling and deconflicting the various uses of a marine environment, such as boating, fishing, tourism, scientific research, and military use.

Yet, MFZs were experimental concepts in China at first and not actually established at scale until about the 1998–9 period.[14] MFZs in China became a national-level, State Council focus following passage of a 2001 *Law of the People's Republic of China on the Administration of the Use of Sea Areas*, which also provided for provincial and municipal-level MFZs to be established by 2010.[15] China's State Council followed with a new *National Marine Functional Zoning (2011–2020)* plan that covers all coastal provinces in China.[16]

China's national-level MFZs today have six objectives: "(1) protecting the marine environment; (2) maintaining sustainable fishery activities; (3) reining in the scale of sea reclamation; (4) reserving marine space resources; (5) conserving natural mainland shoreline; and (6) repairing and restoring coastal and marine areas."[17]

Similarly, a review of marine environmental governance documents indicates that it was only around 2001, with the 10th Five-Year Plan (2001–5), that Chinese authorities began to focus not only on addressing existing marine environmental concerns but also on preventing further environmental degradation.[18] This latter period also saw increased attention paid to science and technology as a means of solving current issues as well as preventing future environmental problems.[19]

By the time of the 11th Five-Year Plan (2006–10), marine environmental governance had expanded to focus specifically on islands, the idea of ecosystems, and marine protected areas (MPAs).[20] By 2010, *the Law of the People's Republic of China on Island Protection* entered into force. This law includes a particular focus on "Special Purpose Islands." The latter "include islands used as base points for designation of the territorial sea, islands used for national defense and islands located within marine nature reserves."[21]

Subsequent Five-Year Plans have also included elements of marine environmental protection measures, but these are clearly not Beijing's top priority. China's *13th Five-Year Plan for the Development of the National Marine Economy* issued in May 2017, for instance, emphasizes economic development, marine, and maritime industrial development, improved maritime services and infrastructure, major scientific and innovation efforts, and opportunities presented by the Belt and Road Initiative, among other issues, all before addressing marine environmental protection and conservation efforts.[22] Other plans and related reports similarly place marine protection and conservation discussions *after* considerations related to economic and industrial aims. Although the above plan and other Chinese Communist Party policy and planning documents indicate that economic development and marine environmental protection are to be given equal weight, Beijing's continued emphasis on advancing marine and maritime industrial development and innovation is unlikely to lead to equal treatment.

Despite the growing list of concerns that loom in China's marine environment, including water shortages in Northern China, over-fished waters, and polluted coastlines, as well as rivers and streams around the country contaminated with industrial waste, it has become clear over time that China's conception of the Blue Economy prioritizes maritime industrial development and technological innovation over and above marine environmental conservation and preservation, even though the latter remain a part of the PRC's conception.[23] While Beijing focused on improving China's marine environment from the 1980s through the 2000s, and it remains an objective today, a clear shift emerged in the early 21st century toward an emphasis on prioritized development of China's marine economy and maritime industries that, in turn, became a focus on development of a Blue Economy in China.

China Shifts to Developing a Blue Economy

The People's Republic of China under the leadership of the Chinese Communist Party does not do much without a plan. This is why those trying to understand modern-day China spend copious amounts of time analyzing and comparing Chinese strategy, policy, and planning documents. These documents are useful to officials and others inside China to know what Beijing's agreed-upon plan is. The plans are useful as well to outside observers seeking to understand where China intends to go, sometimes also why, as well as how far over a given period of time.

One of the tricky aspects of assessing Chinese planning documents as an outside observer, however, is determining what are PRC aspirations and what is it that the PRC can actually achieve by the end of a particular planning cycle. Since 1953, China's Communist Party has issued regular "Five-Year Plans" that encompass the national economy as well as derivative five-year plans that address specific industry sectors and efforts at the provincial, regional, and local levels. Major initiatives tend to have lofty goals and deadlines, such as China's latest *Outline of the 14th Five-Year Plan (2021–2025) for National Economic and Social Development and the Long-Range Objectives through the Year 2035* plan. Similarly, China's goal for its military is to achieve by 2035 basic modernization. But this does not mean that China will be able to actually achieve these goals or do so by their stated deadlines, although it might. What is pretty certain about assessing Chinese strategies and plans is that they lay out at least what China *intends* to try to achieve over a set period of time.

In 2003, China's State Council (the top civilian, state decision-making body) published "An Outline of the Planning of National Marine Economy Development." The document detailed plans to achieve a Marine Economy that would contribute four percent to China's gross domestic product by 2005 and up to five percent by 2010.[24] Contemporary Chinese reports of having achieved a Marine Economy that contributes nearly ten percent of Chinese GDP suggest those goals might have been met, though the basis for the latter calculations is not entirely clear or transparent to outsiders and might well be exaggerated. What is certain is the Chinese leadership's intention to develop a robust marine economy.

In 2012, the State Council issued a new document, published in English as well as Chinese, that similarly laid out lofty goals for China's Marine Economy but also recognized challenges raised by continued marine environmental concerns.[25] The discussion of marine environmental challenges in this plan provides some explanation for where China's marine economic development might be lacking or has fallen short of Beijing's goals. As the report notes,

> The constraint of the marine ecological environment is becoming more and more apparent, and the increased effects of global climate change, marine disasters, and other problems are becoming more and more prominent. These factors have raised serious challenges to China's marine economic development.[26]

The document reflects the then-focus in China on "Scientific Development' as the guiding philosophy for national economic development and seeks to take advantage of what was viewed as favorable expanding global investment and trade dynamics. The report concludes with a chapter on marine environmental protection, but the emphasis and priority are clearly on developing China's marine and maritime industry, both at home and abroad.

It was between the time of these two reports, in 2009, that China's State Council approved five coastal development zones as a pilot-program specifically focused on advancing China's ocean and marine economies in select provinces. In doing so, China's modern leaders were applying to the Blue Economy the same, experimental approach to economic development that dates back to the Deng Xiaoping era of opening China to foreign investment via planning strategically designed Special Economic Zones (SEZ). It is at this point that China can be said to have demonstrably adopted a Blue Economy development concept.

Distributed from north to south, the provinces selected for what were termed initially pilot "Blue Economy development zones" were Shandong, Tianjin, Zhejiang, Fujian, and Guangdong.[27] This experimental zone-based development approach has since expanded further, to include ten named areas of Blue Economy development domestically and related efforts internationally, in ways that are important to understanding China's Blue Economy concept and how to cooperate and compete with it.

Despite decades of effort, however, progress toward advancing China's marine economy (meaning here both marine and maritime industries) and fostering innovation in these sectors while also improving the country's marine environment has been mixed, with the latter remaining a largely separate effort.[28] This lack of systemic progress overall is due in large part to Beijing's continued de facto emphasis on promoting economic growth often at the expense of other objectives, such as marine environmental protection. A 2013 assessment of China's ocean development was frank in its conclusions that although China's marine and maritime industries had developed rapidly, marine science and technology had only "somewhat improved" and the marine "pollution situation is still grim" while future prospects were "far from optimistic."[29] Chinese planners likely viewed the Blue Economy concept as a way to pull these efforts together into a more holistic and successful as well as sustainable endeavor. The innovation element of the Blue Economy concept, however, fit best with Chinese planners' efforts to advance the PRC's commercial maritime industrial development as well as naval and other defense-related capabilities.

By the time of the 13th Five-Year Plan (2016–20), China's Marine Economy development plan issued in 2017 included a continued focus on marine conservation and giving this effort priority yet also listing such concerns following economic, industrial, and innovative priorities.[30] The plan indicates continued and novel efforts to strengthen, improve, and promote greater marine conservation, protection, and restoration but nothing that appears to constitute a major effort to address China's extensive marine pollution challenges. Rather, the intent appears in this plan to be mainly on controlling the marine environment and its resources generally and to focus in only select areas on water pollution control and marine environmental restoration. Among the latter initiatives is China's "Blue Bay" program, which is being implemented in key strategic locations: Jiaozhou Bay (Qingdao region), Liaodong Bay (Bohai Sea area, near China's border with North Korea), Bohai Bay (near Tianjin and Beijing), Hangzhou Bay (south of Shanghai), Xiamen Bay (across from Taiwan), and Beibu Bay (Gulf of Tonkin).[31] Lastly, China's Marine Economy 13th Five-Year Plan, which is dubbed the "Blue Economy" in the official press release, focuses again on offshore islands, citing concerns about their marine ecosystems but also noting their importance in terms of promoting China's maritime rights.[32] Based on PRC activities in recent years, it is likely that the latter concerns will outweigh any Beijing might have about damaging the islands' marine environment.

China's latest, 14th Five-Year Plan (2021–5) came out in the midst of the COVID pandemic and, given this, is likely more of an indication of what China hopes to achieve rather than what the country is likely to be able to accomplish during this particular time period. Most societies and economies around the globe were severely affected by the global pandemic, China's longer than many. Thus, the goals outlined in this particular plan (and its derivative plans) are unlikely to be fully achieved, which would be understandable given the unusual circumstances. At the same time, China's regular FYPs during the Xi era, when compared with those of recent past PRC leaders, tend toward more ideological language and lofty goals than the broad strategic and industry-sector guidance of earlier plans written by a generation of PRC "technocrats" and engineers. For these two reasons, expectations for rapid achievement in the maritime realm ought to be lowered generally in the near-term. Yet, based on the rapid recovery and industry sector growth in the US case and China's pre-COVID rapid maritime and naval development,

China might also see fast-paced advances in the medium-term. This presumes, however, that ideological concerns do not hamper such progress, which is a possibility given Xi Jinping's priorities and proclivities.

Like its predecessors, the 14th Five-Year Plan includes goals for marine conservation, maritime industry, and military modernization, the latter via programs following China's military-civil fusion approach to development. This dual-use and dual-development approach is described, in part, in the document as plans to

> deepen military-civilian S&T collaboration and innovation, strengthen military-civilian overall development planning for maritime, aerospace, cyberspace, biotech, new energy, AI, quantum technology, and other fields, promote resource sharing between military and civilian S&T facilities, and promote the two-way transformation and application of military and civilian scientific research results and the development of key industries. We will strengthen the co-construction and common use of infrastructure, strengthen the overall planning and construction of new infrastructure, and increase the intensity of economic construction projects to implement national defense requirements.[33]

The section on marine environmental efforts, in contrast, consists of one, rather short paragraph emphasizing continued and expanded marine ecological efforts.

China's Contemporary Blue Economy Emphasizes Innovation

China's shift from focusing on development of a marine economy, albeit in a somewhat more environmentally friendly and sustainable way, to adopting a more systemic, holistic, and strategic approach represented by the Blue Economy concept appears tied to both international developments and to domestic reforms. China can be considered a relatively early adopter of the Blue Economy concept, as it became an increasingly popular term of art in international development circles. For China, the concept's emphasis on innovation was key to its appeal. As reportedly described at the 2009 Qingdao International Blue Economy Summit Forum, innovation was an important factor for China in shifting from a focus simply on marine development to adopting a more strategic, scientific, and innovative approach:

> Compared with traditional [sic] ocean economy, the blue economy is more scientific and profound and covers a wide range of subjects. It attaches more importance to development of high-level marine industries, balanced utilization of ocean and land resources and scientific innovation as well as protection of the marine ecosystem.[34]

As outlined in Chapter 2, the PRC's concept of the Blue Economy is similar to the US and international conceptions, in comprising three main components:

- A **marine** focus on environmental conservation and sustainable development efforts. This component includes ocean and marine science and technology research, exploration, and conservation activities.
- A **maritime** component focused on economic and industrial development across a wide array of industries (e.g., fishing, aquaculture, shipbuilding, shipping, port development, oil and gas, alternative energy such as wind and solar, bio-tech and pharmaceutical sectors, as well as tourism and recreation).
- A **naval** and defense-related component that seeks to leverage Blue Economy advances and opportunities for purposes of China's innovation spillovers to naval and other military ambitions. This component focuses on achieving dual-use and commercial-to-naval spin-on and spin-off technology innovations, for instance through development of a "Blue Silicon Valley" set amid a Blue Economy development zone in the northern port city of Qingdao.

Akin to the US approach to industrial and technology cluster innovation, China's Blue Economy concept similarly seeks to promote development of Blue Economy ecosystems or clusters that include specific, regional blue tech clusters and industrial zones. Beijing's approach, however, is mainly based on top-down directives and planning rather than driven mainly by local-area market dynamics, as found in the United States.

China's Blue Economy concept also aligns with other states' in adopting an innovation ecosystem- and cluster-oriented approach to development in which actors, activities, and advances in each sector affect—ideally in a benign way—the actors, activities, and advances achieved in the others. As noted earlier, this ecosystem approach is emphasized in China due to its innovative opportunities as well as lessons learned from past decades of rapid industrial growth that led to extensive environmental damage to China's air, land, water, and coastlines. In pursuing a Blue Economy, ecosystem-oriented approach to development today, Beijing hopes to maintain robust economic and industrial growth while limiting the negative environmental impacts. Althoughpromoting more sustainable models of economic development, China is looking anew to the ocean as an area of economic, innovative and strategic opportunity.

In short, the environmental considerations encompassed in China's Blue Economy concept are once again *not* Beijing's top priority. The primary focus instead is on industrial development and, in particular, advancing scientific and technological innovation in the maritime sphere. While environmental concerns are included in China's Blue Economy plans, policies, and strategies, the implementation of environmental objectives thus far has lagged behind the rhetoric and remains a distant third priority among the three core components, according to environmental experts residing in China as well as critics overseas.[35]

Rather, China's main objective in establishing a domestic Blue Economy is promoting scientific and technological innovation spurred on by dual-use commercial maritime and defense (mainly naval) industrial development. Science and technology innovation has been the top priority for Chinese economic development plans, effectively, since Jiang Zemin led China in the 1990s and officially since Hu Jintao identified science and technology innovation as the main driver for advancing China's overall development (via a doctrine of "Scientific Development and Harmonious Society") in 2004. China's 11th Five-Year Plan (2006–10), implemented during Hu Jintao's era, was the first to identify ocean development as a key concern, although efforts at marine economic development in China date back to the 1990s.[36] Xi Jinping has since expanded the Blue Economy concept as a tool in Chinse foreign policy as well as a means of domestic development.

China has long implemented a dual-use (joint civil and military) development model, a strategy that has gone by different names in different eras but remains fundamentally the same. This approach is referred to presently as military-civilian integration (MCI) and is particularly relevant to China's naval ambitions and maritime industrial capabilities. According to China's State Council,

> China encourages joint building and utilization of military and civilian infrastructure, joint exploration of the sea, outer space and air, and shared use of such resources as surveying and mapping, navigation, meteorology and frequency spectra. Accordingly, military and civilian resources can be more compatible, complementary and mutually accessible.[37]

As in the United States, the Chinese government expects technological spillovers to come from commercial-sector research and technologies that advance military technological developments (known as "spin-on" technology) as well as the reverse (military technology "spin-offs" that impact commercial or private-sector innovation). California's Silicon Valley best reflects this dual-use, spin-on-spin-off approach to commercial and defense technology innovation, as in the case of the area's historic development of semiconductor chips.

In both US and Chinese economies (as elsewhere), regional industry and technology clusters are viewed as optimal mechanisms for promoting technology spillovers. A key difference in the US and Chinese approaches to developing industry and technology clusters, however, is Beijing's top-down emphasis on developing regional economic zones in which industry and technology clusters are strategically planned as compared to the more free-market-driven, organic, bottom-up dynamic experienced in the United States. For China, economic development via establishment of experimental SEZs has been the key to its historically unmatched, rapid economic development over the past 40 years. It is not surprising, therefore, that the economic development zone model has been adapted by Beijing for more specialized purposes, including development of the Blue Economy.

China is not alone in employing SEZs as a means of fostering economic development, but the PRC is at the forefront of this trend and relatively successful compared to other states trying to do the same. According to the United Nations, "we are seeing explosive growth in the use of special economic zones (SEZs) as key policy instruments for the attraction of investment for industrial development."[38]

As discussed in more detail below, the northern port city of Qingdao was selected to be the site for China's first Pilot Blue Economy Development Zone, in large part due to the region's prospects for, and investments in, ocean scientific and technological innovation in both commercial and naval sectors. Beijing has plans, as noted earlier, to develop Blue Economies in other cities along China's long coastline. The site of China's first SEZ, Shenzhen, appears now to be a priority for development and is playing an increasing role in Xi Jinping's plans for the Blue Economy.

China's Blue Economy Connects Domestic and Cross-Regional Strategic Development Plans

China's emphasis on innovation as the focus of its Blue Economy development efforts is not only a domestic consideration. In order to continue growing its economy, China has had to shift its economic attention beyond the domestic marketplace to seek new market opportunities overseas for Chinese exports, including maritime or Blue Economy-based products and services. China has pursued variations of a "Go Out" or "Go Global" strategy to invest in and export overseas since 2003. Beginning with the 12th Five-Year Plan (2011–15), these efforts also have included expanding Blue Economy-related overseas investments, exports, and aid.

The Blue Economy represents an attractive export both in its conception as a more sustainable means of marine and maritime development as well as in terms of services, innovations, and the economic, industrial, and technological spillover effects it promises to generate where adopted. Other countries interested in developing their own Blue Economies in Africa and elsewhere have sought guidance and advice from China on its Blue Economy development efforts and as an alternative to US or Western aid.

As China's global trade is expanding, so are China's power projection, interests, and capabilities, driven in part by a desire to provide security for its citizens' overseas activities. Moreover, for China to achieve its aim of becoming a strong military country and regional (or global) maritime power, Chinese leaders expect its navy (the People's Liberation Army Navy or PLAN) to have the capacity and capabilities to extend its reach and maritime power beyond China's own shores. As one author explains Beijing's thinking, for China to become a strong maritime country means "a developed Blue Economy, strong innovation capacity in maritime science and technology; success in protecting the maritime environment; and a powerful navy."[39] China's Blue Economy development plans are both a strategic end as well as a means to developing the country's commercial and military capabilities.

The connection between China's domestic development and ambitious, geostrategic aims is most clearly apparent in Xi Jinping's BRI announced in 2013 and, in particular, the Maritime Silk Road (MSR), the sea-based component of the BRI. This bold plan serves China's strategic economic and naval expansion objectives and will be an important impetus for the expansion of China's Blue Economy concept and related capabilities far beyond the PRC's own shores. How China's domestic development and foreign strategic aims related to becoming a maritime power have merged is evident in the evolution and implementation over time of China's Blue Economy concept, as explained below.

Conceptual Evolution, Expansion, and Phases of Development in China's Blue Economy

In order to understand the strategic significance of China's Blue Economy development efforts and where they might lead, as well as how effective they might prove, it is important to understand how China's concept of the Blue Economy has evolved over just a short period time (2009–23). It has been a bumpy ride, for it was not at all clear for some time whether the concept would continue to be promoted as a serious driver in Chinese domestic or foreign development. Following a period of uncertainty, however, the Blue Economy has become a more highly visible and critically important strategic component of Chinese domestic and foreign policy.

China has been pursuing development of a Blue Economy for over a decade. Even over this short period of time, Beijing's enthusiasm for the concept has waxed and waned due to various factors, including the leadership transition from Hu Jintao to Xi Jinping in 2012. The latter's focus on implementing a far-reaching anti-corruption campaign, instituting changes to top leadership and processes of policy formulation, executing institutional reforms of China's maritime forces, and more meant that Blue Economy development plans continued to be implemented under

Xi Jinping's government but with increasing uncertainty initially as to their continued prospects.

While China's change in leadership meant new and distinct priorities, Xi Jinping appears to have since overcome his reputed initial skepticism of his predecessor's Blue Economy idea to now wholly embrace the concept—in particular by tying it to the maritime component of his own, signature Belt and Road Initiative. Xi's *Vision for Maritime Cooperation* strategy announced in June 2017 makes clear that China plans to continue to develop a Blue Economy domestically as well as to extend these efforts abroad as an ambitious, central element of Xi's envisioned Maritime Silk Road.

To understand China's contemporary conception of the Blue Economy and its strategic implications, a brief history of the concept's evolution is instructive. The past decade and a half or so has witnessed four distinct phases in the evolution and expansion of China's Blue Economy concept.

Phase 1: Hu Jintao Initiates the Blue Economy Concept and Plans Blue Economy Development Zones (2009–11)

Chinese leader Hu Jintao's ten years in office (2002–12) are remembered mainly for the difficulties he encountered in trying to reform the Chinese state and in attempting to reduce the role of state enterprises, efforts that largely failed to meet stated, ambitious objectives. But Hu might well come to be remembered over the long term more positively as the Chinese leader who initiated a shift toward instituting more environmentally aware and sustainable PRC development strategies and policies while also continuing to prioritize China's market-driven economic and technological reforms. This approach now appears in stark contrast to his successor's ideological priorities and shift away from market-oriented reforms.

After decades of fast-paced industrial growth with little, if any, consideration given to environmental consequences, by the early years of the 21st century, China's land, water, and air had become toxic. The level of pollution had become so bad that it had begun to affect economic growth prospects, which itself was viewed as a serious threat to the Chinese Communist Party's continued leadership. China's 11th Five-Year Plan (2006–10) is identified as the period when Beijing became serious about trying to address the country's environmental challenges.[40]

Having ushered in an era of more environmentally conscious, sustainable development-oriented policies, Hu Jintao's efforts marked a turning point not only for himself but also for China. The rest of the globe, too, was struggling with how to begin to address climate change and other growing environmental challenges.

Late into his second five-year term as China's president, Hu Jintao made the first official mention of the "Blue Economy" concept in a 2009 speech.[41] As noted earlier, Hu's address appears to coincide roughly with a broader, international discussion about this new, "blue" concept outlined in Gunther Pauli's 2010 *Report to the Club of Rome* on the Blue Economy. That same year, China's State Council approved the country's first Blue Economic Development Zone.

It was under Hu Jintao's leadership also that China's regular Five-Year Plans first included the specific, strategic objective of developing an "ocean" economy. China's 12th Five-Year Plan (FYP), issued in March 2011 and covering state strategic development and spending priorities for the years 2011–15, was the first to include "developing the ocean economy" as a "key national development strategy."[42]

Phase 2: Implementation of Blue Economy Development Zones and Blue Technology Innovation Clusters (2011–12; Ongoing Zone Development)

Moving beyond the initial conceptual and planning stage, the next phase in the evolution of China's Blue Economy development model was the implementation of specific Blue Economy-themed economic and investment zones as well as specific Blue Economy industry and innovation clusters. These initial implementation efforts took place during the latter years of Hu Jintao's time as China's leader and continue today.

As noted earlier, China's long-established economic-zone-based development model has been adapted toward the goal of promoting the development of a Blue Economy. Although initially spurred on by an interest in promoting more sustainable development, China's first, pilot Blue Economy-themed zone focused mainly on innovation as the means of attaining a more sustainable, environmentally friendly form of economic and maritime development.

China's State Council selected the northeast port city of Qingdao on the Shandong Peninsula as the site of China's first Pilot Blue Economic Development Zone. Qingdao is known for its maritime industry and naval history, its deep-water port, numerous universities, and well-kept beaches as well as the city's famous *Tsingdao* brewery.[43] Qingdao is a leading marine and ocean science center as home to several shipyards as well as Qingdao University and Ocean University of China. Other universities and businesses have affiliate organizations located in Qingdao as well, including satellite campuses of Sichuan University (Qingdao), Tianjin University (Qingdao), and the Institute of Wuhan University of Technology (Qingdao), among others. Qingdao, is also the headquarters of Haier, a now-well-known, worldwide commercial enterprise and consumer brand of home appliances. China's lead information technology firm, Huawei, also has a presence in Qingdao, further indicating the area's importance in China's economic and development plans. In addition, Qingdao serves as the headquarters for the PLA Navy's North Sea Fleet and is home to a naval submarine academy.

Notably, the port city of Qingdao is also today the home of China's first aircraft carrier, the *Liaoning*, which Beijing purchased in 1998 from Ukraine and put into service in 2012. As China's first aircraft carrier, the *Liaoning* is designated as a PLAN carrier *Type 001*. The *Liaoning* serves mainly as a training vehicle and was refurbished in the port city of Dalian, which sits north of the Shandong peninsula, in Liaoning province, hence the ship's name.[44]

Finally, the choice of Qingdao seemed apt given that the city had demonstrated already an unusual degree (in China) of environmental awareness, being the first city in the PRC to institute a policy of recycling. Qingdao has long stretches of white-sand beaches and notably was chosen as the site for the sailing competition in the 2008 Olympics hosted by China. The sailing race is remembered, however, mainly for the vast quantities of green algae that obstructed the racers. While supporting environmental and conservation objectives was a key objective for establishing the first pilot Blue Economy Development Zone in Qingdao, fostering innovation was, and remains, the zone's priority focus.

In order to promote scientific and technological innovation as well as commercial-military science and technology spillovers, a key part of Qingdao's Blue Economy Development Zone included what planners dubbed initially as a "Blue Silicon Valley." The State Council approved this blue tech industry cluster in 2011, although the word "silicon" appears to have been dropped since then. The initiative's aim was to co-locate Chinese enterprises, researchers, and universities (both commercial and military, domestic and foreign) in a single regional cluster north of downtown Qingdao, hoping to realize the same type of innovative dynamic, industry cluster, and ecosystem dynamic as had emerged in California's Silicon Valley, an area renowned for having advanced innovation in the information technology sector. This zone-within-a-zone approach is common across China, particularly in the more developed coastal regions, where numerous specialized development and investment zones are often nested within one another.

As depicted in Figure 3.1, beyond Qingdao, China's State Council approved several additional Blue Economy Development Zones along China's entire eastern coast. From north to south these zones are located in Liaoning Province (Dalian), the municipality of Tianjin, Hebei Province, Shandong Province (Qingdao, Yantai, Weihei, Dongying, and Rizhao), Jiangsu Province, Shanghai (Pudong) municipality, Zhejiang Province, Fujian Province (Xiamen), Guangdong Province (Zhanjiang), and Guangxi Province.[45] These now ten zones represent an expansion from the initial five provinces and municipalities identified in state plans earlier in 2009 (Fujian, Guangdong, Shandong, Tianjin, and Zhejiang). Not all of these zones appear to have adopted the term Blue Economy, however, as in the Zhejiang Marine Economy Development Demonstration Zone and Fujian's Marine Economic Pilot Zone, as cited in a later 2015 state plan.[46]

Notably, the cities of Qingdao and Zhanjiang are locations for both Blue Economy Development Zones and the China's People's Liberation Army Navy (PLAN) Northern Theater Navy headquarters (HQ) and Southern Theater Navy headquarters, respectively. (The PLAN's third, Eastern Theater Navy HQ, is located in Ningbo, south of Shanghai.) As noted above, Shanghai is among the Blue Economy Development Zones identified and

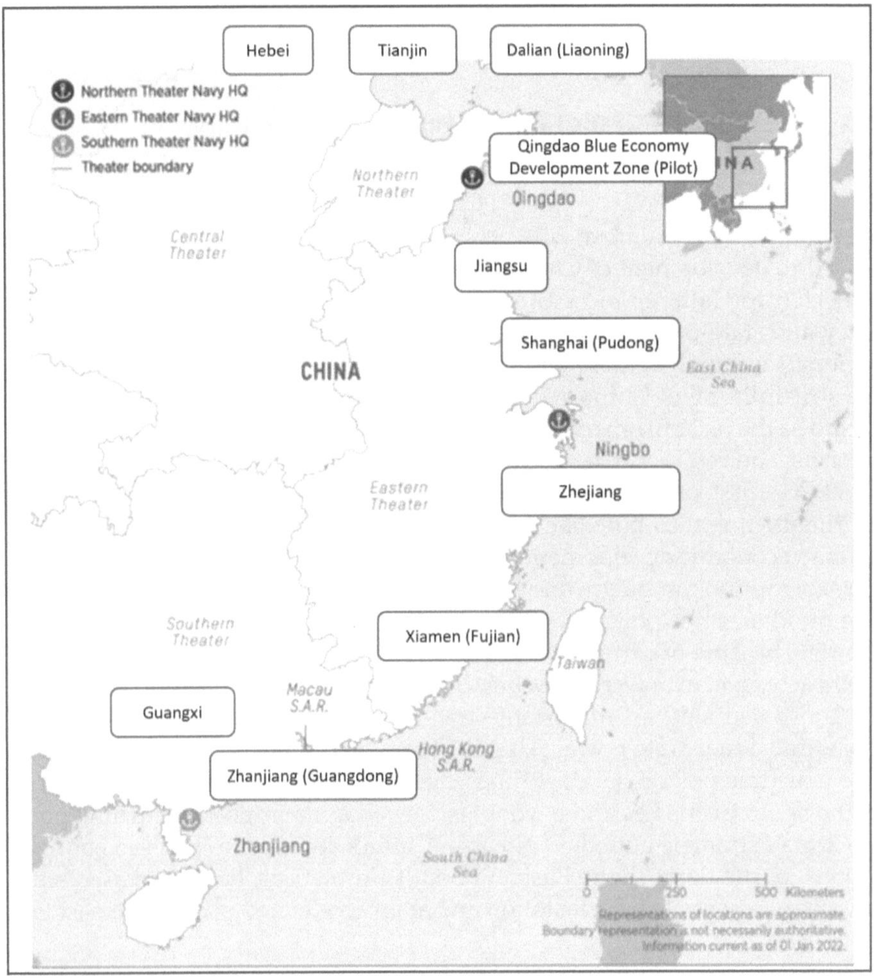

FIGURE 3.1
China's Blue Economy development zones. *Source*: Adapted from Office of the Secretary of Defense, 2023, 58.

is also home to major shipbuilding facilities for both commercial and naval ships. Shanghai is just over 130 miles (216 kilometers) or an approximately two and a half-hour drive from Ningbo.

Of the ten Blue Economy zones, at least six (Shanghai, Tianjin, Zhanjiang, Qingdao—and nearby Yantai—Dalian, and Xiamen) are among those subsequently designated as important Chinese coastal port areas whose development is to be prioritized as part of China's Belt and Road Initiative.[47]

As the clustering of Blue Economy-oriented development zones with commercial, academic, government, and naval assets makes clear, China's plans for its Blue Economy Development Zones are meant to bolster China's maritime industrial, scientific, and technological development, as well as its naval capabilities.

Phase 3: Leadership Transition and Period of Uncertainty on China's Blue Economy Plans (2012–17)

The transition period between Hu Jintao and his successor, Xi Jinping, announced in November 2012, ushered in a period of uncertainty with regard to development of China's Blue Economy. Following a period widely criticized for failures to institute long-needed reforms of China's bureaucracy and state-owned enterprises, Xi Jinping came to office with a determination to accomplish these and many other reforms. Among Xi's efforts was the streamlining of China's ocean bureaucracy, which occurred in 2013 and included the establishment of China's Coast Guard, among other initiatives, reforms, and restructuring efforts.

Yet, Xi's first priority would be fighting corruption, which he viewed as a primary threat to both the Chinese Communist Party leadership and to China's economic development. Xi implemented a robust and wide-reaching anti-corruption campaign, one that continues today. As a result, however, the fate of other, prior policy priorities—including Blue Economy development efforts—became uncertain.

Xi's accession to power following China's 18th Party Congress in November 2012 also signaled an important strategic shift: toward a focus on China becoming a maritime power. This shift toward a more ambitious and assertive maritime posture (and, at times, aggressive, as in operations conducted in the South China Sea and beyond) is viewed as an important turning point in China's strategic outlook.[48] Notably, China's activities and at-sea confrontations, particularly in the East and South China Seas, have increased since this change in strategic orientation and at an accelerated pace in the past two years.[49]

In March 2013, Xi Jinping formally took over as president of China. Prior to this, Xi had taken over other, more important official titles from his predecessor, namely as General Secretary of the Chinese Communist Party and Chairman of the Central Military Commission (head of China's Armed Forces). Xi Jinping thereby had attained essential Party, state, and military leadership titles, some of which had not been conferred as quickly to Xi's predecessors. As such, Xi Jinping possessed early on the formal authority and power to press his own—rather than his predecessors'—agenda and proceeded to do so.

As noted earlier, included in Xi's reform agenda has been a major re-organization of China's ocean bureaucracy. This was an ongoing endeavor into Xi's second term (and due to recent changes to China's Constitution, no longer necessarily his final term as president). The main proponent and lead agent for planning and promoting Blue Economy development at home and abroad in the Hu Jintao years had been China's State Oceanic Administration (SOA).

Since then, SOA has undergone several major re-organizations, raising questions particularly during the early Xi years about where the Blue Economy concept ranked vis-à-vis other priorities, programs, and missions.[50] During the early Xi years, in fact, there was little mention in the Chinese press about Blue Economy development plans and programs or initiatives, although these efforts appeared to continue nonetheless, due perhaps to momentum from earlier spending plans and programs. The lack of public enthusiasm for Blue Economy projects during this transition period, however, was in stark contrast to the earlier Hu era, when such projects were heralded regularly in the Chinese media.

In addition to Xi's own priorities and reform agenda, part of the explanation for the lack of public attention paid to Blue Economy efforts during this period is due possibly to Xi's adverse view (if any) of the Blue Economy as being his predecessor's signature initiative. It is also possible Xi Jinping was uncertain as to what the Blue Economy concept was, particularly given that even some SOA officials were less-than avid proponents of the concept given SOA's then-broad organizational mandate and their possible preference for, or prioritization of, more traditional maritime industrial concerns.[51]

Consequently, the tapering off or lack of continued enthusiastic official or public support for Blue Economy programs appeared to slow the pace of existing projects. Repeat visits to Qingdao in 2014–15 by the author, for instance, revealed unusually slow (for China) progress in attracting investors (domestic and foreign) to the city's Blue Economy Development Zone and the Blue Silicon Valley cluster within it. Building of the planned subway connecting downtown Qingdao with the Blue Economy Development Zone located north of the city also appeared to have slowed or stalled during this time. The Line 11 subway extension connects downtown Qingdao to the Jimo District, where Ocean University and other parts of Qingdao's Blue Economy Development Zone are located about an hour north. The subway line has since become operational, but long after being started.

Nonetheless, Qingdao continues to be among favored locations for China's state-funded ocean, maritime, and Blue Economy research programs. Qingdao's National Laboratory for Marine Science and Technology (QNLM) Pilot Laboratory, approved in December 2013 and officially in operation by mid-2015, is home to China's first indigenously built, manned deep-water submersible, the *Jiaolong*.[52] QNLM is reportedly working also on several other important research endeavors. These projects include the construction of a new ocean drilling ship and the "Haiyan," a 10,000-meter-capable, long-distance, underwater glider.[53] An additional project reported in the media includes something called the "Transparent Ocean Project" (reportedly a sophisticated, real-time, marine data collection and "smart" observation system) that has been likened to the US Defense Department's Defense Advanced Research Projects Agency (DARPA) "Ocean of Things" project.[54] As described on its website, DARPA indicates that the Ocean of Things project "seeks to enable persistent maritime situational awareness over large ocean areas by deploying thousands of small, low-cost floats that form from a distributed sensor network". Such an ocean-based, "smart" sensor network would have myriad defense, scientific, and commercial applications.

The several-year period of uncertainty and apparent slow-down of development efforts, yet continued spending related to Blue Economy plans, appeared to come to an end by mid-2017. What changed? As discussed below, Chinese leader Xi Jinping announced as part of his own signature strategic and foreign policy initiative—the Belt and Road—an ambitious new *Vision for Maritime Cooperation* that incorporated several geostrategic and specifically Blue Economy-related initiatives. If effectively implemented, these programs potentially could have long-lasting impacts on China's engagements in and with the region. In other words, Xi had made the Blue Economy concept his own.

Phase 4: Xi Expands the Blue Economy Concept, Connecting It to the Belt and Road Initiative's Maritime Silk Road (2017–present)

Hu Jintao's introduction of the Blue Economy concept into Chinese strategies, plans, and policies was essential to what has happened since: Xi Jinping's eventual embrace of the idea as a vehicle for his own historic initiative, the Belt and Road. This connection between China's domestic Blue Economy development efforts and Xi's BRI is what marks the Blue Economy concept as not only an important economic and innovation element of China's domestic development strategy but also as a novel geostrategic element, in China's quest for maritime power, and one that is particularly relevant to the Indo-Pacific region and the US–China relationship.

In 2015, Xi Jinping announced a "new development concept" for China's domestic economic development. This concept emphasizes what is commonly referred to in Communist Party rhetoric as being "innovative, coordinated, green, open and shared" development efforts. This novel approach to advancing economic development is in line with China's ongoing domestic Blue Economy development activities, including Blue Economy-themed industry clusters and technology development zones, even if not citing the term or concept specifically.

Also in 2015, the Chinese government published an "Action Plan" for implementing the Belt and Road Initiative.[55] The document, entitled *Vision and Actions on Jointly Building Silk Road Economic Belt and 21st-Century Maritime Silk Road*, makes no mention of the Blue Economy but outlines Beijing's intentions to establish industrial parks, economic development and investment zones, industry clusters, and more domestically and along the Maritime Silk Road. Notably, the document indicates Beijing's interest in making such interactions, investments, and development environmentally friendly.

The year 2017 marked a clear change in Xi's approach, as evidenced in two additionally important strategic and policy declarations. The first was

China's *13th Five-Year Plan for the Development of the National Marine Economy*, jointly issued in May 2017 by the National Development and Reform Commission and the State Oceanic Administration. This plan clearly emphasized development of the Blue Economy as an essential element of China's domestic economic, industrial, and technological development. The plan stresses in the introductory paragraph that expanding the Blue Economy, along with strengthening development of the marine economy, are essential to realizing the "Chinese dream" and the "great rejuvenation of the Chinese nation," which Beijing expects to accomplish by 2049 (the 100th anniversary of the founding of the People's Republic of China). The inclusion of the Blue Economy in China's "centenary goals" indicates its importance. Similarly, the plan specifically links development of the Blue Economy with Xi Jinping's signature Belt and Road Initiative, which he expanded also in 2017 to include Latin America.

In addition, what appeared to Western and Chinese observers to be a clear statement of official support from Xi's government for the concept of developing the Blue Economy arrived with no apparent advance notice in the summer of 2017 in the form of a newly announced *Vision for Maritime Cooperation*. While it is not apparent what prompted the publication of this new vision statement (conveniently published in English, suggesting it was meant to be read abroad), to foreign audiences the document made a clear connection between continued Chinese national development of a Blue Economy and Xi's own geostrategically ambitious Belt and Road Initiative and, in particular, as a component of the BRI's Maritime Silk Road. In this way, Xi adopted his predecessor's idea but made it his own by tying it directly to his own historic efforts to develop China's economy and by expanding these efforts outward in ways that were meant to bolster China's maritime power. The details of this latter document, paired with the 2015 Action Plan (both are discussed in more detail in Chapter 4), outline China's strategic plan to employ the Blue Economy development concept as a means to bolster the PRC's maritime and naval development, integrate China's economy with countries situated along the MSR, and project Chinese power overseas. Promotion of the Blue Economy concept as part of the BRI, and specifically MSR, will play a critical role in whether China can enhance its maritime power and win over regional economies diplomatically while also deepening China's economic, technological, military, and strategic integration with the region.

Subsequently, it appears that the center of gravity for China's own domestic development of the Blue Economy might have shifted from the northern city of Qingdao to the southern city of Shenzhen. Indications of a potential shift in strategic and policy priorities include the convening of a growing number of international conferences, forums, and expos in Shenzhen on the Blue Economy or on related maritime and marine sectors. The most prominent such event is an annual China Marine Economy Expo (CMEE) held in Shenzhen. Another indication of the city's importance is the development in Shenzhen in 2017 of a new Blue Economy-themed industrial park (the product of a partnership agreement between the European Union and the PRC), and other innovation- and maritime-oriented development projects.[56] The strategic location of Shenzhen as tied to the southern-oriented Maritime Silk Road component of Xi Jinping's key Belt and Road Initiative is likely also a key factor in the shift toward focusing Blue Economy development efforts on Shenzhen.

Shenzhen's place in Chinese history as the initial experimental Special Economic Zone that served to open the door to foreign investment in China (an effort led, in fact, by Xi Jinping's father as Communist Party head of Guangdong Province in 1978–80) is likely also a factor. It was Shenzhen's development via its SEZs that sparked the PRC's subsequent economic rise to power, giving the choice of Shenzhen as the center for China's emergence as a center for Blue Economy development and as a maritime power a certain appeal, particularly to China's leader. It is not clear, as yet, however, whether such a shift has taken place in a formal manner or whether Beijing's preferences are simply being considered in planning efforts. Wherever the center of gravity in China's Blue Economy efforts lies, there are numerous other clusters where China is endeavoring to achieve similar results.

Conclusion

When taking into account details of how China's conception of the Blue Economy has changed over a short period of time, it becomes clear that the Blue Economy is viewed by Beijing today as an important new policy tool and a strategic approach to developing China's own economy as well as serving Xi Jinping's ambitious foreign policy objectives. In short, the Blue Economy is a means to an end or, rather, several ends.

As the following chapters lay out, China is adopting and implementing Blue Economy policies and strategies to bolster the country's diplomatic, economic, industrial, and military development and exporting its Blue Economy concept abroad. In these ways, the Blue Economy is meant to be an important strategic means of China becoming once again a maritime power.

Notes

1. Douglas Main, "No, People Don't Have to Watch the Sunrise on TV in China," *Popular Science* (January 21, 2014), https://www.popsci.com/article/science/no-people-dont-have-watch-sunrise-tv-china/.
2. Main, "No, People Don't Have to Watch."

3. Ying Wang and David G. Aubrey, "The Characteristics of China's Coastline," *Continental Shelf Research* (1987), 329–49, https://seagrant.whoi.edu/wp-content/uploads/2015/01/WHOI-R-87-011-Ying-Wang-and-David-Au.pdf.
4. Jane Perlez, "At Mao's Beach, China's Leaders Still Make History as Lifeguards Hide from the Sun," *The New York Times* (August 22, 2019), https://www.nytimes.com/2019/08/22/world/asia/china-beidaihe-beach-communist-party-mao.html.
5. Tabitha Grace Mallory, Andrew Chubb, and Sallie Lau, "China's Ocean Culture and Consciousness: Constructing a Maritime Great Power Narrative," *Marine Policy* (August 15, 2022), https://doi.org/10.1016/j.marpol.2022.105229.
6. Walsh, "Understanding China's Blue Economy Concept."
7. This section is based on author research of the CNKI database (June 2022).
8. Information Office of the State Council of the People's Republic of China, *The Development of China's Marine Programs*, White Paper (Beijing: State Council, 1998).
9. Zong He, "Maritime Economy Is the Main Focus at Qingdao's Xihai'an New District: The State Council Approves the Establishment of the 9th National-Level New District," *China Ocean News (Zhongguo Haiyang Bao)*, trans. Claire Bilden (June 11, 2014).
10. He, "Maritime Economy."
11. Kathleen A. Walsh, "CMSI Workshop on US and Chinese Perspectives on the Blue Economy December 11–12, 2014," *CMSI Bulletin No. 2* (Newport, RI: China Maritime Studies Institute, 2015), 14.
12. Fuwen Wei et al., "Ecological Civilization," *National Science Review*, 8, 7 (July 2021), https://doi.org/10.1093/nsr/nwaa279.
13. Wenjing Bi and Yinkai Yi, "Evolution of Marine Environmental Governance Policy in China," *Sustainability*, 11, 18 (September 17, 2019), 2, https://doi.org/10.3390/su11185076.
14. Xin Teng et al., "Implementing Marine Functional Zoning in China," *Marine Policy* (March 25, 2019), 2, https://doi.org/10.1016/j.marpol.2019.02.055.
15. Teng et al., "China Marine Strategy," 2.
16. Teng et al., "China Marine Strategy," 2.
17. Teng et al., "China Marine Strategy," 4.
18. Bi and Yi, "Evolution of Marine Environmental Governance."
19. Bi and Yi, "Evolution of Marine Environmental Governance."
20. Bi and Yi, "Evolution of Marine Environmental Governance."
21. Jinyuan Su and Yiwei Lu, "Current Legal Developments People's Republic of China: The Law of the People's Republic of China on Island Protection 2009," *The International Journal of Marine and Coastal Law*, 25, 3 (August 1, 2010), 425–36, DOI: 10. 1163/157180810X520318.
22. National Development Reform Commission (NDRC) and State Oceanic Administration (SOA), *13th Five-Year Plan for the Development of the National Marine Economy* (Beijing: NDRC & SOA, 2017).
23. An analysis of critical discourse of mainly Chinese-language literature on the Blue Economy conducted for a multi-authored article confirmed the author's similar conclusion (that addressing environmental concerns was not a top priority in China's Blue Economy concept), a finding reached through prior field research and outreach to PRC and other contacts knowledgeable on China'

marine environmental and Blue Economy efforts. See Michael Fabinyi et al., "China's Blue Economy: A State Project of Modernisation." *The Journal of Environment & Development* 30, no. 2 (2021): 127–48.
24. Rui Zhao, Stephen Hynes, and Guang Shun He, "Defining and Quantifying China's Ocean Economy." *Marine Policy*, 43, 164–73, 165.
25. Information Office of the State Council, "Notice of the State Council on Issuing the National Marine Economic Development Program During the 'Twelfth Five-Year Plan' Period" (Beijing: State Council, 2012).
26. Information Office of the State Council, "Notice."
27. Zhao, Hynes, and He, "Defining and Quantifying China's Ocean Economy."
28. Xinhua (Qingdao) International Ocean Information Center, *Xinhua Ocean Development Index 2013* (Qingdao: State Financial Information Center Index Research Institute, 2013), 6.
29. Xinhua (Qingdao), *Xinhua Ocean Development Index 2013.*
30. NDRC and SOA, *13th Five-Year Plan for the Development of the National Marine Economy.*
31. NDRC and SOA, *13th Five-Year Plan for the Development of the National Marine Economy.*
32. NDRC and SOA, *13th Five-Year Plan for the Development of the National Marine Economy.*
33. Xinhua News Agency, *Outline of the People's Republic of China 14th Five-Year Plan for National Economic and Social Development and Long-Range Objectives for 2035*, trans. Etcetera Language Group, Inc. for Center for Security and Emerging Technology, Georgetown University (March 12, 2021), https://cset.georgetown.edu/wp-content/uploads/t0284_14th_Five_Year_Plan_EN.pdf.
34. Wen Quan, "Blue Economy: From Concept to On-the-Ground." Presentation to the *Symposium on Blue Economy Experience Sharing Report.* Xiamen (November 11, 2015).
35. Chinese non-governmental environmental volunteers interviewed by author, Dalian (2014).
36. Tabitha Mallory, "Preparing for the Ocean Century: China's Changing Political Institutions for Ocean Governance and Maritime Development." *Issues & Studies* (Taipei: Institute of International Relations, National Chengchi University), 51, no. 2 (2015): 111–38.
37. Information Office of the State Council, *China's Military Strategy*, White Paper (May 27, 2015), http://english.www.gov.cn/archive/white_paper/2015/05/27/content_281475115610833.htm.
38. United Nations Conference on Trade and Development (UNCTAD), *World Investment Report 2019: Special Economic Zones Key Messages and Overview* (Geneva: UNCTAD, 2019), iv, http://unctad.org/en/PublicationsLibrary/wir2019_overview_en.pdf.
39. Jia Yu, "Opportunities and Challenges for China's Maritime Development Strategy," in *Maritime Development Strategy: A Collection of Studies*, Jia Yu, ed. (Beijing: Maritime Press, 2017).
40. Yuan Xu, *Environmental Policy and Pollution in China: Governance and Strategy* (New York, NY: Routledge, 2021).
41. Quan Wen, "Blue Economy: From Concept to On-the-Ground."
42. Zhao, Hynes, and He, "Defining and Quantifying China's Ocean Economy."

43. The pilot development zone also encompasses the nearby cities of Yantai, Weihei, Dongying, and Rizhao.
44. Ronald O'Rourke, *China's Naval Modernization: Implications for US Navy Capabilities – Background and Issues for Congress*, RL33153 (Washington, DC: Congressional Research Service, 2023), 22. Notably, the port city of Dalian also served as the building site of China's second, but first indigenously built, aircraft carrier, named the *Shandong* (*Type 002*), which was commissioned in late 2019. The *Shandong* is home ported in the southern island province of Hainan, part of the PLAN's Southern Theater. A third aircraft carrier, the *Fujian*, is expected to be operational in 2024 or 2025, with additional carriers also in development (Office of the Secretary of Defense 2022, 51, 110). Office of the Secretary of Defense (OSD), *Military and Security Developments Involving the People's Republic of China* (Washington, DC: US Department of Defense, 2022), 51, 110.
45. Author interview of State Oceanic Administration official (Beijing, 2014).
46. Information Office of the State Council, "Vision and Actions on Jointly Building Silk Road Economic Belt and 21st Century Maritime Silk Road," *One Belt One Road Action Plan* (Beijing: Xinhua News Agency, March 2015).
47. The 2015 BRI Action Plan lists the following as areas of priority: "strengthen the port construction of coastal cities such as Shanghai, Tianjin, Ningbo-Zhoushan, Guangzhou, Shenzhen, Zhanjiang, Shantou, Qingdao, Yantai, Dalian, Fuzhou, Xiamen, Quanzhou, Haikou and Sanya." Information Office of the State Council, "Vision and Actions on Jointly Building Silk Road Economic Belt and 21st Century Maritime Silk Road."
48. Thomas Bickford, "Chapter 1: China and Maritime Power: Meanings, Motivations and Strategy," in *Becoming a Great "Maritime Power": A Chinese Dream*, Michael McDevitt, ed. (Arlington, VA: Center for Naval Analyses, 2016), 7–20.
49. According to the latest DoD report, *"Between the fall of 2021 and fall of 2023, the United States has documented over 180 instances of PLA coercive and risky air intercepts against US aircraft in the region—more in the past two years than in the previous decade. Over the same period, the PLA has conducted around 100 instances of coercive and risky operational behavior against US Allies and partners, in an effort to deter both the United States and others from conducting lawful operations in the region."* Office of the Secretary of Defense, *Military and Security Developments Involving the People's Republic of China 2023* (Washington, DC: US Department of Defense, 2023), X (emphasis in original text), https://media.defense.gov/2023/Oct/19/2003323409/-1/-1/1/2023-MILITARY-AND-SECURITY-DEVELOPMENTS-INVOLVING-THE-PEOPLES-REPUBLIC-OF-CHINA.PDF.
50. Ryan Martinson, "Chapter 4: The China Coast Guard—Enforcing China's Maritime Rights and Interests," in *Becoming a Great "Maritime Power": A Chinese Dream*, Michael McDevitt, ed. (Arlington, VA: Center for Naval Analyses, 2016), 53–61.
51. Author interview of State Oceanic Administration official (Beijing, 2014).
52. Subsea World News Staff, "China's Sub Jiaolong Completes Another Deep-Sea Expedition," *Offshore Energy Biz* website (July 14, 2016), https://www.offshore-energy.biz/chinas-sub-jiaolong-completes-another-deep-sea-expedition/.
53. Ocean News, "China's Underwater Glider Sets Endurance Record," *Ocean News & Technology* website (January 16, 2019), https://www.oceannews.com/news/science-technology/china-s-underwater-glider-sets-endurance-record.

54. Ryan D. Martinson and Peter A. Dutton, *China Maritime Report No. 3: China's Distant-Ocean Survey Activities: Implications for US National Security*, CMSI China Maritime Studies Reports (Newport, RI: US Naval War College, November 2018), fn 50, https://apps.dtic.mil/sti/pdfs/AD1148881.pdf.
55. Information Office of the State Council, "Vision and Actions on Jointly Building Silk Road Economic Belt and 21st Century Maritime Silk Road," *One Belt One Road Action Plan* (Beijing: Xinhua News Agency, March 2015).
56. The author is grateful to Ryan Martinson for his insights also on the possibility of a strategic shift toward Shenzhen. This state-run, national-level forum began in 2012, just prior to Xi's announcement of the BRI.

References

Bi, Wenjing, and Jinkai Yu. 2019. "Evolution of Marine Environmental Governance Policy in China." *Sustainability*, September 17. https://doi.org/10.3390/su11185076.

Bickford, Thomas. 2016. "Chapter 1: China and Maritime Power: Meanings, Motivations and Strategy." In *Becoming a Great "Maritime Power": A Chinese Dream*, edited by Michael McDevitt, 7–20. Arlington, VA: Center for Naval Analyses.

China State Oceanic Administration Official, interview by author. 2014. Beijing.

Chinese Non-Governmental Environmental Volunteers, interview by Kathleen A. Walsh. 2014. Dalian.

Defense Advanced Research Projects Agency. n.d. *Ocean of Things (Archived)*. Accessed June 2023. https://www.darpa.mil/program/ocean-of-things.

Fabinyi, Michael, Annie Wu, Sallie Lau, Tabitha Mallory, Kate Barclay, Kathleen Walsh, and Wolfram Dressler. 2021. "China's Blue Economy: A State Project of Modernisation." *The Journal of Environment & Development* (Sage) 30 (2): 127–148. https://journals.sagepub.com/doi/10.1177/1070496521995872.

He, Zong. 2014. "Maritime Economy is the Main Focus at Qingdao's Xihai'an New District: The State Council Approves the Establishment of the 9th National-Level New District." *China Ocean News*. Translated by Claire Bilden. State Oceanic Administration, June 11.

Information Office of the State Council. 2015. *China's Military Strategy, White Paper*, May 27. Accessed June 25, 2018. http://english.www.gov.cn/archive/white_paper/2015/05/27/content_281475115610833.htm.

Information Office of the State Council. 2012. *Notice of the State Council on Issuing the National Marine Economic Development Program During the "Twelth Five-Year Plan" Period*. Beijing.

Information Office of the State Council. 1998. *The Development of China's Marine Programs*. White Paper, State Council, Beijing: Information Office of the State Council of the People's Republic of China. https://policy.asiapacificenergy.org/sites/default/files/White%20Paper-%20The%20Development%20of%20China's%20Marine%20Programs%20%28EN%29.pdf.

———. 2015. "Vision and Actions on Jointly Building the Silk Road Economic Belt and the 21st Century Maritime Silk Road Vision and Actions on Jointly Building the Silk Road Economic Belt and the 21st Century Maritime Silk Road." Xinhua News Agency, March.

Main, Douglas. 2014. "No, People Don't Have to Watch the Sunrise on TV in China." *Popular Science*, January 21. https://www.popsci.com/article/science/no-people-dont-have-watch-sunrise-tv-china/.

Mallory, Tabitha Grace, Andrew Chubb, and Sallie Lau. 2022. "China's Ocean Culture and Consciousness: Constructing a Maritime Great Power Narrative." *Marine Policy*, August 15: 12. https://doi.org/10.1016/j.marpol.2022.105229.

Mallory, Tabitha. 2015. "Preparing for the Ocean Century: China's Changing Political Institutions for Ocean Governance and Maritime Development." *Issues & Studies* (Institute of International Relations, National Chengchi University) 51 (2): 111–138.

Martinson, Ryan D. 2016. "Chapter 4: The China Coast Guard--Enforcing China's Maritime Rights and Interests." In *Becoming a Great "Maritime Power": A Chinese Dream*, edited by Michael McDevitt, 53–61. Arlington, VA: Center for Naval Analyses.

Martinson, Ryan D., and Peter A. Dutton. 2018. *China Maritime Report No. 3: China's Distant-Ocean Survey Activities: Implications for US National Security*. CMSI China Maritime Reports, Newport: US Naval War College. https://apps.dtic.mil/sti/pdfs/AD1148881.pdf.

National Development Reform Commission and State Oceanic Administration. 2017. *13th Five-Year Plan for the Development of the National Marine Economy*. Beijing: National Development Reform Commission and State Oceanic Administration.

Ocean News. 2019. *China's Underwater Glider Sets Endurance Record*, January 16. https://www.oceannews.com/news/science-technology/china-s-underwater-glider-sets-endurance-record.

Office of the Secretary of Defense 2023. Military and Security Developments Involving the People's Republic of China 2023 (Washington, DC: US Department of Defense), X. https://media.defense.gov/2023/Oct/19/2003323409/-1/-1/1/2023-MILITARY-AND-SECURITY-DEVELOPMENTS-INVOLVING-THE-PEOPLES-REPUBLIC-OF-CHINA.PDF.

O'Rourke, Ronald. 2023. *China's Naval Modernization: Implications for US Navy Capabilities -- Background and Issues for Congress*. RL33153, Washington, DC: Congressional Research Service. https://crsreports.congress.gov.

Perlez, Jane. 2019. "At Mao's Beach, China's Leaders Still Make History as Lifeguards Hide from the Sun." *The New York Times*, August 22. https://www.nytimes.com/2019/08/22/world/asia/china-beidaihe-beach-communist-party-mao.html.

Su, Jinyuan, and Yiwei Lu. 2010. "Current Legal Developments People's Republic of China: The Law of the People's Republic of China on Island Protection 2009." *The International Joural of Marine and Coastal Law*, August 1: 425–436. http://doi.org/10.1163/157180810X520318.

Subsea World News Staff. 2016. *hina's Sub Jiaolong Completes Another Deep-Sea Expedition*, July 14. https://www.offshore-energy.biz/chinas-sub-jiaolong-completes-another-deep-sea-expedition/.

Teng, Xin, Qiwei Zhao, Panpan Zhang, Liang Liu, Yue'e Dong, Heng Hu, Qi Yue, Ling Ou, and Wei Xu. 2019. "Implementing Marine Functional Zoning in China." *Marine Policy*. March 25. https://doi.org/10.1016/j.marpol.2019.02.055.

United Nations Conference on Trade and Development (UNCTAD). 2019. *World Investment Report 2019: Special Economic Zones Key Messages and Overview.* Geneva: UNCTAD, 31. http://unctad.org/en/PublicationsLibrary/wir2019_overview_en.pdf.

Walsh, Kathleen A. 2015. "CMSI Workshop on US and Chinese Perspectives on the Blue Economy December 11–12, 2014." *CMSI Bulletin No. 2.* Newport: China Maritime Studies Institute, US Naval War College. 14.

———. 2014. "Understanding China's Blue Economy Concept." *The Bridge.*

Wang, Ying, and David G. Aubrey. 1987. "The Characteristics of China's Coastline." *Continental Shelf Research,* 329–349. https://seagrant.whoi.edu/wp-content/uploads/2015/01/WHOI-R-87-011-Ying-Wang-and-David-Au.pdf.

Wei, Fuwen, Shuhong Cui, Ning Liu, Jiang Chang, Xiaoge Ping, Tianxiao Ma, Jing Xu, Ronald Swaisgood, and Harvey Locke. 2021. "Ecological Civilization." *National Science Review,* July. https://doi.org/10.1093/nsr/nwaa279.

Wen, Quan. 2015. "Blue Economy: From Concept to On-the-Ground." Presentation to the *Symposium on Blue Economy Experience Sharing Report.* Xiamen (November 11, 2015).

Xinhua (Qingdao) International Ocean Information Center. 2013. *Xinhua Ocean Development Index 2013.* Annual, State Financial Information Center Index Research Institue, Qingdao: Xinhua (Qingdao) International Ocean Information Center, 87.

Xinhua News Agency. 2021. "Outline of the People's Republic of China 14th Five-Year Plan for National Economic and Social Development and Long-Range Objectives for 2035." *Center for Security and Emerging Technology, Georgetown University.* Edited by Inc Trans. Etcetera Language Group. March 12. Accessed June 2023. https://cset.georgetown.edu/wp-content/uploads/t0284_14th_Five_Year_Plan_EN.pdf.

Xu, Yuan. 2021. *Environmental Policy and Pollution in China: Governance and Strategy.* New York: Routledge. https://www.taylorfrancis.com/pdfviewer/.

Yu, Jia. 2017. "Opportunities and Challenges for China's Maritime Development Strategy." In *Maritime Development Strategy: A Collection of Studies,* edited by Jia Yu, 7–23. Beijing: Maritime Press.

Zhao, Rui, Stephen Hynes, and Guang Shun He. 2014. "Defining and Quantifying China's Ocean Economy." *Marine Policy* (Elsevier) 43: 164–173.

4

The Blue Economy and Chinese Maritime Power

On a remote island off the Shandong Peninsula there is a naval museum featuring a once-forgotten 15th-century, Ming Dynasty-era Chinese admiral whose name was Zheng He. A massive statue of this historic figure overlooks the rocky shore on which the museum rests. The dramatic image of Zheng He, which is the museum's distinguishing feature, is of the admiral's profile facing into the wind, spyglass in hand, as his cloak billows behind.

Disembarking from the ferry that brought us to the island, it was hard not to notice that I and my American colleagues were the only apparent non-Chinese visitors to this then-new attraction off the coast of Weihai and among the few not in uniform (the museum was clearly a destination for area maritime and naval forces to visit). Nevertheless, back in 2008, we were free to roam the museum and to take photos of some of the more interesting exhibits. China is understandably proud of this part of its naval history and happy to have foreigners know Zheng He's story. Zheng He's history contrasts, however, with the museum's actual focus, which is on the Sino-Japanese War of 1894–5. The latter exposed China's then-imperial navy, though a superior fleet in terms of size, as being far inferior to Japan's naval modernizations and capabilities at sea.

Zheng He is now more famous even outside of China as Beijing celebrates his legacy of seven historic sea voyages during the early 15th century that brought an impressive Chinese naval fleet of "Treasure Ships" to receive tribute from and visit parts of the globe that are today known as Southeast Asia, the Middle East, and the Horn of Africa. Zheng He's historic feat and perceived diplomatic successes are viewed today in Beijing as positive messaging, helpful in promoting China's modern-day maritime ambitions and development of its naval power. The not-too-subtle message to foreign audiences is that they need not fear China's growing and increasingly global maritime and naval power based on Zheng He's example.

Zheng He's voyages are a matter of considerable academic debate, however. But as aptly noted by one historian of this era,

> Much of the contention regarding the objective of the voyages stems from a misguided search for a single motive behind a complex and ambitious enterprise spanning a generation. The expeditions, however, were

DOI: 10.1201/9781003396116-4

> simultaneously diplomatic displays, military exercises, and trading ventures, with emphasis on these aspects shifting in response to both Chinese intentions and circumstances abroad.[1]

China's contemporary efforts toward becoming a maritime great power are similarly varied in purpose.

China's Growing Naval and Maritime Power

When examining China's quest to become a modern maritime power, analysts point to and evaluate various elements that are necessary for states to possess in order to be considered maritime powers. These capabilities include the following: naval capability (which is resident today mainly in China's People's Liberation Army Navy or PLAN), coastal and other maritime law enforcement agencies (i.e., the Chinese Coast Guard and maritime militia), maritime industrial development (shipbuilding, fishing, aquaculture, energy, shipping, marine services, etc.), and maritime infrastructure (ports, shipyards, communications, and so forth).[2] As many contemporary studies can attest, China has made rapid and impressive progress in developing all of these elements of maritime power.

A brief overview of China's maritime and naval advances over the past three decades shows that the People's Republic of China has come a long way in a short period of time in its development of its naval and maritime capabilities. China today possesses the world's largest naval, coast guard, and fishing fleets, is one of only a few countries able to project power via a fleet of its own aircraft carriers, and is the world's largest shipbuilder. In addition, China has demonstrated a willingness to use its naval and maritime powers to deter and coerce foreign maritime and naval vessels that Beijing views as violating its extensive maritime claims. China's Blue Economy development concept is meant to further these advances.

China's Fast-Paced Naval Development and Capabilities

China's Navy is today considered to be the largest in the world when measured by its fleet size. The US Department of Defense counts China's naval warships in 2023 as numbering 340 platforms (surface vessels and submarines) as compared to the United States' approximately 290 or so naval vessels.[3] China's naval fleet size surpassed that of even the United States in recent years in large part due simply to the PRC's ability to rapidly produce ships. Some Chinese shipyards can produce both naval and commercial ships, providing long-term viability for these mostly state-owned enterprises, at least in terms of maintaining shipbuilding orders on their books.

Although China has more ships available to sail, this is no guarantee of their ships' quality or sailors' abilities. Nor is fleet size the only measure of China's ability to effectively project naval power. Among the areas where China's Navy is considered to be comparatively weak is in terms of its experience at sea, conducting joint operations, and in terms of having overseas bases, logistics, and supply capabilities.[4] For all of these reasons, the United States is still viewed as being the world's most capable, experienced, and globally deployed naval power.

Whether leaders in Beijing will be willing to use Chinese naval power to pursue its interests does not appear to be in question, however. The Chinese Navy is increasingly involved in naval operations and encounters at sea and in the air that are viewed as troublingly dangerous by China's neighbors and others in the Indo-Pacific region. These operations include People's Liberation Army Navy Air Force (PLANAF) fighters regularly involved in air incursions into Taiwan's air defense identification zone as well as PLAN ships involved in what was effectively (if not formally declared) a blockade of Taiwan following US House Speaker Nancy Pelosi's visit in the fall of 2022.[5] In May 2023, the US military's Indo-Pacific Command issued a statement and shared a dramatic video of what it called an unsafe encounter at sea that involved a Chinese warship maneuvering in front, and within 150 yards, of a US destroyer transiting the Taiwan Strait as part of a US-Canadian joint operation. This video-taped encounter followed similar reports of unsafe encounters by PLA Air Force assets with US planes days earlier and a day after what Beijing found to be remarks overly critical of China made by the US Secretary of Defense at the annual Shangri-La Dialogue in Singapore. China's naval and air forces have been conducting these sorts of highly dangerous, at-sea and in-air near-collisions for many years, despite international condemnations and PRC obligations not to do so. Such encounters also take place beyond the Taiwan Strait, including in the East and South China Seas.

China's Growing Maritime Militia, Coast Guard, and Maritime Law Enforcement Forces

China is distinct in naval terms by supplementing its naval and law enforcement assets and operations with what is called a Chinese "Maritime Militia." China's Maritime Militia paramilitary force is composed of what are normally, or ostensibly, commercial fishing vessels that have been deployed at times for military and maritime security or enforcement purposes (separate from China's other military reserve forces).[6] The Maritime Militia has grown over the past two decades such that today the force includes both somewhat ordinary fishing vessels that normally conduct commercial fishing trips but can be diverted to Maritime Militia operations as described above, as well as a fleet of professional Maritime Militia ships.[7]

A large part of the reason for rising concerns in the Indo-Pacific region about China's growing naval capabilities is actually due to Beijing's use of these non-regular Maritime Militia forces as part of at-sea operations meant to deter, coerce, or prevent actions by other navies or maritime forces. This activity by China's non-naval forces for what are normally naval purposes is called "gray zone" activity or gray-zone forces. The term "gray" is used to indicate that the activity is not a clear use of military force but also indicates the use of non-military forces to achieve what are clearly military and strategic ends (with non-military forces often backed up by actual military forces). China's purpose in using gray-zone forces is clearly to complicate foreign navies' responses, given that the rules of war and of peacetime are distinct and constrain what foreign militaries, coast guards, or other maritime forces can do legally or without potentially provoking a military escalation with China.

China's Maritime Militia dates back to the 1970s, but it has become a regular and controversial presence in the Indo-Pacific region since the 2000s.[8] China's Maritime Militia are deployed regularly in parts of the South China Sea, particularly around the Spratly Islands, as well as anywhere that Beijing views as important to its protection of claims to sovereign territory, whether these are areas of land or sea. China's distant-water commercial fishing fleet is estimated today to be in the thousands of vessels, with an estimated 300 or so operating as Maritime Militia in the South China Sea alone.[9]

Some PRC sovereignty claims, such as China's "Nine-Dash Line" that covers nearly the entire South China Sea, are contested by other states and have been deemed illegal under international law. This makes the presence and aggressive actions by China's Maritime Militia in these waters both controversial and problematic. Their presence, when blocking lawful transit by foreign vessels, oil and gas or underwater scientific explorations, or simply fishing is intended to assert PRC sovereignty claims, to deter or coerce perceived foreign interlopers, or, at times, to protect or facilitate illegal, unregulated, and unreported (IUU) fishing, is illegal under international law.[10]

China's neighbors have been increasingly vocal about aggressive PRC activities at sea and within their own claimed Exclusive Economic Zones (EEZ), with Indonesia, Malaysia, Vietnam, and the Philippines among those making public complaints.[11] In the United States, the Biden administration, too, is further publicizing PRC actions in an attempt to deter China's aggressive maritime activities, whether by military or paramilitary forces.

In addition, according to the US Department of Defense, China's Coast Guard is "the largest maritime law enforcement fleet in the world. Its newer vessels are larger and more capable than older vessels, allowing them to operate further off shore and remain on station longer."[12] The China Coast Guard (CCG) often operates alongside the PLAN and the Maritime Militia in its mission to defend PRC sovereignty claims. The CCG, established in 2013 following a major restructuring of China's maritime forces, also acts as a law enforcement agency, conducting operations to counter illegal fishing and smuggling and addressing other maritime security concerns. The CCG is part of China's internal security forces, answering bureaucratically to the People's Armed Police (PAP), an armed force responsible for domestic security and protection of the Chinese Communist Party.

As the above brief descriptions make clear, China's naval and maritime forces—including military, paramilitary, and law enforcement forces—have grown rapidly and, in the instance of its naval fleet and coast guard, to become the world's largest (at least in terms of numbers of vessels). In addition, these forces are often deployed jointly in order to provide Beijing with a gray zone of deniable use of military force, though the PLAN is often lurking behind China's other maritime forces when confronting foreign vessels. China has shown itself to be quite willing to employ its naval and maritime powers in an aggressive manner in service to Chinese foreign policy and maritime ambitions, and Beijing has a growing capacity to do so.

China's Continuing Maritime Industrial Development

Another traditional measure of maritime power is maritime industry. China's maritime industrial development also has grown substantially and over a generally short period of time. China's shipbuilding industry, for example, is now the world's largest and most productive. This progress has led to advances in other industry sectors such as fishing, energy, and aquaculture. China also has invested considerable funds into its own maritime infrastructure (shipyards, ports, marine communications, etc.) both at home and abroad.

Since the turn of the century, China has focused on shipbuilding as a key strategic industry, resulting in the PRC becoming the world's top shipbuilder by around 2010.[13] According to the latest estimates available (April 2023) as reported in the *South China Morning Post* (SCMP) newspaper, China maintains its overall lead over South Korea in the shipbuilding sector.[14] As the *SCMP* outlines, the PRC currently makes up 39 percent of the world shipbuilding industry, while the Republic of Korea constitutes 33 percent, based on market research conducted by the British firm Clarkson Research Services. The PRC, South Korea, and Japan, taken together, make up over 90 percent of the world's shipbuilding market, when calculated by tonnage.[15]

Much like its naval capabilities, however, while the PRC maintains a lead in terms of the total number of commercial ships built and on order, China lags its competitors in terms of the quality and level of advanced ship technology, the reporting notes. This general observation tracks with personal experience. Having had the opportunity to visit both US and PRC shipyards, it was easy for even an untrained observer to see a qualitative difference in machinery, quality controls, and safety measures employed.

In shipbuilding, South Korea is considered to be dominant in more high-tech ship building capabilities as well as in terms of building more eco-friendly ships, even though China has more ship orders overall on its books.[16] It remains to be seen which country will dominate the future shipbuilding market. Who prevails in this competition could depend on whether customers value quality or quantity and more advanced and eco-conscious ships over lower-cost vessels.[17]

If the future market is focused on more advanced technology, China might be at a disadvantage, at least in the near-term. Experts on shipbuilding cited in the *SCMP* report indicate that China faces an innovation hurdle if seeking to compete on building more advanced and eco-friendly ships, especially if ports around the globe impose more strict environmental regulations on the types of ships able to enter as part of Blue Economy or other maritime and environmental programs. China has published industrial plans that indicate efforts to develop smart, autonomous, and more eco-friendly vessels, but these efforts are likely to lag those of more advanced economies like South Korea, at least for a period of time.[18] Nevertheless, Shanghai's Jiangsu New Yangzi Shipbuilding is reported recently to have delivered a zero-emission containership vessel to Maersk that meets the International Maritime Organization's new environmental standards, indicating the time lag might not be terribly long.[19]

China was able to advance its shipbuilding capabilities in much the same way as it did in the information technology and other key industrial sectors deemed to be strategically important in Beijing. China has been able to achieve, at least in some key sectors, rapid technological advancement mainly through industrial plans (including the *Made in China 2025* plan) that incentivize development and attract foreign investment and foreign technology transfers, through mandated (formally and informally) foreign-joint ventures and collaborative research efforts, by learning from industry-leading foreign partners about industry development, production, processes, services, and repair, as well as by producing at-first simple components that, over time, lead to the production of more advanced parts at lower cost and higher production scale than China's foreign competitors can produce. A key element of being able to progress in this fashion, of course, is infrastructure, which China has been investing in for decades at home and now also abroad. China's inherent economies of scale and adept use of its market advantage in competing with foreign enterprises apply to the maritime sector as they have the information technology domain.

Development of China's shipbuilding industry yields benefits also for the development of other maritime industrial sectors, such as offshore energy (e.g., oil and gas exploration or offshore wind and solar energy), deep sea exploration platforms and vessels, and even aquaculture platforms and vehicles. China has witnessed technological and industrial advances in all of these sectors, based in part on its expanded maritime industrial capabilities from building a world-leading shipbuilding industry.

According to the United Nations Conference on Trade and Development, China's ownership of merchant marine commercial vessels is ranked number two in the world, as of early 2022. The PRC trails Greece (18 percent) with

13 percent ownership of the global total, with Japan (11 percent), Singapore (6 percent), and Hong Kong (5 percent) rounding out the top five.[20]

China's overall fishing fleet is even larger. According to the United Nations, China has the largest fishing fleet in the world, estimated at over half a million vessels (564,000), even after a Beijing-ordered fleet reduction from what had been over a million vessels just a decade ago.[21] As reported by *The New York Times*, China's deep-water, distant fishing fleet is also the world's largest, numbering "nearly 3,000 ships," although estimates vary.[22]

China's distant-water fishing practices are now well-known given the prominence of its controversial and, at times, illegal activity in locations around the globe, spanning the South China Sea to the Galapagos Islands. At the same time, China leads the world in terms of aquaculture, as measured by overall tonnage.[23] China's demand for fish as a food staple is driving much of the country's distant-water fishing, thereby depleting fish stocks around the globe, much as they have been depleted already on and around the Mainland. It is not simply the number of Chinese distant-water fishing vessels that has become problematic, however, but also their practices, including indiscriminate fishing practices and equipment that can undermine the sustainability of fish stocks and do harm to the marine environment.

Finally, China's maritime industrial development has led to an increase in domestic marine and maritime service capabilities, including the establishment of new marine and maritime service organizations and logistics capabilities, as well as industry data services. Developing industry sector service organizations, processes, and logistics is an essential part of developing an industry cluster and for providing various means of information sharing. The PRC is not known for being transparent in terms of sharing data with outside experts, but data collection and analysis of marine and maritime activities as well as services helpful in advancing a strategic industry sector such as this are valued internally as means of China's domestic industrial and technological development.

While aimed at enhancing China's domestic capacity and, in part, a response to international maritime rules, China's investments in its maritime infrastructure, communications, and services at home are also meant to serve the Party's interests overseas. For example, according to Chinese media, China's maritime services have aided port expansion efforts in Mauritania "making it an important logistics node along the 21st Century Maritime Silk Road."[24]

China's Maritime Infrastructure Restructuring and Investments

Investment in Chinese shipyards, ports, bases, and other maritime infrastructure has been a priority for planners in Beijing since before Xi Jinping took over leadership of the Chinese Communist Party. A key part of Xi's plans to expand and advance China's maritime infrastructure, capabilities, and capacity has been to connect development efforts at home with investments overseas as part of the Belt and Road Initiative.

China's shipyards once numbered in the several hundred. Following Beijing's restructuring of this sector over the past decade—a strategy designed to eliminate many of the smaller-sized, privately owned shipyards—the number of Chinese shipyards is now approximately 100 (totaling 117 in 2019).[25] For comparison, the United States has 154 private shipyards for new builds, more than 300 that are doing ship repair, and, of these, 4 shipyards that primarily build and repair ships for the US Navy.[26]

A reduction in the overall number of Chinese shipyards is believed to have reduced redundancies and other inefficiencies in China's shipbuilding industry, while allowing the remaining shipyards to focus on Beijing's priority development plans. Of China's top 100 shipyards, nearly half (45) are State-Owned Enterprises, 49 are privately owned domestic firms, while 5 are foreign-owned.[27] Jiangsu, Zhejiang, and Guangdong Provinces dominate as locations for Chinese domestic shipyards due to their locations near the mouths of the Yangtze and Pearl Rivers. The Yangtze River Delta is, in fact, home to China's largest shipbuilding industry cluster, according to the OECD, connecting shipyards in Jiangsu Province and in Shanghai with those located in Anhui and Hubei Provinces.[28]

China's shipbuilding capabilities include the production also of dredgers, which are essential platforms for conducting land reclamation and in constructing deep-water ports, among other uses. Land reclamation is a cause of serious concern related to China's island-building activities in the South China Sea, in particular. China's extensive island-extending efforts there have raised security alarms across the Indo-Pacific region and resulted in tremendous marine environmental damage to the area.

Dredgers are also used in establishing and expanding deep-water ports. According to the World Shipping Council, China is home to a third of the top 60 ports in the world by trade volume (20 ports of the top 60), constituting 6 of the top 10 and 4 of the top 5 ports in the world.[29] Notably, none of these top listings including Hong Kong. As offshore energy opportunities grow and the need for larger-sized vessels to transport these capabilities does as well, ports around the world are being expanded and harbors dredged for greater depths in order to accommodate larger-sized ships such as Very Large and Ultra Large Crude Carriers as well as super-size cruise ships and other large-size platforms (e.g., platforms transporting offshore wind turbines). Chinese dredgers are likely to be in high demand both at home and abroad for some time.

Chinese dredging vessels are also causing security and environmental concerns, however, for nearby states and particularly Taiwan. PRC dredging vessels in recent years have been encroaching on areas around islands administered by Taiwan to scoop sand for construction projects on the Mainland. Taiwanese authorities view these acts as provocative actions and gray zone tactics intended to bolster PRC claims to sovereignty over these islands and the seas surrounding them.[30] At times, the number of Chinese dredgers involved in these near-island operations have been reported to be in the hundreds.[31] In addition to environmental damage and security concerns leading to Taiwan's Coast Guard responding repeatedly to such incidents, the dredging activity is reported to have damaged marine life as well as undersea communications cables.[32]

In what appears to be a more cooperative activity, China is reported also to be involved in dredging efforts to expand (perhaps deepen) Cambodia's Ream Naval Base, where China's military could establish a presence.[33] The US Defense Department's latest annual report notes that Cambodia is likely to be the site of China's first overseas military base in the Indo-Pacific region.[34]

As these brief examples indicate, China's shipbuilding and related capabilities are sizeable and growing. To the degree that offshore energy and other at-sea business expands, the demand for Chinese vessels, platforms, and services is likely to grow.

At present, there is only limited detailed and public information available to outside observers about what China is building domestically and what activities its maritime representatives are involved in overseas. With regard to China's Belt and Road Initiative, in particular, and PRC investments therein, transparency also is lacking given PRC government opacity plus the fact that there is no centralized institution to collect, much less share, comprehensive data on BRI activities and investments. This task is left to private-sector, academic, and government analysts to discern. An investigation conducted by the *Nikkei Asia* news site indicates that China has invested in at least 25 overseas ports or wharves in 18 countries, spanning Central and South America, Europe, Africa, the Middle East, and Southeast Asia during a ten-year period (2010–20).[35] These investments amounted to $11 billion at the time of the report (January 2020) or $12.6 billion in real dollars in mid-2023.[36] According to *Nikkei Asia*'s findings, two Chinese State-Owned Enterprises dominate these investments, with China Merchant Group investing in 11 ports and COSCO Group in another 9.

The United States and other governments have raised concerns about some of the PRC's overseas port investments, given China's dual-use development model and technology transfer practices amidthe PRC's quest to become a maritime power, as well as cyber surveillance practices and other infrastructure-related concerns. Where China invests in port infrastructure abroad, Chinese-made cyber infrastructure (typically the installation of Chinese-origin Huawei technology) has followed at times as part of these agreements. Such concerns are magnified where foreign investment does not appear to make financial sense (e.g., Sri Lanka's Colombo port), suggesting that China's interest is more geostrategic than economic and risking host countries owing bills to the PRC that they cannot repay, potentially ending up in China's debt in every sense of the word.

In addition to Colombo's port project, PRC port investments in the Greek port of Piraeus (Greece being a NATO member) and the establishment of the

PLA's first overseas support base very near to where US Navy vessels dock in the African port of Djibouti also are notable concerns for the United States and its allies. The 2022 annual report on China's military capabilities by the US Department of Defense noted, too, that "The PRC has likely considered Cambodia, Myanmar, Thailand, Singapore, Indonesia, Pakistan, Sri Lanka, United Arab Emirates, Kenya, Equatorial Guinea, Seychelles, Tanzania, Angola, and Tajikistan, among other places, as locations for PLA military logistics facilities."[37]

In addition to ports and development zones, China's infrastructure investments overseas also include building roads and highways. Roads built by China in recent years include Papua New Guinea's Independence Boulevard and Tonga's national roadway.[38] Highways include Vanuatu's Malakula Island Highway and Micronesia's Pohnpei Highway.[39]

China's rapid expansion of its domestic naval and maritime capabilities plus its expanding overseas investments, access, and presence in strategic places (possibly also future military bases) amount to substantial Chinese maritime power and influence. These efforts are strategic in nature, not merely investment or export opportunities being pursued abroad. According to US Defense Department testimony to Congress in 2019, China's military has explained to US officials that their aim is "'safeguard[ing] China's overseas interests' and … need to build its far seas forces and a need for 'overseas logistical facilities'."[40] Citing China's official *Science of Military Strategy* volume, the US Defense Department official noted that China's "military strategists have also long been concerned with safeguarding China's maritime industry and the ability of Chinese ships to transit strategic sea lines of communication."[41]

By Most Measures, China Is Already a Maritime Power

According to all of the traditional measures of maritime power outlined above, China can today be considered a maritime power. The term "maritime power" can be viewed through various lenses and interpretations and, at times, interchangeably with the word "seapower." Naval historian Geoffrey Till defines the latter in two dimensions: "Seapower as an input" and "Seapower as an output." By the first category, Till means "navies, coastguards, the marine or civil-maritime industries broadly defined and, where relevant, the contribution of land and air forces." In explaining the notion "Seapower as an output," Till notes that

> Seapower is not simply about what it takes to use the sea … It is also the capacity to influence the behavior of other people or things by what one does at or from the sea. This approach defines seapower in terms of its consequences, its outputs not the inputs, the ends, not the means. It is, moreover, about the sea-based capacity to determine events both at sea and on land.[42]

As an ingredient that supports and enhances maritime and naval development (inputs) and that can be exported as a concept and platform for diplomacy, trade, and investments (outputs), the Blue Economy concept is viewed here as a tool by which China (and others) can enhance its own maritime development, capabilities, and power while, at the same time, influencing others'. As such, the Blue Economy can be considered an important element of seapower in a contemporary sense.

China's goal, however, is not simply to be a maritime power; it is to become a *maritime Great Power*, on par with other Great Powers with global maritime (including naval) capabilities, power projection, and presence, especially the United States. China's stated goal is to be by 2050 a maritime Great Power (*hǎiyáng qiángguó*, which can be translated literally as "ocean strong country" or as "ocean superpower"). Chinese leader Xi Jinping articulated this goal in conjunction with the 18th Chinese Communist Party Congress in 2012 and has re-iterated it subsequently, as in the current 14th Five-Year Plan (2021–5).[43]

But as China analyst Andrew Chubb notes, this larger goal actually predates Xi's ascendance. Chubb points out that Xi's predecessor, Jiang Zemin, also called for China to be a maritime great power back in the year 2000.[44] This history indicates that China's quest to become a maritime great power is not a new initiative under Xi's leadership, but something Party leaders have sought to achieve for over two decades. A long article outlining Xi's views on China's strategy for building maritime power also dates his efforts back to 2000, when he was governor of Fujian Province, and indicates that Xi's views today are a natural extension of past CCP development strategies and policy.[45] China's maritime industrial and naval development efforts over the past two decades support this conclusion, that Beijing has been working toward this larger goal for a long time as a matter of strategy.

A traditional nuts-and-bolts-only overview of China's burgeoning naval and maritime capabilities, however, leaves out other essential aspects of being a modern maritime great power. As outlined in 2014 by a Senior Advisory Committee Member to China's National Maritime Development Commission, in order for China to become a maritime great power by 2050, the PRC would need to complete 12 essential tasks. Among these are boosting China's status in international maritime cooperation, the advancement of China's ocean science and technology innovative capabilities, and establishing a popular marine culture.[46] These are the sorts of capabilities that traditional measures of maritime power at times ignore. Yet, capabilities such as ocean science, technology, and exploration are essential as well as other geostrategic components critical for developing, employing, and projecting maritime power in the modern age: diplomacy and modern information capabilities, global maritime economic and trade relations, and the projection of military—particularly naval—force through presence and power projection overseas. China's Blue Economy concept provides the PRC potentially with the means to further develop traditional measures of maritime power in more sustainable and innovative ways while also providing Beijing with additional, non-traditional elements of maritime power, which also likely would be attractive to China's neighbors in the Indo-Pacific region.

The Blue Economy's Role in China's Development as a Maritime Great Power

Beyond the military (primarily naval) and civil-maritime dimension of maritime power addressed above, there are other vital, if perhaps more "soft" forms of power, such as diplomacy and economic, industrial, scientific, technological, and informational (including cyber) powers, that together comprise geostrategic dimensions of maritime power in the 21st century.[47]

As the originator of the term "soft power" defines it, "Soft power is the ability to obtain preferred outcomes by attraction rather than coercion or payment."[48] Applying this term to the PRC, Nye notes that,

> As China dramatically developed its hard power resources, leaders realized that it would be more acceptable if it were accompanied by soft power. This is a smart strategy because as China's hard military and economic power grows, it may frighten its neighbours into balancing coalitions. If it can accompany its rise with an increase in its soft power, China can weaken the incentives for these coalitions.[49]

Yet Nye acknowledges that although Chinese leaders have specifically identified China's need for soft power (citing Hu Jintao and Xi Jinping specifically), their interpretation of the term leaves out important political and ideological (i.e., liberal democratic) aspects that Nye, as an American, includes in his definition. In fact, China's interpretation of soft power appears to include attraction *mixed with* a degree of coercion as well as payment (indicating differences in how these terms are typically conceived of in the West as opposed to in China).[50] China's Blue Economy concept helps to build the PRC's soft power (in all these dimensions) and to connect the additional, non-traditional aspects of being a regional and global maritime great power to China's rapidly growing maritime and naval capabilities.

The following section outlines the ways in which China's pursuit of Blue Economy development at home and abroad can contribute to broader measures of maritime power and could provide Beijing with an ability to compete with the world's greatest naval and maritime power, the United States of America. As outlined below, China has articulated detailed plans on how it aims to achieve its goal of becoming a maritime Great Power by 2050 and the role that the Blue Economy will play in these efforts.

Diplomatic Outreach and Economic Integration through the Blue Economy

China has found that exporting its Blue Economy concept represents a new diplomatic and economic tool at its disposal, representing a somewhat unique and influential form of soft power, which is something that is typically in short supply for the Communist-ruled People's Republic of China.[51] In addition, distinguishing China's contemporary Blue Economy development conception and activities from its past conception is the extension of China's "blue" efforts, via strategic planning and foreign policy initiatives beyond PRC borders and as part of Beijing's efforts to expand its global economic and maritime power.

Under Xi Jinping's leadership, China's concept of the Blue Economy has shifted from its origins as being primarily a domestic economic priority (emphasizing innovation in domestic maritime endeavors) to also being a key strategic component of Belt and Road diplomacy. In support of this new strategy was Beijing's announcement of a new *Vision for Maritime Cooperation* in mid-2017, which built upon Xi's earlier-announced *Belt and Road Action Plan*, published in 2015.[52] These two documents, in particular, provide a blueprint of China's plans to develop an integrated global maritime industrial production, supply, and technological development and innovation chain across the MSR by leveraging the Blue Economy concept of development.[53] Consequently, China's Blue Economy concept has evolved to serve as a core component underpinning Beijing's overall strategy of becoming a *global* maritime Great Power.

China views its ambitions to become a maritime great power as being thwarted, however, by the existence of US alliances, partnerships, naval power, and presence in the Indo-Pacific region, as well as by neighbors suspicious of Beijing's strategic intentions. As an element of Xi's Maritime Silk Road and maritime strategic vision, Beijing intends overseas development and export of its Blue Economy concept as a benign way for China to connect to and integrate with its neighbors in the region and beyond by expanding maritime cooperation across multiple dimensions. These emerging international activities and aspirations are outlined briefly below. In this way, Xi's expanded Blue Economy concept constitutes a new and potentially highly significant, holistic tool to be employed in China's efforts to compete with the United States for influence, access, leverage, and presence across the Indo Pacific and beyond.

As described by Chinese state media,

> The Belt and Road Initiative aims to promote the connectivity of Asian, European, and African continents and their adjacent seas, establish and strengthen partnerships among the countries along the Belt and Road, set up all-dimensions, multi-tiered, and composite connectivity networks, and realize diversified, independent, balanced and sustainable development in these countries.[54]

As will be analyzed below, China's export of its Blue Economy concept and planned establishment of blue zones, clusters, passages and more along the Maritime Silk Road and beyond as part of the BRI have the potential to contribute to China's soft power via diplomatic, informational, economic, and technological components of maritime power while also providing dual-use military (particularly naval) hard-power opportunities as well.

The most immediate contribution the Blue Economy concept provides China is to its public diplomacy. As a rising and increasingly assertive (and, in the case of the South China Sea, demonstrably aggressive) power, Chinese diplomats are given the difficult task of making the PRC's intentions and overseas investments and activities appear benign as well as welcome in the region and beyond (or, at least *not unwelcome*). While the PRC does not typically impose formal public preconditions on the economic aid it offers to other states, in contrast to Western practice, past Chinese economic aid practices have proven to be controversial on other grounds, leading some foreign officials to be wary of accepting Chinese loans or assistance. At least part of such headline-grabbing stories is likely overblown.[55] Yet the perception of China as interested in aid (or lending in the form of loans) only for its own economic and strategic gain persists, notwithstanding Xi Jinping's "win-win" and related foreign policy rhetoric.

The expansive BRI and its MSR component, in particular, have done little to assuage such concerns.[56] What the Blue Economy concept provides, however, is a potentially more positive message for Chinese foreign investment and economic assistance efforts, given its promised economic, innovative, and environmental sustainability benefits. In other words, who wouldn't want a Blue Economy of their own or assistance in developing one? China already has become a leading exporter of its own Blue Economy concept, particularly to parts of Africa, and can be expected to further this promising form of diplomacy and economic assistance over time.

The Blue Economy concept is seen also in Beijing as a means of expanding Beijing's role in the development of global ocean governance more broadly. As Xi Jinping's Belt and Road Initiative is an essential element in making China a maritime Great Power in a new international order, so is the Blue Economy seen as an opportunity for China to shape anew the rules, norms, laws, standards, and practices in the modern maritime realm.

Chinese authors tie development of the still-nascent Blue Economy concept, in which China is already playing a leading role, with the potential for China to make an important and influential contribution to how the ocean, maritime, and marine economies will develop internationally and as part of expanding global ocean governance activities related to these efforts.[57] Xi Jinping's catch-all for this ambition is referred to as "Building a maritime community with a shared future."[58]

China's development of the Blue Economy concept is viewed also as a key part of Xi Jinping's more recent campaign to have China be seen as a global leader and contributing "global public goods" in the international arena, as the Belt and Road Initiative is also being characterized by its advocates. Xi Jinping's address to the United Nations in September 2021 announcing China's Global Development Initiative (GDI) is one such example. The GDI seeks to lead other countries to cooperate on meeting the United Nations Sustainable Development Goals by 2030.[59]

Furthermore, Xi's *Vision for Maritime Cooperation* and the earlier-announced *Belt and Road Action Plan* together make clear that China's domestic and international Blue Economy development efforts are intended to be strategically and closely integrated. The 2015 *Belt and Road Action Plan* "suggests promoting policy coordination, connectivity of infrastructure and facilities, unimpeded trade, financial integration and people-to-people bonds, adhering to the principle of achieving shared growth through discussion and collaboration in propelling the Belt and Road construction." As then-PRC State Councilor Yang Jiechi in 2015 explained:

> The 21st Century Maritime Silk Road will present a rich and colorful program of cooperation. In addition to maritime transport and resource development, it will involve research, environmental protection, tourism, disaster reduction and prevention, law enforcement cooperation and people-to-people exchanges on the sea. Not only will it look at the development of the Blue Economy and building of oceanic economic demonstration zones offshore, it will also build onshore industrial parks, marine science and technology parks and training bases for ocean-related personnel. Not only will we go utilizing the oceanic resources, we will also protect well our oceanic environment. Not only should we deliver a good life to our people along the coast, we should also bring about an interconnected development of the hinterland and coastal regions to achieve common prosperity.[60]

Beijing's 2015 *Action Plan* also outlines intentions to "form an infrastructure network connecting all sub-regions in Asia"; plans to establish facilities and network "connectivity" as a priority; promotes standardized transportation, maritime customs, logistics, info-technology, and technical standards; puts forward the concept of an "Information Silk Road" (sometimes referred to as the "Digital Silk Road") of "cross-border optical cables and other communication trunk line networks" (transcontinental submarine and satellite); "promote[s] green and low-carbon infrastructure construction and operation management"; and promotes the establishment of maritime cooperation centers and cooperation on ocean engineering, exploration, environmental protection industries, and hydropower; among other "blue"-themed efforts.[61]

The 2017 *Vision for Maritime Cooperation* further envisions "synchronizing development plans and promoting joint actions amongst countries along the Maritime Silk Road."[62] Specifically, Xi's maritime vision includes what are called "Blue Partnerships," "Blue Corridors," "Blue Passages," and a "Blue Carbon Program." These initiatives effectively expand and inter-connect China's domestic Blue Economy Development Zone model resident on the

Chinese Mainland and seeks to extend their reach overseas, as outlined below.

1. *China's Blue Partnerships along the Maritime Silk Road*

In a speech marking the 70th anniversary of the PLA Navy, Xi Jinping explained the purpose behind the MSR's Blue Partnerships, stating

> The reason for China to propose jointly building the 21st Century Maritime Silk Road … is to facilitate maritime connectivity, pragmatic cooperation in various fields, and the development of the "blue economy," as well as to promote the integration of maritime cultures and to improve maritime well-being.[63]

Over the past few years, China has established "Blue Partnerships" with the European Union, 12 island countries (including Antigua and Barbados, Samoa, Cape Verde, the Maldives, Sri Lanka, and Sao Tome and Principe), Mozambique, the Seychelles, and Portugal.[64]

China's Blue Partnerships initiative promotes a list of 16 principles that countries and organizations involved in the affiliated Sustainable Blue Partnership Cooperation Network commit to pursue. This network includes several Chinese and US foundations.[65] While public information is thin and further information is needed, the partnerships thus far announced appear to have been administered initially on the Chinese side by the State Oceanic Administration, though this role has since been taken up since by China's Ministry of Natural Resources following restructuring of the maritime sector.

Chinese officials claim the Blue Partnerships are mainly tied to cooperation on instituting policies and actions related to the United Nations Sustainable Development Goal 14 on oceans and to commitments made under the Paris Climate Agreement. The EU–China Blue Partnership agreement builds on annual bilateral summits and provides more details, including that the agreement is

> to support the development of a thriving and sustainable Blue Economy by exploring possibilities to foster closer business-to-business interaction and exchanges of information between stakeholders such as enterprises, research institutes, financial institutions and industry associations … Cooperation will also extend to improving knowledge of the oceans through better ocean literacy, enhanced ocean observation and open science and data.[66]

In 2017, the European Union and China announced an agreement to jointly develop a one square kilometer-sized China–EU Blue Industry Park in the Baoan district of Shenzhen, scheduled to be fully completed by 2025.[67] According to the English-language *China Daily* article, "Plans call for the demonstration program to take advantage of Europe's expertise in high-end intelligent marine equipment and Shenzhen's high-tech manufacturing capacity to develop deep-sea submersibles, seabed robots and marine mineral exploitation devices for the international market."[68] Recent tensions in EU–China relations, however, could potentially thwart these efforts.

China's most recent Blue Partnership with Portugal, for which there is even less public information, reportedly includes "collaboration between the two countries' governments, science and technology sectors, businesses and the general public in such fields as maritime governance, marine ecology, marine renewable energy and marine culture."[69]

2. *China's Blue Economic Corridors along the Maritime Silk Road*

China's Blue Economic Corridors are intended to link, integrate, and standardize China's domestic Blue Economy Zones with those located in neighboring states, whether connected by land or by sea. Three of China's six regional economic corridors (see Figure 4.1) are connected by sea: the China–Pakistan Economic Corridor (CPEC), the Bangladesh–China–India–Myanmar Economic Corridor, and the China–Indochina Peninsula Economic Corridor.[70] Infrastructure development, whether railways or ports, is a key part of these plans, as will be the information technology network architecture that serves to connect these various Sino-foreign corridors.

3. *China's Blue Passages Connect Blue Economic Corridors along the Maritime Silk Road*

Establishing cross-border economic "corridors" is not an entirely new approach for Beijing, since China has for many years exported its SEZ-development economic model among developing states in Africa and elsewhere and sought to connect these efforts with those on the Mainland.[71] What is new is the *Vision for Maritime Cooperation*'s plan to further *integrate* China's domestic and overseas development efforts from the local to regional to broader MSR-levels, the latter of which is how the "Blue Passages" are conceived.

Three Blue Passages are envisioned to "jointly build the blue economic passage of China-Oceania-South Pacific, travelling southward from the South China Sea into the Pacific Ocean" along with a "China-Indian Ocean-Africa-Mediterranean Sea Blue Economic Passage" and "another blue economic passage ... envisioned leading up to Europe via the Arctic Ocean."[72]

Beijing's notion of establishing a "Blue Passage" across strategically vital sea lanes remains somewhat amorphous as yet but represents a bold new, strategic, and near-global approach to expanding China's maritime power via

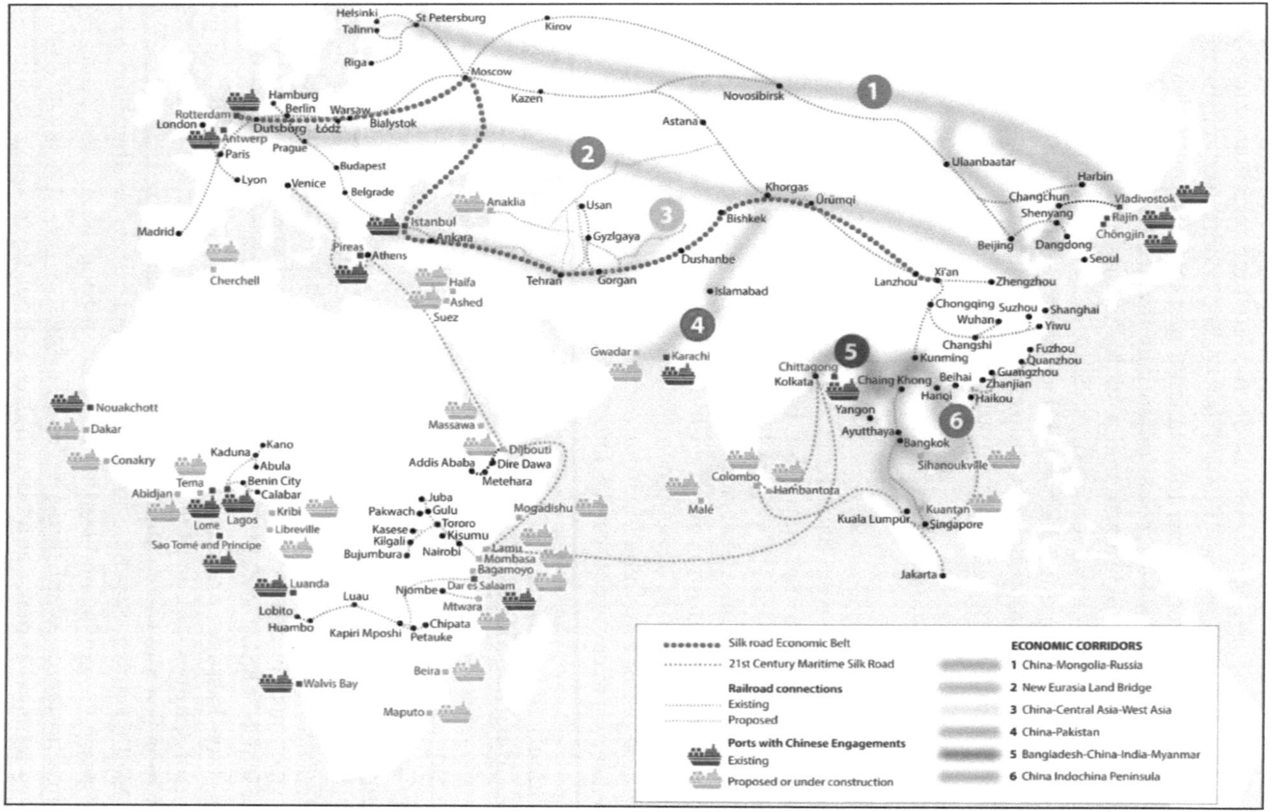

FIGURE 4.1
China's Blue Economic Corridors along its Maritime Silk Road. *Source*: OECD, 2018, 11, research from multiple sources, including HKTDC, MERICS, Belt and Road Center, Foreign Policy, The Diplomat, Silk Routes, State Council Information Office of the People's Republic in China, WWF Hong Kong (China).

the Blue Economy concept. If realized, China's "Blue Passages" would allow Chinese maritime and potentially naval projection that would make Ming Dynasty-era Admiral Zheng He's voyages seem modest by comparison.

4. ***China's Blue Carbon Program***

In addition to the three afore-described "Blue" initiatives is another that China has adopted and is emphasized in Xi's 2017 *Vision*: Blue Carbon. The concept of Blue Carbon refers to the amount of carbon that is found in coastal waters or ocean ecosystems. The idea is to promote healthy marine environments, since carbon emissions arise from unhealthy marine environments and contribute to climate change.

Xi's 2017 *Vision* promotes joint efforts aimed at combatting climate change, including via a proposed new "21st Century Maritime Silk Road Blue Carbon Program to monitor coastal and ocean blue carbon ecosystems, develop technical standards, and promote research on carbon sinks" along with more environmental conservation and sustainable development via joint or collaborative "Blue Carbon" programs.

China is involved in other international blue carbon efforts, as well, but clearly intends to establish its own programs also. Efforts to explicitly include "blue" environmental initiatives in the *Vision* and as part of broader international environmental engagements is likely to make China's Blue Economy plans more attractive to foreign partners and to afford China with the ability to claim progress also toward achieving internationally shared conservation and climate change goals.

In order to implement all of China's ambitious, "blue"-themed plans in a coordinated and cohesive manner, Xi's *Vision* also seeks to integrate marine and maritime industry development across the Maritime Silk Road. According to the 2017 *Vision* document, in this regard:

> China is prepared to provide technical assistance to countries along the Road in drafting plans for sustainably utilizing marine resources. Enterprises are encouraged to participate in marine resource utilization in a responsible way … China will join in efforts by countries along the Road in establishing industrial parks for maritime sectors and economic and trade cooperation zones, and promote the participation of Chinese enterprises in such endeavors. Demonstration projects for developing the Blue Economy will be implemented and developing countries along the Road will be supported in mariculture to improve livelihoods and alleviate poverty. China will also work with countries along the Road in developing marine tourism routes and high-quality tourism products, and in setting up mechanisms for tourism information sharing.

Beyond its scope and ambition, what is striking in reading the 2017 *Vision* document is the extent to which the tone is similar to China's own domestic five-year and strategic plans, reflecting an expectation that Beijing's strategic intentions will be acted upon even by China's neighboring (yet sovereign and independent) states. For instance, the *Vision* goes on to explain that

> Countries along the Road are encouraged to enhance cooperation through pairing sister ports and forging port alliances. Chinese enterprises will be guided to participate in the construction and operation of ports. Projects for the planning and construction of submarine cables will be jointly advanced to improve connectivity in international communications.

As the latter passage suggests, Xi's *Vision for Maritime Cooperation* intends to extend Beijing's economic, industrial, technological, and financial development model and security interests via the promotion and Chinese-led development of maritime industry and infrastructure in a way designed to enhance and interconnect China's domestic and overseas Blue Economy and maritime capabilities across the entire Indo-Pacific region and beyond. In more recent years, Xi Jinping has taken to espousing the need for cooperation in building a "maritime community for a shared future" or, as it is sometimes referred to, a "maritime community for common destiny." Xi's *Vision* makes clear that maritime cooperation and community will be led and defined by Beijing.

What this *Vision* means in practice is already becoming apparent in plans and activities related to China's overseas initiatives, some under a "Blue" umbrella. In addition to China's foreign investments generally, Beijing's plans for the MSR involve establishing various types of PRC-invested overseas investment and development zones, leveraging China's long and relatively successful experience since opening its first SEZ in Shenzhen 40 years ago. For instance, accompanying China's first overseas military base in Djibouti was an agreement to build a Free Trade Zone (FTZ) to be jointly managed by the Djibouti government and three Chinese enterprises.[73] PRC investment in the port of Gwadar, Pakistan, also featured an SEZ for foreign investment. Blue Economy-themed overseas development zones would follow this same logic and appeal to potential foreign hosts. Some of China's overseas maritime investments, however, have led to concerns over military (mainly naval) intentions plus charges of unfair financial practices, including the creation of "debt traps" for developing countries unable to pay back substantial or high-interest Chinese loans.

A second key component in developing a Chinese maritime network along the MSR is the networking or upgrading of overseas zones, ports, or places by installing Chinese-developed infrastructure technology, particularly telecommunications. For example, upon gaining a controlling share in the Greek company operating the port of Piraeus, the Chinese enterprise China COSCO Overseas Shipping Group reportedly replaced the port's entire network infrastructure with Chinese-brand Huawei telecommunications technology.[74] New, "Bluetech" innovative capabilities are likely to be part of future such efforts and could prove more attractive to host countries if promising to be more innovative and sustainable as well as already being lower cost than existing infrastructure and Western-sourced upgrades offer.

Imported Chinese labor and managers constitute a third common component of MSR investments to date. At times China's practice of bringing its own citizens overseas for labor purposes has been a cause for concern among local populations where domestic job opportunities are viewed as being threatened or imported labor affects local skills development, thereby raising brain drain concerns where talented job hunters are pushed to look elsewhere. The promise of new jobs plus more innovation capabilities and opportunities through China's Blue Economy initiatives and investments could offset some of these common concerns among host countries.

Taken as a whole, it's clear that China's MSR as conceived by Xi Jinping is far more than a series of foreign maritime investments but is, rather, a geostrategic and digitized logistics network of connected Chinese-invested places, bases, zones, and nodes intended in Beijing to be interconnected to each other and to the PRC's own economy, infrastructure, technology, and government. The "blue" component of China's overseas investments thus far serves mainly as an incentive for foreign governments to view such prospective Chinese investments as a positive proposition by promising enhanced maritime industry, innovation, and infrastructure capabilities while also sustaining, rather than degrading, the region's marine conservation as might otherwise be expected. Whether any of these promises, particularly those related to environmental conservation, are realized and in a way that serves local as well as PRC interests remains to be seen.

China's record to date, however, on marine conservation has received serious international criticism where its infrastructure development, and particularly island building via land reclamation in the South China Sea, has proven destructive to the marine environment. In 2016, an International Tribunal declared the following judgement:

> [having] considered the effect on the marine environment of China's recent large-scale land reclamation and construction of artificial islands at seven features in the Spratly Islands and found that China had caused severe harm to the coral reef environment and violated its obligation to preserve and protect fragile ecosystems and the habitat of depleted, threatened, or endangered species. The Tribunal also found that Chinese authorities were aware that Chinese fishermen have harvested endangered sea turtles, coral, and giant clams on a substantial scale in the South China Sea (using methods that inflict severe damage on the coral reef environment) and had not fulfilled their obligations to stop such activities.[75]

These sorts of overseas activities by China have been justified under various rationales that sound benign and could be welcomed in the region.

Testifying before the Senate Foreign Relations Committee in 2015, then-US Assistant Secretary of State Daniel Russel observed that,

> Beijing has offered multiple and sometimes contradictory explanations as to the purpose of expanding these [PRC] outposts and constructing facilities, including enhancing its ability to provide disaster relief, environmental protection, search and rescue activities, meteorological and other scientific research, as well as other types of assistance to international users of the sea.

He concluded that "far from protecting the environment, reclamation has harmed ecosystems and coral reefs through intensive dredging of the sea bed."[76]

In order to try to negate some of this bad press, China's state-run media announced in 2019 an initiative to promote "ecological protection and restoration" by placing additional facilities in the South China Sea reportedly to study the delicate coral reefs.[77] Based on China's abysmal ecological record in these contested waters to date, however, many observers are likely to remain skeptical that this initiative and others like it are more than an effort at public relations. To the extent that such efforts can be bolstered, as tied to Blue Economy-themed development activities, such a campaign could aid in improving China's ecological and environmental image, or at least mitigate further damaging regional perceptions of China's reputation.

Through more extensive, "blue"-themed diplomatic, informational, and economic exchanges with states across the Indo-Pacific region, Beijing hopes to establish a more inviting atmosphere for China's growing maritime and naval capabilities to be engaged in regional development and security matters. In this, Beijing is not relying on rhetoric alone, but seeking concrete ways in which the region's shared interest in the Blue Economy can lead to the integration of China's domestic Blue Economy development zones, clusters, technologies, infrastructure, and more with that established throughout the region. This more "soft" approach to expanding maritime power, by employing an idea to which other states are naturally attracted, is something arguably new for Beijing and represents an important way of potentially gaining influence in the region, thereby contributing to China's comprehensive maritime power.

China's Blue Economy, Ocean Science, and Technology Innovation as a Core Component of Maritime Power

China's shift from pursuing myriad marine economy-related development and environmental efforts over many years to a more cohesive, strategic, and sustainable approach to development in all marine, maritime, and naval capabilities under the Blue Economy rubric is driven mainly by China's decision announced in 2012 to become a "maritime Great Power" by 2050.[78] For China to become a maritime Great Power on par with the United States and others, Chinese plans acknowledge that not only is a strong marine and maritime domestic economy essential, but so too is a robust ocean science, technology, research, and business environment, which in turn is fed and sustained by implementing environmental protections that help to draw more investors, industries, innovators, tourists, students and others to marine or coastal areas, resulting in more sustainable development prospects.[79] It is pursuit of this more systems-oriented approach and emphasis on maritime or blue innovation clusters that is intended to enhance China's overall maritime capability (including marine, maritime, and naval interests).

Advances in China's overall maritime power will depend on the extent to which China can be successful in establishing collaborative, world-leading ocean science research institutions. According to a 2017 study on marine science,

> territories that publish the most are places hosting one or more world renowned marine scientific institutions … More broadly, the multidisciplinary nature and the diversity of academic contributors have emerged as key elements in the creation of major marine scientific centres.[80]

Recent studies on innovation clusters generally find similar dynamics at play: technology innovation tends to lead to still-more technology innovation in the same area given the talent pool, resources, funding, and other key elements that exist there.[81]

Beijing continues to promote greater collaboration among China's own ocean science community while also seeking to expand collaboration with overseas ocean researchers. In February 2018, China announced plans for a new "Center for Ocean Mega-Science" to be "located in a science and education park in Qingdao."[82] Among this center's projects is constructing "a marine big data management and application service system," an artificial intelligence-enhanced and Chinese-developed decision-support system for collecting, standardizing, and analyzing marine research data.[83] The latter, Center for Ocean Mega-Science, is part of the Chinese Academy of Sciences (CAS). The authors of a recent paper detailing this particular project indicate that this project will help meet the United Nation's Sustainable Development Goals (SDGs) as well as those of the UN Decade of the Ocean.[84]

The authors of the above paper notably acknowledge at the end of the article their use of US data as compiled and shared by the National Oceanic and Atmospheric Administration's National Centers for Environmental Information (NOAA/NCEI). According to its website, the NCEI provides free access to its "archive of global coastal, oceanographic, geophysical, climate, and historical weather data."[85] This acknowledgment matches what more than one PRC interlocutor has said to me, each expressing that they could not do their own ocean research without access to NOAA's online data. China recognizes that the ability to collect, store, and share such valuable research data is key to further understanding of the ocean. Having confidence in and unencumbered, uncensored access to such data, however, is an open question in terms of establishing a Chinese equivalent.

China's efforts to develop research partnerships in its domestic Blue Economy clusters and development zones with world-renowned oceanographic institutions are another indication of how the PRC has sought to enhance its own ocean science and research. Sino-foreign joint research and development (R&D) arrangements such as with the Woods Hole Oceanographic Institution in Massachusetts (since cancelled by the US partner) fit China's long-time development strategy. China's decades-long technology development strategy seeks to advance domestic high-technology industries via foreign technology transfer, joint R&D, and other ways of learning from foreign investment and research collaborations.[86] Concerns over the potential for advanced technology transfer, a phenomenon now more fully understood by Western partners dealing with China, are likely to limit the extent of these sorts of Sino-foreign joint R&D in the future. Yet, collaborative ocean data sharing and international and multilateral fundamental ocean scientific research collaboration are commonplace, essential to our understanding of the ocean, and something that China can be expected to continue and pursue further.

Moreover, China's comparatively more advanced ocean science and technologies plus sizeable research budget and other available resources exceed most others in the region and provide the PRC with an additional form of maritime and potentially naval power. This asymmetry in ocean scientific research and technological capabilities, as well as Beijing's potential willingness to exploit its advantages at other states' expense (as already demonstrated in the South China Sea), poses serious concerns about regional security and marine conservation with regards to issues such as deep-sea mining and other deep-water resources, interests, and activities.

At the same time, the PRC's comparatively robust ocean science and technology capabilities make China a potentially attractive partner to smaller-sized neighbors who possess fewer ocean science and technology capabilities. Beijing has sought in recent years to establish Sino-foreign ocean research collaborations with neighboring states to promote China's growing maritime powers through a more positive lens. China's joint maritime research arrangements include reported agreements with the Philippines, Malaysia, and Burma.[87] As China's Blue Economy development efforts advance, the PRC could become a more attractive research partner to other, smaller, or less-developed states in the region and beyond.

In fact, China's 2017 *Vision on Maritime Cooperation* strategy includes plans for cooperation on marine science, technology, and innovation. The *Vision* announced, for instance, a new Marine Science and Technology Cooperation Partnership Initiative to be developed "together with countries along the [Maritime Silk] Road" (which, notably, does not include the United States).[88] In addition, the *Vision* seeks cooperation to "jointly survey and research the key waters and passages along the [Maritime Silk] Road ... intensify cooperation in the fields of marine survey, observation technologies, renewable energy, seawater desalination, marine bio-pharmacy, seafood technology, drones and unmanned vessels."[89] Importantly, the document specifies, too, that "Cooperation in mutual recognition of marine technological standards and technology transfer will also be boosted. Scientific research institutions are encouraged to develop partnerships with enterprises in establishing oversea[s] bases for the demonstration and promotion of marine technology."[90] Finally, numerous regional cooperation and joint research centers are proposed such that, "Together with countries along the Road, China will build platforms for sharing of marine research infrastructure, data and technic [sic] resources, and marine technological cooperation parks."[91]

Lastly, China's maritime and naval power can be measured to a degree by the extent to which it credibly deters other states from conducting ocean research in marine areas, particularly regions that the PRC contests and claims as its own. While ocean scientific research is taking place across much of the globe, where it is made more difficult, if not impossible (other than by PRC researchers or those sanctioned by the PRC government), is in areas claimed or contested by Mainland China. In discussions with ocean researchers and experts, this area includes at least part of the South China Sea and the Taiwan Strait and could extend further as China's maritime and naval power expands.

Reasons for not conducting ocean scientific research in such areas, even where such activity is legal under commonly accepted interpretations of the United Nations Convention on the Law of the Sea (UNCLOS), include diplomatic and security concerns (if PRC vessels were to intercede) and financial considerations and expense (including insurance costs). Much of this uncertainty is due to the fact that the PRC has promoted a re-interpretation of UNCLOS terms to disallow certain activities in what it claims as an expansive Exclusive Economic Zone. Thus, China has, in effect, expanded its maritime power by denying and deterring others' ocean scientific research and exploration in areas that the PRC claims as its own but that the United States and other states do not view as lawful.

By developing more advanced ocean scientific research and technological capabilities through innovation and research partnerships as part of domestic and overseas Blue Economy plans, China has the potential to substantially expand its maritime capabilities. Preventing or deterring others from doing the same in certain strategic locations also advantages China's relative maritime power. At the same time, the inability to conduct ocean science in key parts of the globe is likely to impact efforts to stem climate change and our understanding of other natural hazards.

Maritime Power, Projection, and Security via the Blue Economy

As outlined above, maritime power in the modern age includes not only possessing domestic capabilities such as sizeable and technologically advanced hard power in the form of naval, coastguard, and law enforcement forces but also the ability to influence matters at sea and beyond through soft powers related to projecting naval and civil maritime capabilities. The Blue Economy concept, as pursued by China, is a tool by which the PRC (and presumably others) seeks to enhance its own maritime development and capabilities while, at the same time, influencing others'. China's Blue Economy plans and maritime strategies combine in ways that Beijing hopes will help shape the way maritime security in the Indo-Pacific region and beyond develops in terms of governance structures, ocean science, scientific exploration and collaboration, maritime industry and technology, as well as economic integration. As such, the Blue Economy concept is meant to aid China's development efforts at home as well as to project overseas its maritime power and influence.

China's regional economic, environmental, and scientific endeavors discussed above are driving Beijing, in turn, to promote maritime security as "a key assurance for developing the blue economy."[92] China's 2017 *Maritime Vision* document declares that

> Efforts will be made to promote the concept of common maritime security for mutual benefits. Cooperation in maritime public services, marine management, maritime search and rescue, marine disaster prevention and mitigation and maritime law enforcement will be strengthened in order to enhance capacities for minimizing risks and safeguarding maritime security.[93]

By employing the Blue Economy concept as a soft power tool, Beijing hopes to be able to conduct outreach to countries that might otherwise be wary of China's military and particularly naval ambitions. It is one thing to seek military alliances or lesser types of military agreements with states that are allied with other powers (particularly the United States), who view military agreements as complicating such critical relationships or are simply not interested in establishing military relations. These are among the reasons why China's international outreach to Indo-Pacific states has focused more on establishing "places" rather than strictly military "bases" overseas. Establishing Blue Economy-oriented places adds an attractive element to this notion for the PRC as well as for potential foreign hosts.

An important component of China's MSR *Vision* and Blue Economy diplomacy is the dual-use nature of Chinese overseas investments and development zones. The Chinese-invested ports in Djibouti, Piraeus, Gwadar, Hambantota, Sri Lanka, and elsewhere host both Chinese commercial and naval vessels, for instance. There is little reason to think that a Chinese Blue Economy Development Zone or other type of "blue" presence, place, or base established overseas would be a commercial-only endeavor.

As outlined above, Xi Jinping's *Vision for Maritime Cooperation* and subsequent domestic and diplomatic outreach present an entirely new diplomatic, informational, scientific, economic, environmental, security, and strategic framework for the region's maritime development and security. Under this framework, "China encourages countries along the [Maritime Silk] Road to align their strategies, further all-around and pragmatic cooperation, and to jointly build unobstructed, safe, and efficient maritime transport channels," all of which are intended to be linked and integrated with China's domestic economy through Blue Economy Development Zones, Blue Economic Corridors, Blue Passages, and other "Blue" collaborative initiatives as well as a newly conceived "Information Silk Road" meant to connect these efforts via cyber infrastructure.[94]

The extent to which China can actually integrate regional economies via Blue Economy development with Mainland-based zones, clusters, partnerships, and cross-border corridors and passages, etc., remains to be demonstrated. Nevertheless, the plans outlined to date make clear Xi's intentions to do so. Such efforts will impact regional military and security concerns, particularly vis-à-vis US allies, partners, and friends, especially in the Indo Pacific, if they have not already.

According to an earlier US Department of Defense annual report on China, which employed the original One Belt, One Road (OBOR) term for what is now referred to as the Belt and Road Initiative,

> While some OBOR projects appear to be motivated by economic considerations, OBOR also serves a greater strategic purpose. China intends to use OBOR to develop strong economic ties with other countries, shape their interests to align with China's and deter confrontation or criticism of China's approach to or stance on sensitive issues.[95]

China's domestic development of the Blue Economy and blue-themed investments, developments, and connections made along the Maritime Silk Road are intended to facilitate the achievement of these geostrategic aims and in a more appealing manner.

At the same time, China's export of its Blue Economy concept and its support services, logistics infrastructure, advice, and investment offers to others developing their own Blue Economies provides the PRC with a potential source of soft power that is both novel and attractive. Earlier efforts to show China doing good acts around the globe as it expands its maritime and military footprint have tended to rely on what others view as nationalistic demonstrations of Chinese military power. PRC efforts include a multitude of films and television series, often touting China's military capabilities in ways that arouse PRC patriotism but can be seen abroad as worrisome signs of China's military might. The Blue Economy offers a more subtle and potentially more powerful image of China exporting sustainability, innovation, and maritime industrial opportunity—exports that other states generally find attractive—along with the projection of China's maritime force. Study of this form of Chinese soft power has been largely neglected to date but will prove important as part of US–China strategic competition.

While all of the above has been going on in Beijing and beyond, the United States, too, has been active in its own Blue Economy development efforts to promote more sustainable and innovative marine, maritime, and naval development. As with many other important issues, US–China relations and their recent turn for the worse are affecting how the Blue Economy is pursued and defined and in ways that will contribute to US–China strategic competition.

Notes

1. Finlay, Robert. "The Voyages of Zheng He: Ideology, State Power, and Maritime Trade in Ming China." *Journal of the Historical Society* 8, no. 3 (2008): 327–47, 330–1.
2. Michael McDevitt, "Chapter 9: Findings and Conclusions" in *Becoming a Maritime Power: A Chinese Dream*, ed. Michael McDevitt (Arlington, VA: Center for Naval Analyses, 2017), 117–35, 127.
3. Ronald O'Rourke, *China's Naval Modernization: Implications for US Navy Capabilities – Background and Issues for Congress*, RL33153 (Washington, DC: Congressional Research Service, 2023).
4. Ronald O'Rourke, *China's Naval Modernization*, 4.
5. Institute of International Strategic Studies, *The Military Balance 2022: The Annual Assessment of Global Military Capabilities and Defence Economics* (London: IISS, 2023), 235.
6. Although commonly called the "Maritime Militia," this force is formally called the People's Armed Forces Maritime Militia (PAFMM), as outlined in Office of the Secretary of Defense, *Military and Security Developments Involving the People's Republic of China* (Washington, DC: US Department of Defense, 2022).
7. Greg Poling et al., *Pulling Back the Curtain on China's Maritime Militia* (Washington, DC: Center for Strategic and International Studies Asia Maritime Transparency Initiative, 2021), https://csis-website-prod.s3.amazonaws.com/s3fs-public/publication/211118_Poling_Maritime_Militia.pdf?VersionId=Y5iaJ4NT8eITSlAKTr.TWxtDHuLIq7wR.
8. Poling et al.
9. Poling et al.
10. For rich detail on China's naval and maritime forces and strategy, see Martinson, Ryan D. *Echelon Defense: The Role of Sea Power in Chinese Maritime Dispute Strategy* (Newport, RI: China Maritime Studies Institute, US Naval War College, 2018).
11. OSD (2022), 17.
12. OSD (2022), 78.
13. OECD, "China's Shipbuilding Industries and Policies Affecting It," OECD Science, Technology, and Industry Papers, 105 (Paris: OECD, 2021), 9.
14. Seong H. Choi, "Can China's Shipbuilding Tech Catch up with South Korea, and What Role Is the Environment Playing?," *South China Morning Post* (April 29, 2023).

15. United Nations Conference on Trade and Development, *Handbook of Statistics 2022* (Geneva: United Nations, 2022).
16. Choi.
17. Choi.
18. OECD, "China's Shipbuilding Industries and Policies Affecting It."
19. Jasmina Ovcina Mandra, "Maersk-Chartered Maersk Biscayne Departs from Yanzgijiang," *Offshore Energy* (February 1, 2023), https://www.offshore-energy.biz/maersk-chartered-maersk-biscayne-departs-from-yanzgijiang/.
20. UNCTAD, *Handbook of Statistics 2022*.
21. Food & Agriculture Organization (FAO), *The State of the World's Fisheries and Aquaculture 2022: Toward Blue Transformations* (Rome: FAO, 2022), https://doi.org/10.4060/cc0461en.
22. Stephen Lee Myers et al., "How China Targets the Global Fish Supply," *The New York Times* (September 26, 2022).
23. FAO, 9.
24. Xinhua, "Xi Focus: Building a Maritime Community with Shared Future for the Blue Planet" (June 7, 2021), http://www.xinhuanet.com/english/2021-06/07/c_139994197.htm.
25. OECD, "China's Shipbuilding Industries," 10.
26. Maritime Administration, *The Economic Importance of the US Private Shipbuilding and Repairing Industry* (Washington, DC: US Department of Transportation, March 30, 2021), p. 2, https://www.maritime.dot.gov/sites/marad.dot.gov/files/2021-06/Economic%20Contributions%20of%20U.S.%20Shipbuilding%20and%20Repairing%20Industry.pdf.
27. OECD, "China's Shipbuilding Industries," 12.
28. OECD, "China's Shipbuilding Industries," 14–15.
29. World Shipping Council, "The Top 50 Container Ports" website (2021), https://www.worldshipping.org/top-50-ports.
30. Yimou Lee, "Troubled Waters: China's Latest Weapons against Taiwan: The Sand Dredger," *Reuters* (February 5, 2021), https://www.reuters.com/graphics/TAIWAN-CHINA/SECURITY/jbyvrnzerve/.
31. Yimou Lee, "Troubled Waters."
32. Lee.
33. OSD (2022), 145.
34. OSD (2022), 145.
35. Watanabe, "China Drops $11bn Anchors to Expand Maritime Silk Road," *NikkeiAsia* website (January 5, 2020), https://asia.nikkei.com/Spotlight/Belt-and-Road/China-drops-11bn-anchors-to-expand-Maritime-Silk-Road.
36. Watanabe.
37. OSD (2022), XII.
38. Ministry of Foreign Affairs (PRC), "Fact Sheet: Cooperation between China and the Pacific Island Countries" (May 17, 2022), https://www.fmprc.gov.cn/mfa_eng/wjdt_665385/2649_665393/202205/t20220524_10691917.html.
39. Ministry of Foreign Affairs (PRC), "Fact Sheet: Cooperation between China and the Pacific Island Countries."
40. Sbragia, Chad, "Testimony before the US Congress Subcommittee on Coast Guard and Maritime Transportation Hearing on China's Maritime Silk Road Initiative" (October 17, 2019), https://www.congress.gov/116/meeting/house/109805/witnesses/HHRG-116-PW07-Wstate-SbragiaC-20191017.pdf.

41. Sbragia.
42. Geoffrey Till, *Seapower: A Guide for the 21st Century* (London: Taylor & Francis, 4th ed.), 24–7.
43. Xinhua, "Outline of the People's Republic of China 14th Five-Year Plan."
44. Chubb, "Xi Jinping and China's Maritime Policy."
45. Jianyou Wang, "A Study of Xi Jinping's Thought of Sea Strategy" [习近平建设海洋强国战略探析]," *Journal of Liaoning Normal* University (Social Science Edition), vol. 42, no. 5, trans. CNKI Database (September 2019), DOI: 10.16216/j.cnki.lsxbwk.201905103.
46. Mingyi Cheng, "By 2050 China Will Have Established Itself as a Maritime Great Power," *China Ocean News (Zhongguo Haiyang Bao)*, trans. Claire Bilden (January 13, 2014), 1–2.
47. The term "soft power" is used here in the sense theorized by Joseph Nye but updated since. See Joseph Nye, "Soft Power: The Origins and Political Progress of a Concept," Comment in *Palgrave Communications* (February 21, 2017), p. 1, DOI: 10.1057/palcomms.2017.8.
48. Nye.
49. Nye.
50. For a discussion of Chinese soft power and how the notion of coercion and payments fits into China's conception, see Jean-Marc F. Blanchard and Fujia Lu, "Thinking Hard about Soft Power: A Review and Critique of the Literature of Soft Power," *Asian Perspective*, vol. 36, no. 4, Special Issue: China and Soft Power (Oct–Dec 2022), 565–89.
51. On other ways China has sought to develop soft power as it expands it maritime and naval power overseas (i.e., supporting multilateral anti-piracy operations in the Gulf of Aden since 2008) but at a time when US–China relations were at a relatively high point, see Andrew S. Erickson and Austin M. Strange, "China's Blue Soft Power: Antipiracy, Engagement, and Image Enhancement." *Naval War College Review*, Winter 2015, 68, no. 1 (Newport, RI, Naval War College Press, 2015): 71–91.
52. See, respectively, Information Office of the State Council, "Vision for Maritime Cooperation under the Belt and Road Initiative" (Beijing, Xinhua News Agency, June 20, 2017), http://news.xinhuanet.com/english/2017-06/20/c_136380414.htm; and Information Office of the State Council, *One Belt One Road Action Plan* (Beijing: Xinhua News Agency, March 2015), https://www.fmprc.gov.cn/eng/topics_665678/2015zt/xjpcxbayzlt2015nnh/201503/t20150328_705553.html. Both documents were available in English-language translations.
53. Kathleen A. Walsh, Testimony before the House Subcommittee on Coast Guard and Maritime Transportation Hearing on "China's Maritime Silk Road Initiative: Implications for the Global Maritime Supply Chain" (October 19, 2019).
54. Information Office of the State Council, "Vision and Actions on Jointly Building Silk Road Economic Belt and 21st Century Maritime Silk Road," *One Belt One Road Action Plan* (Beijing: Xinhua News Agency, March 2015).
55. Deborah Brautigam, *The Dragon's Gift: The Real Story of China in Africa* (Oxford: Oxford University Press, 2009).
56. James Griffiths, "Are the Wheels Coming off China's Belt and Road Megaproject?," *CNN* (December 31, 2018), http://www.cnn.com2018/12/31/asia/china-kenya-belt-road-bri-intl/index.html.

57. Wei Yang and Hao Kong, "The Development of Blue Economy from the Perspective of Global Ocean Governance," *Ocean Development and Management* (February 2019), 33–6.
58. Xinhua, "Xi Focus: Building a Maritime Community with Shared Future for the Blue Planet" (June 7, 2021), http://www.xinhuanet.com/english/2021-06/07/c_139994197.htm.
59. PRC Ministry of Foreign Affairs, "Global Development Initiative-Building on 2030 SDGs for Stronger, Greener and Healthier Global Development," United Nations Sustainable Development Goals website, https://sdgs.un.org/partnerships/global-development-initiative-building-2030-sdgs-stronger-greener-and-healthier-global.
60. Ministry of Foreign Affairs (PRC) website, 2015, http://www.fmprc.gov.cn/mfa_eng/zxxx_662805/t1249761.shtml.
61. State Council, 2015.
62. State Council, 2017.
63. CCTV, "Xiplomacy: Xi Advocates Building Maritime Community with Shared Future."
64. See Xinhua News Agency, "China Promotes Blue Partnership with Island Countries," *ChinaPlus*. Electronic (Beijing, September 22, 2017), http://chinaplus.cri.cn/news/business/12/20170922/30253.html; Xinhua News Agency, *News Analysis: Why Portugal's "Blue Partnership" with China is Win-Win* (December 4, 2018) http://www.xinhuanet.com/english/2018-12/04/c_137650888.html; and "Promoting the Blue Partnership for a Shared Sustainable World" (World Economic Forum website, accessed June 2023), https://www.weforum.org/friends-of-ocean-action/sustainable-blue-partnership-cooperation-network.
65. Friends of Ocean Action, "Sustainable Blue Partnership Cooperation Network."
66. European Commission, *EU and China Sign Landmark Partnership on Oceans* (July 16, 2018), https://ec.europa.eu/fisheries/eu-and-china-sign-landmark-partnership-oceans_en.
67. Zhao Lei, "China-EU Launch Work on Industry Park Plan in Shenzhen," *China Daily* (December 9, 2017), http://www.chinadaily.com.cn/a/201712/09/WS5a2c8756a310eefe3e9a138d.html.
68. Zhao Lei, "China-EU Launch Work on Industry Park Plan in Shenzhen."
69. Xinhua News Agency, *News Analysis: Why Portugal's "Blue Partnership" with China is Win-Win* (December 4, 2018), http://www.xinhuanet.com/english/2018-12/04/c_137650888.html.
70. The mainly land-based economic corridors (tied to the "Belt" of BRI) include connections across the New Eurasian Land Bridge Corridor, a China–Mongolia–Russia Economic Corridor, and a China–Central Asia–West Asia Economic Corridor.
71. Xi's approach is similar to past Chinese foreign policy initiatives to promote overseas development zones and to Deng Xiaoping's approach to promoting foreign aid as an overseas extension of ongoing domestic economic reform efforts. Brautigam (2009).
72. State Council, *Vision* (2017).
73. Walsh, Testimony (2019).
74. Chris O'Dea, "How China Weaponized the Global Supply Chain," *National Review* (June 2019), http://www.nationalreview.om/magazine/2019/07/08/how-china-weaponized-the-global-supply-chain/.

75. Permanent Court of Arbitration (PCA), "Findings of the Permanent Court of Arbitration," PCA (July 12, 2016).
76. Daniel Russel, "Testimony of Daniel Russel, Assistant Secretary of State Bureau of East Asian and Pacific Affairs US Department of State before the Senate Foreign Relations Committee Hearing on Maritime Issues in East Asia" (May 13, 2015), https://www.foreign.senate.gov/imo/media/doc/051315_REVISED_Russel_Testimony.pdf.
77. Xinhua, "China Launches Ecological Protection Facilities on Nansha Islands," *Xinhua News Agency* (January 2, 2019), http://en.people.cn/n3/2019/0102/c9000-9533673/html.
78. Cheng, "By 2050."
79. Xinhua (Qingdao).
80. Charles (2017), 128.
81. Atkinson et al., *The Case for Growth Centers* (2019).
82. Xinhua News Agency, *China to Establish Ocean Science Research Center* (February 8, 2018), http://www.xinhuanet.com/english/2018-02/08/c_136959522.htm.
83. Zhang et al., "Developing Big Ocean System in Support of Sustainable Development Goals: Challenges and Countermeasures," *Big Earth Data*, 5, 4 (London: Taylor & Francis Group and Science Press, September 2021), 557–75, doi: https://doi.org/10.1080/20964471.2021.1965371.
84. Zhang et al., "Developing Big Ocean System."
85. See the NOAA/NCEI website at https://www.ncei.noaa.gov/access/search/index.
86. Kathleen A. Walsh, *Foreign High-Tech R&D: Risks, Rewards, and Implications for US-China Relations* (Washington, DC: Stimson Center, 2003).
87. Ralph Jennings, "Joint Research Projects Help China Consolidate Power, Peacefully, at Sea," Voice of America (January 27, 2018), www.voanews.com/a/joint-reseach-china-south-china-sea/4227514.html.
88. State Council, *Vision* (2017).
89. State Council, *Vision* (2017).
90. State Council, *Vision* (2017).
91. State Council, *Vision* (2017).
92. State Council, *Vision* (2017).
93. State Council, *Vision* (2017).
94. State Council, *Vision* (2017).
95. Office of the Secretary of Defense, "Executive Summary," *Assessment on US Defense Implications of China's Expanding Global Access*. Annual Report (Washington, DC: US Department of Defense, 2018), 26, https://expanding-global-access-report-final.pdf.

References

Atkinson, Robert D., Mark Muro, and Jacob Whiton. 2019. *The Case for Growth Centers: How to Spread Tech Innovation Across America*. Report, Metropolitan Policy Program, The Brookings Institution and Information Technology & Innovation

Foundation, Washington, DC: The Brookings Institution, 93. https://www.brookings.edu/wp-content/uploads/2019/12/Full-Report-Growth-Centers_PDF_BrookingsMetro-BassCenter-ITIF.pdf.

Blanchard, Jean-Marc F., and Colin Flint. 2017. "The Geopolitics of China's Maritime Silk Road Initiative." *Geopolitics* (Taylor & Francis) 22 (2): 223–245. https://www.tandfonline.com/doi/pdf/10.1080/14650045.2017.1291503.

Brautigam, Deborah. 2009. *The Dragon's Gift: The Real Story of China in Africa*. Oxford: Oxford University Press.

Charles, Kevin. 2017. "Marine Science and Blue Growth: Assessing the Marine Academic Production of 123 Cities and Territories Worldwide." *Marine Policy* (Elsevier) 84: 119–129.

Cheng, Mingyi. 2014. "By 2050 China Will Have Established Itself as a Maritime Great Power." *China Ocean News*, January 13: 1–2.

Choi, Seong H. 2023. "Can China's Shipbuilding Tech Catch Up with South Korea, and What Role Is the Environment Playing?" *South China Morning Post*. April 29.

Chubb, Andrew. 2019. "Xi Jinping and China's Maritime Policy." *Global China Series* (The Brookings Institution), January 22. www.brookings.edu/articles/xi-jinping-and-chinas-maritime-policy/.

Erickson, Andrew S., and Austin M. Strange. Winter 2015. "China's Blue Soft Power: Antipiracy, Engagement, and Image Enhancement." *Naval War College Review* (Naval War College Press) 68 (1): 71–91.

European Commission. 2018. *EU and China Sign Landmark Partnership on Oceans*. Electronic, July 16.

Finlay, Robert. 2008. "The Voyages of Zheng He: Ideology, State Power, and Maritime Trade in Ming Chin." *Journal of the Historical Society* 8 (3): 327–347, 330–331.

Food and Agriculture Organization (FAO). 2022. *The State of the World's Fisheries and Aquaculture 2022: Toward Blue Transformations*. Annual, Rome: FAO. https://doi.org/10.4060/cc0461en.

Friends of Ocean Action. n.d. *Sustainable Blue Partnership Cooperation Network: Promoting the Blue Partnership for a Shared Sustainable World*. https://www.weforum.org/friends-of-ocean-action/sustainable-blue.

Griffiths, James. 2018. "Are the Wheels Coming Off China's Belt and Road Megaproject?" *CNN*, December 31. Accessed December 31, 2018. www.cnn.com2018/12/31/asia/china-kenya-belt-road-bri-intl/index.html.

Information Office of the State Council. 2015. "Vision and Actions on Jointly Building the Silk Road Economic Belt and the 21st Century Maritime Silk Road Vision and Actions on Jointly Building the Silk Road Economic Belt and the 21st Century Maritime Silk Road." Xinhua News Agency, March.

———. 2017. "Vision for Maritime Cooperation Under the Belt and Road Initiative." *Full Text: Vision for Maritime Cooperation under the Belt and Road Initiative*. Beijing: Xinhua News Agency, June 20.

Institute of International Strategic Studies. 2023. *The Military Balance 2022: The Annual Assessment of Global Military Capabilities and Defence Economics*. Annual, London: Routledge, 233–243.

Jennings, Ralph. 2018. "Joint Research Projects Help China Consolidate Power, Peacefully, at Sea." *Voice of America*, January 27. Accessed May 2023. www.voanews.com/a/joint-reseach-china-south-china-sea/4227514.html.

Lee, Yimou. 2021. *Troubled Waters: China's Latest Weapons Against Taiwan: The Sand Dredger*, February 5. Accessed June 10, 2023. https://www.reuters.com/graphics/TAIWAN-CHINA/SECURITY/jbyvrnzerve/.

Mandra, Jasmina Ovcina. 2023. "Maersk-chartered Maersk Biscayne departs from Yanzgijiang." *Offshore Energy*. https://www.offshore-energy.biz/maersk-chartered-maersk-biscayne-departs-from-yanzgijiang/.

Maritime Administration. 2021. *The Economic Importance of the US Private Shipbuilding and Repairing Industry*. Washington, DC: US Department of Transportation. https://www.maritime.dot.gov/sites/marad.dot.gov/files/2021-06/Economic%20Contr.

Martinson, Ryan D. 2018. *Echelon Defense: The Role of Sea Power in Chinese Maritime Dispute Strategy*. Newport: China Maritime Studies Institute.

McDevitt, Michael. 2017. "Chapter 9: Findings and Conclusions." In *Becoming a Maritime Power: A Chinese Dream*, edited by Michael McDevitt, 117–135. Arlington, VA: Center for Naval Analyses.

Meyers, Stephen Lee, Agnes Chang, Derek Watkins, and Claire Fu. 2022. "How China Targets the Global Fish Supply." *The New York Times*, September 26. https://www.nytimes.com/interactive/2022/09/26/world/asia/china-fishing-south-america.html.

Minisry of Foreign Affairs (PRC). 2015. *Ministry of Foreign Affairs*. http://www.fmprc.gov.cn/mfa_eng/zxxx_662805/t1249761.shtml.

———. 2022. "Fact Sheet: Cooperation Between China and the Pacific Island Countries." *MOFA website*, May 17. Accessed June 11, 2022. https://www.fmprc.gov.cn/mfa_eng/wjdt_665385/2649_665393/202205/t20220524_10691917.html.

———. n.d. *Global Development Initiative-Building on 2030 SDGs for Stronger, Greener and Healthier Global Development*. Accessed June 17, 2023. https://sdgs.un.org/partnerships/global-development-initiative-building-2030-sdgs-stronger-greener-and-healthier-global.

Nye, Joseph. 2017. "Soft Power: The Origins and Political Progress of a Concept." *Palgrave Communications*, February 21: 1–3. http://doi.org./10.1057/palcomms.2017.8.

O'Dea, Chris. 2019. "How China Weaponized the Global Supply Chain." *National Review*.

OECD. 2018. "Figure 3. One (Land) Belt One (Maritime) Road." OECD Business and Financial Economic Outlook 2018 (Paris: OECD). www.oecd.org/daf/OECD-Business-Finance-Outlook-2018-Highlights.pdf.

OECD. 2021. "China's Shipbuilding Industries and Policies Affecting It." https://www.oecd-ilibrary.org/docserver/bb222c73-en.pdf.

Office of the Secretary of Defense. 2018. *Assessment on US Defense Implications of China's Expanding Global Access*. Annual, Washington, DC: US Department of Defense, 26.

———. 2022. *Military and Security Developments Involving the People's Republic of China*. Annual Report to Congress, Washington, DC: US Department of Defense. https://media.defense.gov/2022/Nov/29/2003122279/-1/-1/1/2022-MILITARY-AND-SECURITY-DEVELOPMENTS-INVOLVING-THE-PEOPLES-REPUBLIC-OF-CHINA.PDF.

O'Rourke, Ronald. 2023. *China's Naval Modernization: Implications for US Navy Capabilities -- Background and Issues for Congress*. RL33153, Washington, DC: Congressional Research Service. https://crsreports.congress.gov.

Permanent Court of Arbitration. 2016. "Findings of the Permanent Court of Arbitration." *PCA*, July 12.

Poling, Gregory B., Tabitha Grace Mallory, Harrison Pretat, and The Center for Advanced Defense Studies. 2021. *Pulling Back the Curtain on China's Maritime Militia*. Washington, DC: Center for Strategic and International Studies Asia Maritime Transparency Initiative, 77. https://csis-website-prod.s3.amazonaws.com/s3fs-public/publication/211118_Poling_Maritime_Militia.pdf?VersionId=Y5iaJ4NT8eITSlAKTr.TWxtDHuLIq7wR.

Russel, Daniel. 2015. "Testimony of Daniel Russel, Assistant Secretary of State Bureau of East Asian and Pacific Affairs US Department of State Before the Senate Foreign Relations Committee Hearing on Maritime Issues in East Asia." *Senate Foreign Relations Committee*, May 13. https://www.foreign.senate.gov/imo/media/doc/051315_REVISED_Russel_Testimony.pdf.

Sbragia, Chad. 2019. "Testimony Before the US Congress Subcommittee on Coast Guard and Maritime Transportation." *Hearing on China's Maritime Silk Road Initiative*. Washington, DC. https://www.congress.gov/116/meeting/house/109805/witnesses/HHRG-116-PW07-Wstate-.

Till, Geoffrey. 2018. *Seapower: A Guide for the 21st Century*. Vol. 4th ed. London: Taylor & Francis.

United Nations Conference on Trade and Development (UNCTAD). 2022. *Handbook of Statistics 2022*. Annual, Geneva: United Nations. https://unctad.org/system/files/official-document/tdstat47_en.pdf.

Walsh, Kathleen A. 2003. *Foreign High-Tech R&D in China: Risks, Rewards, and Implications for US-China Relations*. Washington, DC: Stimson Center.

———. 2019. "Testimony." *House Subcommittee on Coast Guard and Maritime Transportation Hearing on "China's Maritime Silk Road Initiative: Implications for the Global Maritime Supply Chain"*. Washington, DC, October 19.

Wang, Jianyou. 2019. "A Study of Xi Jinping's Thought of Sea Strategy[习近平建设海洋强国战略探析]." *Journal of Liaoning Normal University* (Social Science Edition), September, 1000–1751 (2019) 05-0103-10.

Watanabe, Shin. 2020. "China Drops $11bn Anchors to Expand Maritime Silk Road." *Nikkei Asia*, January 5. https://asia.nikkei.com/Spotlight/Belt-and-Road/China-drops-11bn-anchors-to-expand-Maritime-Silk-Road.

Wei, Yang, and Kong Hao. 2019. "The Development of Blue Economy from the Perspective of Global Ocean Governance." *Ocean Development and Management*, 33–36.

World Shipping Council. 2021. *The Top 50 Container Ports*. Accessed June 10, 2023. https://www.worldshipping.org/top-50-ports.

Xinhua (Qingdao) International Ocean Information Center. 2013. *Xinhua Ocean Development Index 2013*. Annual, State Financial Information Center Index Research Institue, Qingdao: Xinhua (Qingdao) International Ocean Information Center, 87.

Xinhua News Agency. 2017. "China Promotes Blue Partnership with Island Countries." *ChinaPlus*. Electronic. Beijing, September 22.

———. 2018. *China to Establish Ocean Science Research Center*. Beijing, February 8.

———. 2018. *News Analysis: Why Portugal's 'Blue Partnership' with China Is Win-Win*. Beijing, December 4.

———. 2019. "China Launches Ecological Protection Facilities on Nansha Islands." *Xinhua News Agency*. Beijing, January 2.

———. 2021. "Outline of the People's Republic of China 14th Five-Year Plan for National Economic and Social Development and Long-Range Objectives for 2035." *Center for Security and Emerging Technology, Georgetown University.* Edited by Inc Trans. Etcetera Language Group. March 12. Accessed June 2023. https://cset.georgetown.edu/wp-content/uploads/t0284_14th_Five_Year_Plan_EN.pdf.

———. 2021. *Xi Focus: Building a Maritime Community with Shared Future for the Blue Planet.* June 7. http://www.xinhuanet.com/english/2021-06/07/c_139994197.htm.

———. 2022. "Xiplomacy: Xi Advocates Building Maritime Community with Shared Future." *CCTV.com.* June 9. https://english.cctv.com/2022/06/09/ARTIsvgYi0Y5EKiKLkT3lYT220609.shtml.

Zhang, Bin, Fuchao Li, Gang Zheng, Yanjun Wang, Zhetao Tan, and Xiaofeng Li. 2021. "Developing big ocean system in support of Sustainable Development Goals: Challenges and countermeasures." *Big Earth Data* (Taylor & Francis Group and Science Press) 5 (4): 557–575. https://doi.org/10.1080/20964471.2021.1965371.

Zhao, Lei. 2017. "China-EU Launch Work on Industry Park Plan in Shenzhen." *China Daily,* December 9.

5

The Blue Economy in US–China Relations

A "blue economy" is driving technological development, infrastructure growth, and changing patterns of life at sea … all of which creates enormous implications for our maritime forces. – then-US Chief of Naval Operations Admiral Mike Gilday (October 2022).[1]

As outlined in preceding chapters, the United States and the People's Republic of China are each working to develop Blue Economies at home, focusing in particular on fostering "blue" innovative ecosystems and clusters to promote maritime and naval advances. China, however, is also using the Blue Economy concept to enhance its geostrategic advantage overseas, particularly in the Indo-Pacific region. The United States' strategic approach to developing the Blue Economy to date has been less clear.

At the same time, the United States and China are engaged in a contest for power and leadership in the Indo-Pacific region and beyond. The Blue Economy concept is likely to play an increasingly important role in who succeeds in this contest. The competition over the development and diplomatic leveraging of a Blue Economy concept represents an under-appreciated dimension of the current strategic and maritime competition between the United States and China. This competition can be viewed as a new form of the "Great Game," a term coined by Rudyard Kipling to describe late-19th century Great Power competition and carving up of the world map into spheres of influence (the powers then being Great Britain and the Russian empire, each focused on gaining power in Central and Southern Asia). Today's Great Power competition in the Indo Pacific as it involves the Blue Economy can be considered a new "Great Blue Game," and one that has similarly global repercussions.

US–China Cooperation and Competition in the Blue Economy

In the early days of both China's and the United States' entrée into developing a Blue Economy (generally during the Obama–Hu Jintao era), cooperation between the two states was possible, even promising. Bilateral conferences and symposia on the Blue Economy took place as well as maritime industry

DOI: 10.1201/9781003396116-5

events open to both US and PRC attendees. Top US oceanographic institutes such as the Woods Hole Oceanographic Institute (WHOI) established research programs with PRC counterparts in China, and US Government officials from the State Department, the National Oceanic and Atmospheric Administration (NOAA), and elsewhere collaborated with PRC officials on establishing Blue Economy-related initiatives. It was possible for analysts and academic experts to conduct field research in China and in the United States on the Blue Economy without real fears of being accused of espionage. Today, much of this activity is either not possible or advisable given growing tensions in US–China relations.

What does remain possible is collaboration (much of it virtual) on basic scientific research. In fact, cross-national collaboration on scientific research remains a key indicator of a dynamic and world-leading scientific community. According to the *Nature Index* (an online database on cross-national scientific collaborations published in major scientific journals and maintained by the journal *Nature*), the United States remains the top international scientific research collaborator overall. China follows closely behind, ranking second on the list in terms of numbers of collaborative articles (for the period of December 1, 2021, to November 30, 2022). From 2021 to 2022, the overall US share of collaborative scientific articles published declined slightly (perhaps due to challenges related to COVID-19), while China's overall share increased, making the PRC first in terms of country share of collaborative scientific articles.

China's ascendance to the number-two rank overall and number one in terms of share overall of collaborative articles reflects a sharp increase in Chinese international scientific collaborations over the past several years. This increase is in response to Chinese Communist Party plans and programs that promote cross-national scientific research and publication. China's rapid ascendance up the research ladder, at least in terms of quantity of publications, patents, and doctoral dissertations, has set off alarms in Washington and beyond about China's potential to outpace scientific endeavors elsewhere.

The United States is ranked number one overall for scientific research in the four fields monitored in the *Nature Index*: life sciences, physical science, chemistry, and earth and environmental sciences. The latter field includes "water research" and is the smallest share of US contributions by far.

China is ranked number two in the *Nature Index* of global science research collaboration on earth and environmental sciences. As noted, the United States is at the top of this list, with Australia, Germany, and Canada rounding out the top five countries that collaborate on earth and environmental sciences (including water research). In this field, the United States and China are each other's top collaborators, indicating that collaborative scientific research continues in the natural sciences despite an overall downturn in US–China relations over this same time period. Yet, like the United States, earth and environmental sciences is also the smallest category share of China's overall published science research collaborations.

US–China scientific collaborations on ocean- and water-related research are likely to continue to some degree and, based on the small share of collaborations to date, could increase as does interest in the Blue Economy. Cross-national basic or fundamental scientific research tends to continue even during periods of international crisis, as it did in select scientific endeavors between US and Soviet scientists during the Cold War. Other types of research collaboration (applied research, engineering, and technology development), however, tend to become more difficult as international relations sour between states. The United States and China have been in a downward trajectory in terms of bilateral relations for nearly a decade, since soon after Chinese leader Xi Jinping took over in 2012 and took China in a surprisingly different ideological and strategic direction.

Cooperation Yields to US–China Competition

The sharply negative turn in US–China relations in recent years is due in part to several developments. The most consequential development is Xi Jinping's shift away from the modern Chinese concept of "hide and bide" foreign policy as followed by Deng Xiaoping and his successors up until Xi's ascendance. Beijing's shift under Xi's leadership to a more nationally assertive and, in some respects, aggressive stance in international relations, has led the United States to list China as a revisionist power in national security and defense strategies. In the United States' latest National Security Strategy (2022), China—and the complicated conundrum it presents—is aptly described:

> The PRC is the only competitor with both the intent to reshape the international order and, increasingly, the economic, diplomatic, military, and technological power to do it. Beijing has ambitions to create an enhanced sphere of influence in the Indo-Pacific and to become the world's leading power. It is using its technological capacity and increasing influence over international institutions to create more permissive conditions for its own authoritarian model, and to mold global technology use and norms to privilege its interests and values. Beijing frequently uses its economic power to coerce countries. It benefits from the openness of the international economy while limiting access to its domestic market, and it seeks to make the world more dependent on the PRC while reducing its own dependence on the world. The PRC is also investing in a military that is rapidly modernizing, increasingly capable in the Indo-Pacific, and growing in strength and reach globally – all while seeking to erode US alliances in the region and around the world.
>
> At the same time, the PRC is also central to the global economy and has a significant impact on shared challenges, particularly climate change and global public health. It is possible for the United States and the PRC to coexist peacefully, and share in and contribute to human progress together.[2]

A more nationalistic approach to foreign policy arose as a major theme in US–China relations under the Trump administration and has been continued in some respects under the Biden administration. The latter is reflected in increased export controls on advanced technologies and policies supporting strategically important domestic industry and manufacturing, such as domestic production of semiconductor chips. The United States' more assertive strategic trade and technology policy approach to Chinese trade and investment practices is in response, in large part, to China's own policies promoting economic and technological nationalism over decades.

The scourge that the COVID-19 global pandemic laid upon the United States, China, and the rest of the world is also an important factor in declining US–China relations. This challenge is exacerbated due to the ongoing lack of transparency from Beijing on the pandemic's origin, which has been even more obstructive than during the earlier severe acute respiratory syndrome (SARS) outbreak 20 years ago.

In addition to these challenges, Xi Jinping's ambitious domestic and geostrategic plans (such as the Belt and Road Initiative), along with a clearly more ideological approach to governing the PRC and in more aggressively conducting China's international relations in the Indo-Pacific region, has alarmed US and allied powers increasingly over time. These actions reflect Xi's intent to rival the US, the US-led liberal international order, and the post-World War II Western ideals that underlie it. Given the PRC's decades-long military modernization efforts and more recent, formal strategic alignment with Russia, as well as outreach to other states unfriendly to US and Western interests (e.g., Iran), the threat that China potentially poses is perceived to have grown substantially over the past decade. This perception of a growing threat is also now shared in other Western and allied capitals. In the United States, threat perceptions of China have grown even across partisan lines (if for different reasons), making US perceptions of China as a threat an unusually bipartisan issue.

For its part, China has long viewed the United States and the West as both a potential threat (though without naming the United States directly until recently) as well as an economic opportunity since Chinese leader Deng Xiaoping ushered in the reformist "Open Door" policy era in the late 1970s. It is under Xi Jinping's leadership, however, that the ideologically adversarial nature of US–China relations has re-emerged. Xi has abandoned the more pragmatic approach to diplomatic and international relations followed by Deng Xiaoping and his successors prior to Xi's ascendance to top party leader in 2012. In doing so, Xi has upended Deng's grand bargain with the West: to effectively agree to do business and focus on economic prosperity *despite* ideological differences (agreeing to disagree on the latter for the time being), allowing China to focus primarily on economic, technological, and military modernization. For Xi, who aims to fulfill what he terms the "Chinese Dream of National Rejuvenation," among other lofty goals, the United States and its Western allies and ideals stand in the way.

In terms of advancing China's military power and maritime strategy, it is primarily the US military, and particularly the US Navy, that present an obstacle to China's regional or global power projection. Beijing views the US military presence and alliances, partnerships, and friends in the region as aspects of what China calls American hegemony. Xi's return to a more ideological approach to international relations has made contending US–China security and geostrategic concerns more difficult to manage and raised further the potential for open conflict.

The implications for bilateral relations of these trends and each country's efforts to develop Blue Economy clusters suggest competition and even confrontation are more likely in the near term than is cooperation. Yet, both capitals are likely, nevertheless, to find mutual interest in the other's Blue Economy development efforts for economic, scientific, environmental, and military strategic reasons. Both states are also likely to be competing for and with Blue Economy-oriented investments, technologies, and innovations developed elsewhere, particularly across the Indo-Pacific region.

Today's US–China competition over the Blue Economy has several dimensions: (1) in terms of developing and defining the Blue Economy concept, itself; (2) in terms of developing domestic Blue Economies and doing so more effectively, innovatively, and sustainably than the other in order to establish vibrant and sustainable Blue Economy innovative ecosystems; and (3) in terms of exporting these approaches to developing Blue Economies elsewhere while leveraging the Blue Economy concept in the broader geostrategic contest between the US and PRC in bolstering political-military-economic spheres of influence. Each of these levels and types of competition also holds consequences for how the Blue Economy will either aid or slow related efforts to curb marine pollution, overfishing, climate change, and other marine environmental concerns.

US Efforts at Measuring an Ocean or Blue Economy Concept

Having outlined in Chapter 3 the evolution of China's Blue Economy concept, a brief overview of how the Blue Economy has developed in the United States is essential to understand how US and PRC conceptions differ and also share similarities, as well as what it means for future US–China relations and the Blue Economy, itself. For the United States, concerns about marine conservation date back to the early 1970s. But the United States' focus on the Blue Economy began only at the turn of the century as an effort to promote what the US government has preferred at times to call the "Ocean Economy."

The United States' own concept of developing an "Ocean Economy" predates China's concept of a Blue Economy by nearly a decade. United States policy on developing a still-evolving national Ocean or Blue Economy concept has evolved over time but has been continuously coordinated in the White House. These efforts began first under President Clinton who, with then-Vice President Gore, focused national attention on the environment and the oceans, hosting the first *Oceans Conference* and calling for an "oceans commission."[3] Congress mandated the Commission under the *Oceans Act of 2000* (Public Law 106-256), in which the Commission on Ocean Policy was conceived and its task was to "make recommendations for coordinated and comprehensive national ocean policy." President George W. Bush subsequently issued Executive Order 13366, establishing the US Commission on Ocean Policy.

The Commission, chaired by retired US Navy Admiral James Watkins and including world-renowned ocean explorer Robert Ballard, among others, published a final report in July 2004, entitled *An Ocean Blueprint for the 21st Century*. The report emphasizes the importance of what it terms the "Ocean Economy" as a "new approach [that] considers the relationships among all ecosystem components," both natural and industrial.[4]

As tracked today in a satellite account established by the US Department of Commerce's Bureau of Economic Analysis (BEA), the US Marine Economy (though once called the "Ocean" Economy) includes the following ocean-related activities and industrial sectors:

- Living and marine resources
- Offshore minerals
- Coastal and marine construction
- Coastal utilities
- Marine research and education
- Nonrecreational ship and boat building
- Marine transportation and warehousing
- Coastal and offshore tourism and recreation
- Coastal and marine professional and technical services
- National defense and public administration[5]

Notably, this list is similar to the European Union's list in what it calls the Blue Economy, which includes the following seven "established sectors": (1) marine living resources; (2) marine non-living resources (oil and gas, minerals, and support activities); (3) marine renewable energy (offshore wind energy); (4) port activities (cargo and warehousing, port and water projects); (5) shipbuilding and repair; (6) maritime transport (passenger, freight, and services); and (7) coastal tourism.[6]

The EU also recognizes several additional "emerging and innovative sectors" of the Blue Economy, for which data is not fully available but for which indications are promising. Sectors categorized by the European Commission as emerging and innovative include marine renewable energy (which includes ocean energy, floating solar energy, and offshore hydrogen generation), blue biotechnology (algae production and processing), desalination, maritime defense, security and surveillance, as well as research and innovation, plus infrastructure (focused on submarine cables and robotics).[7]

By contrast, the OECD lists 14 "ocean economic activities" in its account, in its effort to standardize measurement of the "Ocean" or "Blue" Economy across multiple European states. These sectors include the following:

1. Marine fishing
2. Marine aquaculture
3. Maritime passenger transport
4. Maritime freight transport
5. Offshore extraction of crude petroleum and natural gas
6. Marine and seabed mining
7. Offshore industry support activities
8. Processing and preserving of marine fish, crustaceans, and mollusks
9. Maritime ship, boat, and floating structure building
10. Maritime manufacturing, repair, and installation
11. Offshore wind and marine renewable energy
12. Maritime ports and support activities for maritime transport
13. Ocean scientific research and development
14. Marine and coastal tourism[8]

The difference in terms of the latter count is likely at least in part due to OECD measures of the value added from six ocean sectors where OECD countries (and East Asia and the Pacific countries) dominate: "marine fishing, marine aquaculture, marine fish processing, shipbuilding, maritime passenger transport and maritime freight transport."[9]

Despite the differences in categorizing as well as the naming of these accounts, the similarities between Western "Ocean" and "Blue" Economy sectors are clear. One area of divergence is where some of the "Ocean" or Blue Economy sectors already exist, while others are emerging in all three regional groupings, making any full accounting of "ocean," "marine," or "blue" activities difficult. Over time, these indexes are likely to become more similar and standardized so as to allow easier and better cross-country comparisons.

China's Blue Economy sector classifications appear to be similar, although formal classifications are difficult to nail down exactly given PRC opaqueness when it comes to sharing data as well as challenges involved in translation. Nevertheless, a rough comparison of US, EU, and PRC Ocean, Blue, and Marine Economy sectors, respectively, shows considerable similarities in ways of capturing the Blue Economy (though with sectors going by different names). A comparison of these classifications is depicted in Table 5.1.

TABLE 5.1

Cross-Regional Comparison of Blue Economy Sectors

Cross-Regional Comparison of Blue Economy Sectors		
China Marine Economy Sectors	**EU Blue Economy Sectors**	**US Ocean Economy Sectors**
Marine fishery	Marine living resources	Living and marine resources
Offshore oil and gas Ocean mining Marine salt	Marine non-living resources	Offshore minerals
Shipbuilding	Shipbuilding and repair	Nonrecreational ship and boat building
Coastal tourism	Coastal tourism	Coastal and offshore tourism and recreation
Marine engineering, architecture, and construction	Port, warehousing, and water projects	Coastal and marine construction; marine transportation and warehousing
Marine electric power	Marine renewable energy	Coastal utilities
Marine communications and transportation	Maritime transport	Marine transportation and warehousing; coastal and marine professional and technical services
Marine biomedecine	*Blue bioeconomy and biotechnology*	Marine research and education
Seawater utilization	*Desalination*	(No direct equivalent to China or EU)
Marine chemical	(No direct equivalent to China)	Coastal and offshore tourism and recreation
	Maritime defense, security and surveillance	National defense and public administration

Sources: adapted from European Commission, "Table 7.5 China vs EU Blue Economy sector equivalents," in Blue Economy Report, 2021 (Luxembourg, Publications Office of the European Union, 2021), p. 160. This report compares EU and PRC Blue Economy sectors, using an academic classification for PRC sectors. The latter compares reasonably well with sectors identified in China's 13th FYP for National Economic Development but does not clearly account for the latter's sectors described as shipping services, marine cultural industry, sea-related financial services, or marine public service industry). Italics are from the original, indicating an EU "Emerging and Innovative" sector. Comparisons are indicated as initially determined by the EU for comparisons of the EU and China, with the US list and last EU sector (maritime defence, security and surveillance) added by this author to compare with US sectors as listed in William Nicolls et al., "Defining and Measuring the US Ocean Economy" (Washington, DC: Bureau of Economic Analysis, US Department of Commerce, June 2020). Comparisons with US sectors were determined by the author using "Table B. Items Used by Activity" in Nicholls et al. (pp. 17–24).

Although many of the sectors are similarly classified, not all of them are easily comparable. What stands out most clearly is the United States' and EU's public classification of defense sectors as part of the Blue Economy, whereas the academic listing for PRC sectors used in the EU's original comparison does not list this sector. There is undoubtedly, however, a defense component of the PRC's Blue Economy concept, as there is elsewhere, yet anything defense-related is very likely to be considered sensitive data by today's Chinese Communist Party leadership.

The United States' classification is, at once, more narrow and broader than that used by the EU or China. Two other sectors that belie comparison are the EU's desalination or China's seawater utilization categories, for which the US classification does not appear to have any equivalent sector. Yet, in two other instances (related to marine construction and warehousing as well as maritime transport), a single Chinese and EU classification can only be captured by two separate US sectors (coastal and marine construction plus marine transportation and warehousing; and marine transportation and warehousing plus coastal and marine professional and technical services, respectively). The United States' more delineated categorizations are likely due, at least in part, to differences in pre-existing, standardized industry codes used in measuring the United States economy as compared to those used by the EU and China.

The sector that is categorized as related to biomedicine or biotechnology by China and the EU, respectively, appears to be narrower than the US category of marine research and education. The latter includes all marine academic instruction, training, scientific research, licensing, and more. Consequently, the US marine research and education sector likely includes biomedicine or biotechnology-related research as well as desalination research, along with many other scientific and technology research fields.

Recognizing the challenges inherent in these different definitions and classifications, the US Congress passed into law in late 2022 a mandate for "Blue Economy Valuation." Under this law, Commerce's BEA and other federal agency heads are charged with developing a "Coastal and Ocean Economy Satellite Account ... [and to] collaborate with national and international organizations and governments to promote consistency of methods, measurements, and definitions to ensure comparability of results between countries."[10] The law also includes a provision mandating the NOAA Administrator report to Congress at least every two years on these efforts. The Executive Branch also is charged with the mission that

> defines the Blue Economy ... makes recommendations for updating North American Industry Classification System reporting codes to reflect the Blue Economy; and provides a comprehensive estimate of the value and impact of the Blue Economy with respect to each State and territory of the United States.[11]

US Ocean Bureaucracy

The US Department of Commerce's National Oceanic and Atmospheric Administration and the State Department's Bureau of Oceans and International Environmental and Scientific Affairs (OES) are the leading US Cabinet agencies implementing and promoting Ocean or Blue Economy-themed programs in the United States and overseas. At least 12 other US government departments and independent agencies also play a role (as coordinated in the White House).[12]

Following a promising start on establishing a Commission on Ocean Policy and its 2004 report, the George W. Bush administration's focus on ocean policy appears to have waned in subsequent years, likely due to what were perceived to be more immediate and pressing concerns following the 9/11 attack, wars in Afghanistan and Iraq, and broader counter-terrorism concerns.

Nevertheless, US Executive Branch efforts to develop a comprehensive Ocean Policy that included elements of an Ocean Economy dynamic continued in President Obama's first term, initially via an Interagency Ocean Policy Task Force established in 2009. Based on the Task Force's recommendations, in July 2010 President Obama signed Executive Order 13547, which established a National Ocean Council to implement and coordinate the new "National Ocean Policy for the Stewardship of the Ocean, Coasts, and Great Lakes." These initial efforts at providing definition, strategic direction, interagency coordination, development principles, and policy objectives were shelved by President Trump in 2018. While US efforts to develop an Ocean Economy continued in some manner, overall efforts slowed and their focus shifted toward marine exploration, mapping, and resource extraction.

President Trump's own 2018 Executive Order 13840 overrode Obama-era policies and replaced the former National Ocean Council with a new Ocean Policy Committee (OPC), also operating from the White House as a shared responsibility once again of the Office of Science and Technology Policy (OSTP) and the Council on Environmental Quality (CEQ), who serve as OPC co-chairs and are both a part of the Executive Office of the President.

The newly formed Ocean Policy Committee held its first meeting on August 1, 2018, and established two OPC Subcommittees on Ocean Resource Management (ORM) and Ocean Science and Technology (OST) (Ocean Policy Committee 2018). Although a second OPC meeting was expected to take place in December 2018, there is no public evidence that it was held at that time; the meeting likely fell victim to the US Government shutdown that commenced in late December 2018.

The OPC's next meeting would take place nearly a year after its inaugural gathering. The OPC's June 2019 meeting focused on easing regulatory restrictions on ocean exploration along the US coast and efforts to limit marine debris. This OPC meeting was followed in November 2019 by a White House "summit" to discuss ocean partnerships and R&D priorities. The "Fact

Sheet" resulting from the latter, however, suggests an ocean policy agenda comparatively limited in scope in contrast to the Obama era. According to a November 2019 Fact Sheet, President Trump directed

> Federal agencies to develop a national strategy to map the US Exclusive Economic Zone (EEZ) and a strategy to map the Alaskan coastline … directing the OPC to recommend actions to increase the efficiency of the permitting process for ocean exploration activities across Federal Agencies.[13]

The OPC released these strategies in June 2020, namely the "National Strategy for Mapping, Exploring, and Characterizing the United States Exclusive Economic Zone," "Recommendations for Increasing the Efficiency of Permitting for Ocean Exploration, Mapping, and Research Activities," and "Mapping the Coast of Alaska: A 10-Year Strategy in Support of the United States Economy, Security, and Environment."[14] To conduct the ocean mapping tasks, OPC established a National Ocean Mapping, Exploration, and Characterizing (NOMEC) Council chaired by NOAA's Director of Ocean Exploration and Research.

Based on public records related to OPC activities over several years, the Trump administration's ocean policy appeared focused mainly on emphasizing an ability to explore the ocean in order to allow drilling in ocean and coastal areas. President Trump also issued a proclamation in September 2020 to mandate reporting and authorization of all foreign marine scientific research in the US EEZ, likely a measure aimed at ensuring against PRC and other potentially malign activities in the US EEZ, which notably extends to 14 US territories in the South Pacific.[15] As such, the Trump administration's ocean agenda fell short of a comprehensive Ocean or Blue Economy strategic concept yet did appear to consider the potential for US–China competition in the marine science space.

What stands out in the preceding timeline is the degree to which all four prior US administrations (Presidents Clinton, Bush, Obama, and Trump) developed and managed US ocean policy from the White House. This bipartisan, top-level management and approach to coordination reflects the still-evolving nature of the Ocean or Blue Economy concept in the United States, its inherent inter-disciplinary nature, and the lack, thus far, of any established Cabinet department or independent agency or office that alone can take the lead in administering and implementing it across the whole of government.

The use of presidential Executive Orders and White House personnel also ensures such efforts are temporary in that they can be overturned as a matter of policy by an incoming administration. These nascent efforts suggest that the Ocean or Blue Economy concept has not yet crossed the threshold of being perceived as important enough to be instituted in a more permanent way, as would be the case with Congress mandating by law a new department, office, or independent agency dedicated to the issue. To date the Biden administration also has led its efforts from the White House, selecting to administer efforts through the OPC and maintaining its role in directing Ocean and Blue Economy efforts rather than once again re-starting efforts under an entirely new White House initiative.

President Biden's administration is pursuing a broader and relatively more holistic approach to developing what is now more frequently referred to in US government documents as a Blue Economy (or "New Blue Economy") than his predecessor. In January 2021, NOAA published a *Blue Economy Strategic Plan for 2021–2025* that focuses mainly on creating jobs and other opportunities in the "New Blue Economy" domestically. In 2023, the White House's OPC also published a *US Ocean Climate Action Plan* that focuses on addressing climate challenges broadly, though only mentioning briefly the concept of a Blue Economy and using the term "sustainable ocean economy" instead. While promising, these documents reflect the continuing challenge the Executive Branch faces on how to define, much less comprehensively and strategically pursue, development of a Blue Economy at home and abroad.

The Biden administration is advancing Blue Economy initiatives at lower levels as well, from the Department of Energy to the Department of Defense and beyond, including substantial funding opportunities for Blue Economy programs, projects, and startup ventures. What appears to be mainly missing, however, is a more comprehensive strategy for developing the Blue Economy at home *and* that promotes US Blue Economy objectives abroad as a prominent part of US diplomacy and as tied to US country-to-country or regional relations, technology development, exports, and more. The OPC's own "Ocean Policy Committee 2022–2023 Action Plan Summary" document includes developing a *National Strategy for a Sustainable Ocean Economy.*[16] But this effort, still in development, appears to focus only on US domestic Blue Economy efforts and does not appear to include also foreign policy considerations. As such, it is a step in the right direction, but a broader, geostrategic outlook is needed.

Notably, OPC's document indicates that

> This initiative results from the United States joining the High Level Panel for a Sustainable Ocean Economy, and the attendant commitment to develop by 2026 a national sustainable ocean plan for the US Exclusive Economic Zone. The United States will first develop a National Strategy to help guide development of the sustainable ocean plan.[17]

This rationale for developing a more strategic approach to developing a Blue Economy is inherently international in that the United States is joining an effort established by US allies, partners, and others back in 2018. US membership only in 2021 also indicates the lack of US global leadership on the issue of the Blue Economy in recent years.

From the start, Congress has played an important role in US efforts to develop a Blue Economy. On the one hand, laws enacted by Congress provide necessary authorities and sometimes also funding for programs that the Legislative Branch deems important. On the other hand, when Congress gets involved in policy matters, this is often a sign of an Executive Branch that is not perceived by Congress and its constituents as moving fast or far enough. Yet, in a Congress that has been dysfunctional over many years, ocean-themed legislation has often been passed only through the authorization and appropriations bills that focus on defense matters, since these bills are typically passed every year into law, unlike many other pieces of legislation.

Congress notably was responsible for passing the *Oceans Act of 2000* (Public Law 106-256) and, more recently, enacted into law the authorities, missions, responsibilities, and other aspects of OPC's mandate, which has been expanding. The National Defense Authorization Act (NDAA) for Fiscal Year 2021 as passed into law (Public Law 116-283) reauthorized the OPC (which had been operating under presidential Executive Order) and also designated OPC as responsible for overseeing the National Oceanographic Partnership Program (NOPP) Office (see Figure 5.1 depicting the current US ocean policy

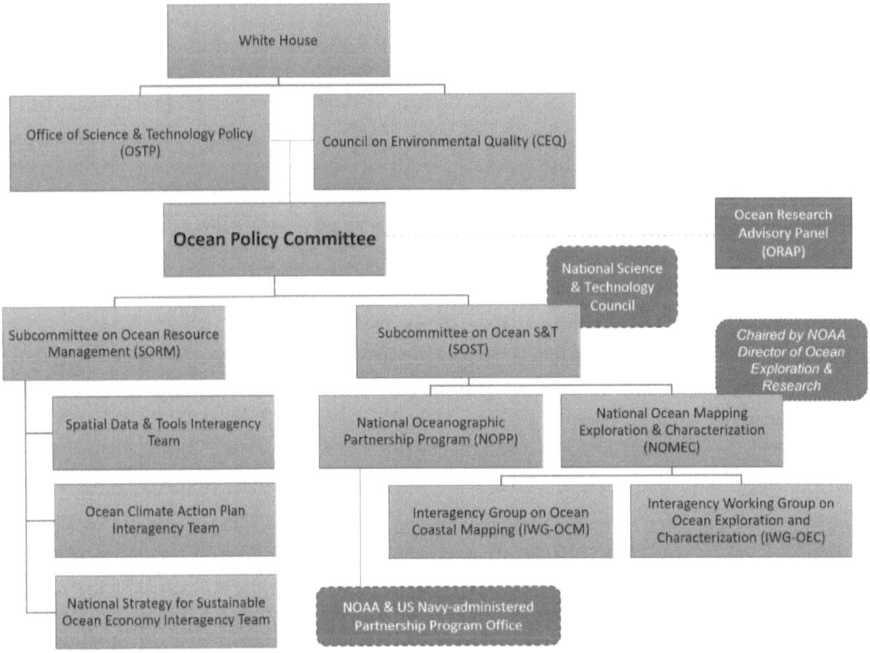

FIGURE 5.1
US Ocean bureaucracy (2023). *Source*: Adapted from National Oceanic and Atmospheric Administration, n.d.b.

bureaucracy). According to its website, the NOPP, itself, was established initially back in the late 1990s and

> facilitates partnerships between federal agencies, academia, and industry to advance ocean science, research, and education. Through this collaboration, federal agencies can leverage resources to invest in priorities that fall between agency missions or that are too large for any single agency to support.[18]

Under the 2021 legislation, the NOPP has been re-designated as an Interagency Working Group (IWG). The US Navy's Office of Naval Research and NOAA Administrator jointly run the NOPP Office as co-chairs of the NOPP-IWG.

Federal agencies involved in NOPP include NOAA, the National Science Foundation, the Environmental Protection Agency (EPA), the National Aeronautics and Space Administration (NASA), the Office of Naval Research (ONR), the US Army Corps of Engineers, the US Interior Department's Bureau of Ocean Energy Management (BOEM), and others. As spelled out in the 2021 legislation, the OPC's oversight of the NOPP under the law includes the responsibility to "prescribe policies and procedures to implement the National Oceanographic Partnership Program, including developing guidelines for review, selection, identification, and approval of partnership projects, in conjunction with Federal agencies participating in the program."

Back in 2009, the US Senate held a public hearing on "The Blue Economy: The Role of the Oceans in Our Nation's Economic Future" chaired by senators from the coastal states of Washington and Maine. The hearing was held by the Committee on Commerce, Science, and Transportation Subcommittee on Oceans, Atmosphere, Fisheries, and Coast Guard, indicating that stakeholders in these sectors likely pressed their senators and staff for this sort of public hearing on issues critical to them. Given the focus of much of the testimony on how the Blue Economy contributes to jobs in the US economy, it is not surprising that senators from Washington state, Maine, and elsewhere would find the Blue Economy issue of interest.

While this Congressional hearing, held in 2009, was timely and arguably even ahead of its time, Congress has since shown only intermittent interest in the topic. A single report by the Congressional Research Service (CRS) on the topic of the Blue Economy—a brief, two-page, "In Focus" overview entitled "What Is the Blue Economy?"—appeared in August 2022 and highlighted the lack of consensus on how to define the term or how to calculate its impact on the US economy.[19] Reports such as this by CRS can be a good indication of the level of interest in issues by members of Congress overall, since CRS is Congress' research bureau and is responsive to their inquiries.

In addition, Congress' Ocean Caucuses are bipartisan groups that members can join if interested in such issues and that are active on Blue Economy and other oceans-related matters. Members of Congress and their staffs also participate in a Capitol Hill Ocean Week (CHOW) event that annually highlights issues related to and sometimes includes Blue Economy topics, though the focus of the event is mainly on marine conservation matters. This event and a related Ocean Awards Gala take place on or near Capitol Hill and are hosted by a non-governmental organization, the National Marine Sanctuary Foundation. According to the group's website, the origins of this event date back to 2001, and its board members have included prominent oceanographers, business leaders, policymakers, and former members of Congress. While likely to highlight issues related to the Blue Economy at times, this effort reflects more of the private sector's and non-governmental organizational interest and advocacy on such issues rather than actual policy or law-making efforts by the US government.

It is China's maritime and naval advances that have caught Congress' attention more broadly, however, with many hearings taking place on these topics and a new House Committee on the Chinese Communist Party established in 2023 to look into a myriad of issues related to China's rise, including matters of defense, the environment, and more.

Concerns over China's expanding maritime interests and capabilities are also likely a major factor in the renewal of an ocean-related expert panel. Under the Fiscal Year 2021 National Defense Authorization Act, Congress acted to re-establish the Ocean Research Advisory Panel (ORAP). According to the legislation, the ORAP is to be comprised of 10–18 experts from the National Academies of Sciences, Engineering, and Medicine, from academia, industry, government (local, state, tribal, and territorial), and "marine science, marine technology, and marine policy, or related fields." In May 2022, the US government published ORAP's charter, indicating its mission is to "provide the Ocean Policy Committee (Committee) of the National Oceanographic Partnership Program with independent scientific advice and recommendations on national oceanographic matters."[20] The ORAP was re-authorized, having been created under the FY1998 NDAA, as was the NOPP's oversight body, the National Ocean Research Leadership Council (NORLC).

These overall limited efforts by Congress to manage and oversee ocean policy by the Executive Branch, however, indicate that progress on implementation has been slow and intermittent, with efforts to coordinate ocean law and policy remaining a challenge even with administrations and members of Congress interested in pursuing a more strategic approach to pursuing an Ocean or Blue Economy.

Continued efforts to develop the Blue Economy have stretched across the past five US administrations and continued despite leadership of the White House and Congress switching back and forth between Democrats and Republicans. This history is testament to the issue's importance to US national interests. Yet, one of the core issues hampering further development of the Blue Economy in the United States and beyond is the debate over what to call it.

Competing Definitions of the Ocean and Blue Economy

As recounted briefly above, what the United States means by the Ocean Economy, Marine Economy, or Blue Economy is not entirely clear. In fact, the issue of terminology and lack of clear and standard definitions for these terms continues to stymie efforts to coordinate development of an Ocean or Blue Economy in the United States and abroad.

The US Government, US Western allies, and members of the OECD prefer generally to use the term "Ocean Economy" to "Blue Economy." As defined by the OECD, "the Ocean Economy can be defined as the sum of the economic activities of ocean-based industries, and the assets, goods and services of marine ecosystems."[21]

Some US Government and non-governmental organization advocates in the United States prefer the term "Ocean Economy" to "Blue Economy" given the former term's implied emphasis on prioritizing marine conservation and sustainable approaches to ocean development while also (if secondarily) seeking to find new ways to leverage economic and innovation opportunities. Advocates of the "Blue" Economy term have argued it means essentially the same thing, while others prefer to focus simply (or more so) on the economic and technology innovation opportunities provided in the blue space (whether environmentally sound or sustainably developed or not).

The term "Bluetech" is also used in the United States and elsewhere, sometimes to mean the Blue Economy though generally considered to be a part of it. Bluetech's focus is primarily (but not exclusively) on commercial and military technology innovation of marine, maritime, and naval capabilities, which is also how some view China's Blue Economy concept. Bluetech does not always factor in notions of sustainable development and environmental conservation, however, and advocates admit those are often secondary considerations to innovation, itself.

Nevertheless, the three main terms—"Ocean," "Marine," and "Blue" Economy—appear to be converging increasingly around the same general innovation and ecosystem-oriented concept of marine conservation-minded sustainable maritime industrial development and, hence, as implicitly concerned about conservation and environmental effects in pursuing maritime economic development and marine science, if perhaps to differing degrees. Some experts advocate using the term "Sustainable Blue Economy" to make the connections explicit.[22] A recent document emanating from the White House adopts the term "sustainable ocean economy," which the report notes is the term used by the World Bank and "is often also referred to as the blue economy."[23]

Earlier divergence in the definitions, however, of an Ocean or Blue Economy—domestically and overseas—was a dispute over more than terminology. This dispute and competition at times impacted US diplomatic efforts in the Asia Pacific region, and possibly elsewhere, to advance the idea of ocean stewardship, at times thwarting international initiatives due to misunderstandings, disagreements, or an inability to agree on basic terms.

As a way of overcoming battles over whose term or which definition to utilize, a working group of the Asia Pacific Economic Cooperation (APEC) forum agreed in 2014 on a "common view" of the Ocean or Blue Economy term, agreeing that

> For the purposes of APEC, the APEC Ocean and Fisheries Working Group views Blue Economy as an approach to advance sustainable management and conservation of ocean and coastal resources and ecosystems and sustainable development, in order to foster economic growth.[24]

This unwieldy, compromise "common view" to which the United States and other states agreed, was pressed by Beijing and viewed in China subsequently as a strategic gain in that the "common view" is referred to as the "Xiamen Declaration" after the APEC forum's then-Chinese host city in 2014.

Since that time, the term Blue Economy has been used more often in the United States, including in both informal and official communications, but not uniformly. The Obama-era US–China Strategic and Economic Dialogues (S&ED), for example, also eventually adopted the APEC common view on the Blue Economy as a practical matter. This is one reason for an apparent shift from the once-common use of "Ocean" Economy to the "Blue" Economy among at least some US experts and officials.

Non-governmental (Track-II) and academic exchanges over recent years also have addressed the distinctions in US and Chinese views on the meaning of the "Ocean" or "Blue Economy" in order to identify potential areas of cooperation or conflict. A 2018 report on one of these non-governmental, bilateral meetings, for instance, recommends the United States and China continue to work to understand these definitional distinctions. The report advocates development of a joint English and Chinese glossary of terms, for example, as a way to further progress and understanding.[25]

Another factor driving confusion in terminology is the growing number of ocean and blue-themed domestic and international conferences. For instance, annual or periodic US or international events with an Ocean or Blue Economy theme include the following:

- The US State Department-led "Our Oceans" conference (initiated under the Obama administration and continued through the Biden administration)
- The United Nations' "Ocean Conference"
- APEC Blue Economy Forums
- The World Ocean Council's annual Sustainable Ocean Summit (SOS)
- *The Economist* magazine's annual "World Ocean Summit"

- The National Marine Sanctuary Foundation's Capitol Hill Ocean Week (CHOW)
- The TMA BlueTech's annual "Blue Tech Week" in San Diego, CA
- The "Blue Innovation Symposium" (formerly called the "Maritime Innovation Symposium") hosted near-annually in Massachusetts or Rhode Island

Notably, an official US State Department list of US commitments made at the most recent 2023 *Our Ocean* conference includes a section on the "Sustainable Blue Economies," which it describes as "sustainable and inclusive blue economic activities that create pathways to long-term blue economic development by addressing the range of stressors threatening ocean health."[26]

The Blue Economy concept and terminology are also gaining popularity in the United States and elsewhere given that the ocean is big "blue" business. According to OECD estimates, ocean-based industries contributed US$1.5 trillion to the global economy in 2010, representing 2.5 percent nominally of then-world gross value added.[27] The majority of this activity was in offshore oil and gas (34 percent), marine and coastal tourism (26 percent), maritime equipment (11 percent), and port activities (13 percent). Other sectors such as aquaculture and offshore wind energy have been on the rise, too, in recent years and can be expected to grow as a share of economic output.[28]

Recent reports on investment opportunities in the Blue Economy by, for instance, Morgan Stanley and Startup Genome, also indicate growing interest by the private sector in the Blue Economy. According to data analysis by the latter "Europe is the global leader in Blue Economy startups, holding 39 percent of the share and producing the highest number of early-stage deals."[29] North America accounts for 31 percent, while Asia is listed as 15 percent, though both regions have been catching up to Europe in recent years.[30] The report concludes that "The Blue Economy is considered to be in the Introduction or Early Growth phase of its lifecycle."[31]

The demand in China for Blue Economy business could be even greater. China's 2019 *China Ocean Economic Development Report Index*, for instance, claimed that the country's "marine GDP" represented 9.3 percent of the PRC's total GDP."[32]

While accurate accounting of exactly how much revenue, jobs, and investment opportunities have been created in Blue Economy-related industries remains a challenge in the United States, China, and elsewhere, it is nonetheless clear that new opportunities are rapidly emerging as the ocean is increasingly looked upon as a source of food, transport, energy, commerce, communication, science, territory (through land reclamation), critical resources, and, ultimately, security.

US data in 2019 show that the Marine Economy (which roughly equates to the Blue Economy) grew faster than the overall US economy. Data published for 2020, however, indicate a relative slow-down in the Marine Economy as a percentage of GDP (down 5.8 percent, inflation adjusted) compared to the overall economy (3.4 percent decline). The latter is likely due to effects from the COVID-19 epidemic. It will be some time before we know the actual growth trend in the US Blue Economy given the lag time in collecting, analyzing, and publishing such data.

Yet, as noted earlier, another driving factor is industry's interest in the United States, China, and elsewhere in pursuing "blue" technology (or "Bluetech") and related innovation opportunities. It seems clear that interest continues to grow in the types of business and other opportunities that the Blue Economy promotes given the rise in events and reports with a "Blue Economy" theme in recent years and despite the epidemic's negative impact.

Finally, President Biden's administration has adopted the terms "Blue Economy" and "Sustainable Blue Economy," along with "New Blue Economy," as reflected in the National Science and Technology Council's report on *Opportunities and Actions for Ocean Science and Technology (2022–2028)*. The latter report builds on the Trump-era *Science and Technology for America's Oceans: A Decadal Vision* but also outlines new initiatives on developing a "Diverse and Inclusive Blue Workforce" and "Blue Carbon" programs.

The Biden-era document defines the Blue Economy in simple terms: "the ocean supports a vast diversity of economic activities, which together compose the 'blue economy'".[33] Also beginning in the Biden administration, NOAA has adopted the term "New Blue Economy" to connote: "new business development framed around an information and knowledge-based approach to support fisheries, transportation, shipping, renewable energy, recreation, and other ocean-based uses."[34]

Thus, it appears that the terms of debate have shifted, from a competition mainly over using the phrase "Ocean Economy" or "Blue Economy" to what sort of "Blue Economy" the United States (and China) is pursuing and exporting. Although US and PRC conceptions are in some ways converging, which definition or approach to developing a Blue Economy dominates will matter. Will it be the United States' and other Western governments' preferred, more holistic, conservation-minded "Ocean Economy"-oriented approach to defining a sustainable Blue Economy or China's more industry- and innovation-oriented "Blue Economy" approach to development? In the area of US–China competition over the concept and what to call it, one might call it a tie. Yet, this competition over terminology has complicated development efforts in the United States and US outreach abroad. China's approach to developing its concept and preference for the term Blue Economy appear to have been overall more successful to date, in part due to the term's popularity in Asia.

Competition in Developing a Domestic Blue Economy

Giving equal priority to all of a Blue Economy's ecosystem components (marine conservation, maritime industrial development, and innovation) is likely to prove challenging for any government or international collaborative effort. Will the pursuit of an Ocean or Blue Economy lead to maritime development at the risk or cost of marine environmental conservation as in the past, or will more sustainable development methods be prioritized even if, in the short term, they are challenging or costly to businesses or could possibly slow down industrial progress? These are questions that US, PRC, and other officials all face.

The rise of a "Bluetech" industry in the United States and elsewhere also raises questions about how important a role marine conservation will actually play in the pursuit of new maritime industry opportunities and innovations. Will development of Bluetech mean simply more marine and maritime industry innovation or will it be truly "blue" by emphasizing also more sustainable, conservation-oriented methods and outcomes? Will, once again, near-term economic and financial gains be pursued at the expense of long-term sustainability?

In fact, during the era of Trump and Xi, US and Chinese priorities with regard to developing the Ocean or Blue Economy appeared to have come into greater alignment, at least in practice, with both emphasizing economic opportunities and science and technology innovation, potentially at the expense of conservation and sustainability. President Trump's Executive Order, issued on June 19, 2018, defined "ocean-related matters" merely as "management, science, and technology matters involving the ocean, coastal and Great Lakes water of the United States (including its territories and possessions), and related seabed, subsoil, waters superadjacent to the seabed, and natural resources."[35]

As with other Trump administration policy initiatives, the Executive Order appeared to prioritize economic and business interests, in the name of national security, similar to Beijing's approach to developing the Blue Economy as a national economic strategy and maritime security priority. While employing the term "Ocean Economy", the Trump-era concept appeared to lack—or downplayed—much of the *conservation* and *sustainability* considerations and the policies and regulations that enforce or promote them—that were considered important under the previous administrations. As such, US and Chinese "Blue" Economy efforts appeared to be aligning yet were more likely to lead to strategic competition than to promote cooperation.

President Trump's Executive Order also newly designated the White House's Director of the Office of Science and Technology Policy (OSTP) and Chairman of the Council of Environmental Quality (CEQ) as co-chairs for ocean affairs. The president's first CEQ nominee was withdrawn due to controversy and the OSTP position went unfilled for a year and a half until President Trump put forward a nominee in August 2018; both nominees were confirmed but not until the end of 2018. Given this apparent lack of urgency, there was little reason to expect ocean affairs would be a priority issue in policy decision-making in the Trump White House.

Given the fact that President Trump would soon be entering his last year in office, White House-led efforts might easily have fallen victim to competing election-year and pandemic priorities or been shelved and ignored by a following administration, as happened to Obama-era policy initiatives under President Trump.

In the early Biden era, however, there have been several indications of a more effusive approach to pursuing the Blue Economy as a strategic interest, both for its own sake and in terms of competition with China. The term "Blue Economy," for instance, was cited specifically by President Biden's National Security Advisor, Jake Sullivan, in remarks related to publication of the administration's National Security Strategy (NSS), which outlines core US national interests.[36]

The State Department also appeared at first to place greater attention and emphasis on understanding and development of the Blue Economy as a matter of foreign policy and outreach, soliciting scholars with relevant expertise to take part in overseas outreach activities (though it is not clear if this program has been executed). Yet, the State Department has since appeared to pay scant public attention to the Blue Economy, perhaps due to the fact that most key decisions in the Biden administration are made at the White House, where the OPC, Special Presidential Climate Envoy John Kerry, and National Security Council Coordinator for the Indo Pacific, Kurt Campbell, all sit.

As noted previously, the National Oceanic and Atmospheric Administration has expanded its focus on Blue Economy and "New Blue Economy" efforts under the Biden administration. Even the US Department of Defense has become active in recent years in the climate change space, identifying climate change as a national security challenge and priority. The latter is in addition to the US Navy's inherent interests and roles, particularly via leadership running the NOPP-IWG and through funding of innovative partnerships among defense, academic, and business communities that are expected to serve both commercial and defense needs in the maritime domain.

What is clearly lacking, however, in US development of the Blue Economy *and* in terms of exporting these ideas abroad, is a comprehensive strategy to do both. Not only are there different terms being used for what is much the same thing, which is confusing and obfuscating, but the White House remains the hub of Blue Economy decision-making, efforts that could be upended entirely in a new administration. The challenge of developing a comprehensive strategy for an interdisciplinary, interagency, and dual domestic and foreign policy issue like the Blue Economy will be difficult, but essential, if the United States is to pursue a Blue Economy development concept in a strategic manner and as an element of US maritime power.

The White House is the central point for interagency decision-making, but this is mainly supposed to be for crisis management, to decide the most difficult issues across the interagency, and to coordinate policy initiatives. The Blue Economy by now is neither new nor a crisis decision. Pursuit of a more permanent development approach to the Blue Economy calls for the delegation of authorities to a single entity outside of the White House (if still coordinating through it the most difficult interagency decisions) with resources and personnel sufficient to accomplish a mission to develop a Blue Economy at home and to expand US influence on the Blue Economy abroad.

As the debate over how to define a Blue Economy is being slowly resolved, a more enduring competition between the United States and China continues: the contest for developing Blue Economy maritime innovation clusters meant to fuel more sustainable maritime (civil-military) and marine development. The current state of US–China relations is impacting this contest and will continue to do so given the still-interdependent economic and trade relations that exist in a globalized economy, atop which these two states sit.

The Contest to Develop Blue Economy Clusters, Technologies, Standards, and More

The United States and China are engaged already in an increasingly fierce strategic competition to advance science, technology, and innovation throughout our economies and on which our respective commercial and military capabilities each rely. Development of the Blue Economy, particularly through innovation-oriented clusters, will play a critical role in the development of both commercial and naval technologies, engineering, and scientific breakthroughs in both countries. The challenge each country faces is that commercial innovation and technology development, as well as science are, in an age of economic globalization, international pursuits. This leads to a situation where US and Chinese businesses, researchers, and scientists must cooperate or collaborate to some degree across borders but must also be cognizant of the inherent hazards in doing so, lest the knowledge be put to industrial or military use against the other or by another competitor or adversary.

While comprehensive data regarding Blue Economy-related development in each country remains, at best, preliminary and limited, US efforts to develop blue innovation clusters appear thus far to maintain the United States' overall innovation advantage over China. A 2017 study examining over 100 cities and territories for their knowledge transfer spillover effects from specifically marine science-oriented academic research centers lists the United States as having two "research territories" among the top five: San Diego, CA, and Woods Hole, MA (where Scripps and Woods Hole Oceanographic Institutions are located, respectively), ranking third and fifth overall.[37] China also makes the list, but is ranked further down at seventh place (Qingdao) and eleventh place (Shanghai); other US cities appear higher (Seattle was listed in sixth place and Washington, DC, in eighth) or lower (Miami was thirteenth and Los Angeles, eighteenth).[38] The study notes

China's emergence on the list as important given the pace of growth and the country's rise in prominence over a short period of time (calculated in terms of both the quantity and quality of China's marine publications for distinct time periods, specifically 2000 and 2011).[39]

In fact, the Chinese Academy of Sciences (CAS) was ranked in another study as the top "producer of high-quality Earth and environmental sciences research" in the journal *Nature*'s citations Index. The journal cites CAS for having "collaborated with almost as many institutions in the United States (249) as CAS researchers did with Chinese institutions (276)" for the years spanning 2015–17.[40] The latest US–China collaborative research was double what it had been dating back to 2012, dominated by the field of chemistry.[41]

Despite this progress and China's focus, particularly since 2013, on pursuing ocean research, concerns remain over the quantity of Chinese scholarship exceeding its quality. Other concerns include the impacts of academic as well as institutional and national pressures to publish or perish, and concerns expressed by Chinese scientists that they are playing less vital or secondary, supporting roles in research collaborations with their Western counterparts.[42] These could be some reasons also why China ranks at the bottom of the earlier-mentioned 2017 study's measure of *quality* marine science publishing. In comparison, the United States is ranked at the top (which generally accords with the *Nature* Index's rankings), suggesting the US lead in marine science could continue for some time and despite the recent increase in the number of Chinese-authored or co-authored marine science publications.

The 2017 study also found that "the marine academic potential of a territory is highly dependent on the diversity of local scientific contributors ... [but] ... Chinese and American cities reflect more self-centered research dynamics."[43] In other words, the United States and China were deemed to be less open and internationally collaborative in terms of marine academic publications than their European counterparts. This tendency is likely due to lurking national security concerns in both countries vis-à-vis the other, among additional factors such as country size.

Though some degree of marine scientific collaboration is in both countries' interests when considered purely in terms of advancing scientific understanding, obstacles to doing so are already appearing and likely to expand in the post-coronavirus era and given rising US–China tensions. Joint US–China marine science research programs, projects, and proposals have been cancelled or scaled back in the past due to national security concerns on the part of US authorities; others have likely not come to fruition due to risk aversion and uncertainty on both sides with regard to the worsening state of diplomatic relations.

Security concerns arising from political uncertainties in the South China Sea also have made ocean exploration especially difficult. It is not clear, for instance, how or from which government(s) one would need permission to do ocean exploration there, which likely leads many to not even attempt doing so. Where attempted, the costs are likely for many to be prohibitively expensive due to compulsory insurance policies necessary for US and international researchers to conduct ocean research in such disputed areas.[44] Neither constraint is necessarily true, however, for PRC scientific researchers given that Beijing claims such waters as sovereign territory and has large fleets of naval, paramilitary, and law enforcement forces to back them up.

Another critical strategic consideration is the impact that the Blue Economy and MSR could have on the future of maritime and naval innovation. Development of the Blue Economy and China's MSR plans are likely to impact technological innovation in the strategically vital maritime space (on the surface as well as below and above the water line) for purposes of commercial dual-use and military applications, particularly naval innovation. The same reasons that the US Navy values a strong maritime industry and emerging Blue Economy clusters such as have developed in San Diego, California, and elsewhere is due to the spillover advantages they afford to naval innovation. This same objective underlies Beijing's interest in developing a strong Blue Economy at home and integrating maritime development overseas.

Similarly, there are important strategic implications of US and Chinese development of Blue Economy-themed capabilities, policies, and strategies arising from issues concerning what investment and technology-related rules, laws, norms, protocols, and technical and engineering standards are being developed for the Blue Economy. Once established and if they become dominant, these standards, protocols, rules, and more are likely to hold sway over the market and across the region for some time. The degree to which the United States or China dominates and defines these practices and in ways that are transparent, inclusive, and free of corruption will determine future maritime development. Monitoring significant Bluetech advances, in particular, will be important in identifying emerging standards and their strategy and policy implications.

Monitoring scientific and technological advances in the Blue Economy, wherever they arise around the globe, can be difficult, as raised in the discussions on terminology and challenges in measuring the Blue Economy. Being involved in part of the development cycle and supporting private enterprise is one way for governments to do so. US domestic investments in the Blue Economy are comparatively transparent when held up against China's, with federal, state, and organizational requests for proposals (RFPs) and other funding opportunities typically published and traceable online. In the US instance, the Department of Defense and US Navy are active in promoting and funding Blue Economy-related activities (if not always named as such). Among these programs are the Defense Community Infrastructure Program (DCIP) under the Office of Local Defense Community Cooperation (OLDCC), and at least 18 "Tech Bridge" programs located in mostly coastal regions around the country plus in the United Kingdom and Japan as sponsored by the Secretary of the Navy. DoD also sponsors innovation promotion offices such as the Defense Innovation Unit (established initially during the Obama administration) and NavalX, a self-described "innovation and agility cell" established in 2019 to serve US Navy and Marine Corps interests specifically.[45]

By comparison, China's Blue Economy-related activities and funding are much more opaque. But as outlined earlier in this volume, Chinese strategies, plans, and policies focused on domestic and overseas Blue Economy development make clear the priority placed on the Blue Economy by leaders in Beijing. These documents also indicate that, at the very least, PRC government support and funding are available for these pursuits. The main challenge in China's case is not so much government involvement and spending, but whether or not Beijing's strategies, plans, and policies will bear fruit at the local level and be implemented in an effective manner. Having in recent years limited or no access to what is happening on the ground in China plus limits to online access to publications in recent years makes it far more difficult for US analysts to discern the level of China's scientific and technological progress in this regard.

As the Blue Economy develops in the United States, China, and elsewhere, new maritime and other "blue" technologies, platforms, and standards will emerge that will compete for influence and market share in each large-size market and across the Indo-Pacific region. Will these new technologies, platforms (including cyber), standards, protocols, and practices be based on distinctly US- or Chinese-dominated specifications or be more universally applicable? This is a key reason why domestic development of the Blue Economy and its many offshoots is important and likely will be a determining factor for international trade and investment in Blue Economy sectors worldwide. Infrastructure development, particularly ports and transportation routes along coastal areas, also will be a key concern in this contest as will be the extent to which new, blue industries and capabilities will be innovative and environmentally sustaining or be further exploitative. China's spending on Blue Economy efforts, particularly its Maritime Silk Road Initiative component, seek to ensure in broad terms China's blue technological influence and, if possible, dominance, in the region.

It is too early yet to assess the effectiveness of China's Blue Economy efforts as tied to the MSR; there is too little credible data available as yet. What is outlined and understood thus far are China's ambitious vision, strategies, plans, and policies. It is not at all certain that Beijing can fulfill these grand ambitions, or do so in an effective, affordable, influential, and sustainable manner. Nor is it certain that China's neighbors in the region and beyond will be interested over the long term in engaging, investing, integrating in, or collaborating with China's Blue Economy-oriented Maritime Silk Road projects despite the potential opportunities presented. Many (138 countries as of 2021) have joined China's BRI but only some have opened their doors to Beijing's investments while others hedge, supporting the BRI in principle but not formally becoming an investment node.[46] It is certain, however, that

Chinese bureaucrats are working to implement the Party's stated strategies, policies, and plans to leverage the Blue Economy as a point of entrée for the MSR across the region.

At present, the outlook for a mutually beneficial Sino-Western collaborative outcome in terms of developing the MSR and Blue Economy is not encouraging, even beyond downward-trending US–China relations. Upon examining opportunities for European economies along the Maritime Silk Road, the European Council on Foreign Relations concluded that, "on balance, the Maritime Silk Road creates more competition than cooperation opportunities in Europe-China relations, including on a fundamental level—the very terms of engagement in Europe-China relations ... a clear mind is needed regarding Chinese power ambitions."[47] Notably, this was the assessment made prior to COVID-19 exploding around the globe and the expansion of Sino-Russian relations amid the war in Ukraine, both of which have substantially soured relations between China, Europe, and other Western states.

Western governments also are increasingly wary of Chinese state-owned, subsidized, or leading technology-oriented enterprises such as Huawei and ZTE, while China remains wary of opening its own markets further or more quickly to foreign competition and technologies in strategically critical sectors. Nevertheless, if China is able to integrate MSR architecture and Blue Economy development efforts with Chinese domestic technology, standards, and infrastructure across the region, this could come at the expense of US and allied interests and capabilities, particularly if US and Western enterprises are not competing in, lack access to, or are unduly subject to espionage or technology transfer requirements where collaborating in such projects.

Overall, however, scientific cooperation between American and Chinese research communities has weathered past downturns in bilateral US–China relations and continued even during periods of crisis. Some degree of scientific (if not technological) collaboration with Chinese scientists in marine and maritime endeavors is likely to continue, but with growing risks to each project or program as tensions persist and political leverage can be found in highlighting scientific or technological cooperation as advancing the other's techno-military-security agenda. Even if relations improve substantially, this will not negate the ongoing contest for maritime innovation and, ultimately, maritime power superiority, which is likely to be determined in part by how the Blue Economy develops in each country.

Despite diplomatic, economic, scientific, and even technological innovation-related incentives for the United States and China to cooperate on issues such as climate science, it is in the military-security realm, specifically the development of naval capabilities, that US–China cooperation is much less likely and competition or even conflict more so. Any prospects for Ocean- and Blue Economy-related cooperation are likely to be negatively impacted by worsening military and security concerns between Washington and Beijing. What this all means for Blue Economy clusters being developed in China, in the United States, and elsewhere is that there is likely to be quite limited cross-investment by the PRC or United States in each other's innovation ecosystems, thereby limiting the scientific, technological, and innovative spillovers that otherwise might be expected. It also means that third-party locations will matter more, as this is where the scientific, technological, and innovative competition will play out in the marketplace.

In terms of the contest for whose Blue Economy clusters will prove most adept and productive, it is as yet too soon to determine whether the PRC or United States is ahead. What will determine this outcome is each country's strategies, policies, and development approaches. China's SEZ development model has proven to be successful in many, though not all, cases. The United States' approach, being far more haphazard and organic, tends to come out on top over time due to free market forces that allow for and drive innovation. But there is no guarantee in either case that these approaches will fare similarly in the case of the Blue Economy, a much more holistic and therefore challenging approach to economic, industrial, and technological development.

Future US–China Relations and the Blue Economy

The basis for increasingly challenging US–China political-economic-security relations has been long in the making due, in particular, to China's rapid economic development that has helped to feed fast-paced military modernization. US–China tensions have recently increased also due to recriminations stemming from the global pandemic, which originated in central China. Chinese Communist Party speeches and propaganda routinely identify the United States (if not always by name, clearly implied) as a strategic competitor or, worse, hegemon; United States rhetoric, too, has taken a similarly critical turn in recent years and has become more contentious in the post-coronavirus era.

Despite decades of expanding foreign investment and trade, Beijing's strategically critical view of the United States has not eased in the post-Cold War era and, in fact, in important ways has worsened under Xi Jinping's leadership. This is especially true in ideological terms, with Xi's emphasis on Chinese Communist Party dictates becoming a growing irritant in Sino-foreign relations, far more so than over the past four decades that have been characterized mainly by a focus on continued economic reform in order to entice greater amounts and higher levels of foreign investment.

In turn, as China's power has grown in a comprehensive manner over the past four decades, the challenges posed to the status quo or ruling power (i.e., the United States) naturally increase, leading some to theorize that conflict between the two powers is highly likely even if not wanted, a theory dubbed the "Thucydides Trap" by Harvard's Graham Allison. Yet, China's rising power is, itself, less of a concern than how China plans to exert its growing powers. Threat perceptions are a combination of capability plus intention; it is the latter that is of particular concern today given Xi's clear intention (and growing capability) to revise the world order to be more Sino-centric and in ways that are perceived to come at the expense of the United States and its Western allies.

Reflecting these growing fundamental tensions in US–China relations, the United States in the Trump administration's National Security Strategy (NSS) listed China for the first time as a "strategic competitor," and the National Defense Strategy (NDS) public summary named China as a "revisionist power." These carefully chosen terms clearly indicated a change in official US policy and strategy vis-à-vis the PRC from one of overall strategic balancing of security challenges and economic opportunities that had dominated in recent decades, to something more security, economically, and technologically risk-averse.

Notably, this strategic shift is supported by a slow-growing but marked shift in US and Western elite attitudes and skepticism toward China, including a far more negative view of modern Chinese governance during the Xi era that is held even among the typically stalwart and optimistic business community. Given the often dual-use (civil and military) potential applications of many US and Western technologies—on which Beijing places priority for trade, investment, and development—commerce with China has always had a military-security dimension but is generally viewed more skeptically now than in the past.

The degree to which the United States' negative shift in attitude toward China is shared among Western governments is evident in the European Union, formally labeling China as a "systemic rival" in March 2019. Similar to the United States, European views are based on long-standing, still-unresolved concerns over China's persistent technology transfer mandates, cyber attacks, and espionage activities, China's aggressive actions in the South China Sea, across the Taiwan Strait, as well as continued constraints and costs incurred by those investing on the Mainland, plus worsening human rights concerns added to other deepening political-ideological differences.[48]

Under the Trump administration, these pre-existing fissures increased substantially, with some even assessing the period to be the start of a new Cold War.[49] The Biden administration has maintained much of the Trump-era policy apparatus vis-à-vis China and has taken a far more skeptical approach toward China than their counterparts during the Obama and previous administrations. This bipartisan shift in attitude toward the PRC is largely in response to Xi Jinping's actions, governance style, and contentious ideological approach to dealing with the United States and other Western powers. Xi's declaration of a "no-limits" strategic partnership with Russia as a sign of solidarity with Russian President Putin's aggression toward Ukraine further set back US–China relations, as did China's response to US House Speaker Pelosi's visit to Taiwan in late 2022, and the early 2023 "spy balloon" incident just before a scheduled trip to Beijing by US Secretary of State Blinken to renew US–China dialogue. Secretary Blinken subsequently visited Beijing, but his visit took place more than two years into the Biden administration, showing how difficult this obviously important relationship has been.

Over the past four decades, the United States to varying degrees has tolerated (if oftentimes reluctantly) China's rising power and, in some cases, sought to include China as a partner, a competitor, and even a leading voice in the liberal international order, if not wholly to Beijing's satisfaction. This hedging strategy remains but is far more tilted today toward addressing security concerns than toward promoting economic trade and investment opportunity. The question going forward, and affecting no less than the future of international relations and of economic globalization in the 21st century, is whether or not the world's top two economies—the United States and China—can continue to tolerate the other's geostrategic influence and ideologies while balancing the risks and opportunities involved in doing so, or whether the relationship will shift to a mutually strategically confrontational position that is likely to lead to conflict and a renewed split in the global order.

What the worsening US–China security dilemma means for the Blue Economy in the United States, China, and beyond is not entirely clear. As US–China bilateral relations have become more challenging in recent years, geostrategic considerations have also grown more complicated. Both countries' pursuit of Blue Economy clusters, zones, and broader development efforts suggests these programs, plans, and strategies will play an important role in determining which country will dominate maritime and naval developments separately as well as in the Indo-Pacific region and beyond. This competition includes who will make the political, economic, scientific, environmental, and security-oriented rules that govern development in the international Blue Economy.

Yet, if both the United States and China seek to limit bilateral Blue Economy trade, investment, cooperative research, science, and innovation due to military-technology-security concerns, both countries will be disadvantaged and progress will be delayed from what otherwise might have been possible via careful collaboration conducted with an informed understanding of the challenges and risks involved. This lack of development would, in turn, impact allied and third-party economies, especially if the latter were forced to choose between cooperating with the United States or with China on new Blue Economy development. In addition, without a comprehensive strategy that incorporates both domestic and international development of the Blue Economy, the United States risks missing critical opportunities that could shape the future Indo Pacific and beyond, particularly with respect to advances in maritime power and if made by China or others.

The implication at present of worsening bilateral US–China relations across both security and economic dimensions is that risk assessments in both capitals and among investors will take precedence and likely limit or foreclose entirely opportunities that might otherwise once have been deemed worth pursuing despite an inherent degree of political-economic-technological risk.

This approach is likely to slow overall development of the Blue Economy in the United States and in China.

At the same time, if US–China relations were to improve due to substantial policy reforms or in the post-coronavirus economy (though this does not appear likely at present), the opportunities for cooperation on a range of Blue Economy-related projects, programs, investments, and collaborative scientific efforts abound. The question is whether the United States and China will collaborate with each other in this regard or only with third parties. In the latter sense, a new phase in the strategic contest already has begun, as the United States and China both pursue development of Blue Economies and blue or ocean innovation clusters in competition with, and potentially at the expense of, each other, as well as with third parties. This emerging "Great Blue Game" is likely to be most apparent in terms of attracting (or repelling) involvement by other economies, particularly those in the Indo-Asia-Pacific region.

In the present contest, China has a head start on the United States in terms of enacting strategies and policies for developing the Blue Economy that seek to foster development both at home and abroad but appears to lag US efforts in developing dynamic, market-driven, innovative Blue Economy ecosystems. It is not clear that China's Blue Economy clusters are as dynamic and growing as rapidly, despite state and Party support of such activity. The United States is well positioned to continue expanding public and private investments in Blue Economy activities at home and abroad but lacks an overall strategy to do so or to expand these gains overseas.

US–China Strategic Competition: Leveraging the Blue Economy for Geostrategic Advantage

As important as the role that the Blue Economy development concept appears poised to play in each country's domestic plans and in US–China relations is how the Blue Economy factors into broader geostrategic interests and aspirations, particularly those in the Indo-Pacific region. As outlined in Chapter 4, China has published expansive plans to employ the Blue Economy concept as part of a larger strategy to become more integrated with neighboring and regional economies across the Indo Pacific and beyond and as a key strategic aspect in China's efforts to become a maritime great power.

For China, the Blue Economy is viewed as an important means of increasing PRC influence and access abroad, particularly along China's conceptual MSR. This ambitious, economic cum geostrategic plan encompasses nearly the entire globe, with the MSR component extending from China's shores through the Pacific and Indian Oceans, across the Mediterranean and the Atlantic Ocean to Latin America, as well as the Arctic and Antarctic (or Southern) Oceans. There is no equivalent US strategy, though the United States maintains and is expanding its global diplomatic, commercial, and military presence overseas as part of the strategic competition with China and in announcing a Blue Pacific Partnership program with several Indo-Pacific allies and partners in 2022.

While the United States' maritime strategy has a global outlook and the US military, via global combatant commands and forward regional presence as well as basing, has the ability to project power around the globe, the latest *US Maritime Strategy* document (2020) makes no mention of the "Ocean" or "Blue Economy," much less strategically emphasizing the Blue Economy concept as a policy lever in expanding US strategic influence. An earlier *Maritime Strategy* (2015) actually was broader in scope.[50]

More recent efforts by the Biden administration, in addition to the new Partners in the Blue Pacific program as part of Indo-Pacific outreach, include the Department of Transportation's Maritime Administration plans to issue its own maritime strategy to address the state of US shipyards and other infrastructure needs.[51] These efforts bode well for potential Blue Economy advances in the United States but do not constitute a holistic and comprehensive strategy for US development of the Blue Economy, much less how to leverage such efforts overseas and in ways that can be implemented across the entire US Executive Branch.

In contrast, China's modern Blue Economy concept, particularly as tied to Xi's *Vision of Maritime Cooperation* and the MSR, is aimed at advancing China's domestic maritime sector as well as all of the hard and soft elements of maritime power. China's attempt to tie its Blue Economy concept to ambitious plans for the Maritime Silk Road will impact existing US strategic alliances and partnerships in the region. As a result, the Blue Economy element of the MSR is likely to introduce significant new diplomatic and strategic considerations to the US–China contest vis-à-vis the Indo-Pacific region, constituting the basis for what can be considered already to be a Great Blue Game.

As conceived here (see Text Box 5.1), a Great Blue Game between the United States and China involves a competition to employ the Blue Economy as part of every element of maritime power and in ways that will affect the region's diplomatic, economic, technological, and security makeup.

TEXT BOX 5.1: THE 21ST-CENTURY GREAT BLUE GAME

Concept

The term Great Blue Game conveys the notion of a geostrategic contest between competing Maritime Great Powers (i.e., the United States and, potentially, the People's Republic of China) for regional and global influence via development of the Blue Economy and the maritime and naval capabilities, access, leverage, and projection necessary to achieve strategic maritime and naval aims.

Elements of National and International Power in the Great Blue Game

- Maritime and "Blue" Diplomacy (including sustainable and innovative marine conservation efforts)
- Maritime and "Blue" Information (including ocean science and research, cyber and information-sharing capabilities, and networks)
- Maritime and Blue Military Power (sustainable and innovative naval, maritime, law enforcement, and paramilitary capabilities)
- Maritime or Blue Economy (including domestic and foreign investment, infrastructure, commercial maritime industry, ocean science, technology and innovation, standards and regulations, foreign aid, etc.)

Who develops these elements of power and wields them most effectively in the Indo-Pacific region is likely to dominate in the US–China geostrategic contest for power and influence.

Leveraging the Blue Economy in the Great Blue Game

The Blue Economy concept plays a formal and fundamental role in China's domestic as well as geostrategic plans. The same cannot be said of the United States at present. As someone engaged in studying the Blue Economy over the past decade, two communications received from the US Government tell the story. The first communication was a telephone call early in the author's initial investigations into China's Blue Economy to explain that the United States government preferred to use the term Ocean Economy over the term Blue Economy and why. The second communication was an email nearly a decade later asking about interest in helping to conduct outreach in the Indo-Pacific region and elsewhere on the issue of the Blue Economy. While readily accepting both communications, the latter, and the years-long gap in between, indicate that the United States has fallen behind China's efforts to develop and leverage its Blue Economy concept, whatever name it goes by.

As a novel, attractive, and more responsible approach to promoting economic, innovative, and sustainable development in the ocean, marine, and maritime domains, the Blue Economy concept has much to offer. If the United States is to win, dominate, or at least not lose the emerging Great Blue Game, it is imperative for the United States to enter the strategic fray. The absence of a comprehensive Blue Economy component of US strategy (as part of its maritime strategy at the very least, and with regard to the Indo Pacific in particular) risks ceding influence over future ocean, maritime, and naval strategic developments to China.

Only in the past year or two has the United States responded to what it views as China's Blue-Economy-themed encroachments into critical strategic territory in the South Pacific, in particular, with a new Blue Pacific Partnership and other initiatives that have Blue Economy components. The following section lays out how a small island state in the South Pacific has become a playing field for the two powers' Blue Economy competition and how this competition has spurred on additional domestic and international Blue Economy activities, initiatives, and agreements.

It was Washington's reaction to news of a reported draft Memorandum of Understanding (MOU) between the PRC and the Solomon Islands (SI) in early 2022 that sparked a new level of interest in the United States and elsewhere in the region in the Blue Economy and as a geostrategic competitive matter vis-à-vis the PRC. The next section provides a brief overview of the US–China strategic competition to influence the Solomon Islands—and, by these actions, the broader Indo-Pacific region—via contending visions of the Blue Economy.

Case Study: The United States and China Vie for Influence in the Solomon Islands

Following strategic declarations that went effectively unrealized over many years, US national security strategy has in fact finally pivoted or "re-balanced" in real terms away from Middle Eastern challenges toward Asia to focus increasingly on Great Power and strategic competition, mainly centered on China. The reason for this shift is due to opportunities and challenges presented by the rapid and increasingly aggressive rise of China, particularly the PRC's fast-paced technological and military modernization, as well as "wolf-warrior"-style coercive diplomacy, revisionist legal efforts, and provocative paramilitary, gray-zone activities. Amid this shift toward Great Power politics and focus on China, however, small islands in the South Pacific appeared to have become relatively less central to US strategic interests.

Long before being officially announced, the eventual shift in US strategic attention toward Great Power politics that occurred in the Trump and Biden administrations was evident in a change in how the United States military command with responsibility over areas of the Pacific altered its public description of its geographic area of responsibility (AOR). Somewhere around 2009–10, the US military command then called Pacific Command (PACOM), and since 2018 known as Indo-Pacific Command (INDOPACOM), changed the way it counted the number of entities its AOR encompassed. Before the update, PACOM public releases listed 43 countries or nations as being in its AOR (along with 20 territories and 10 US territories); by fall 2010, the number had changed in official descriptions to 36 nations. What happened to the others?

While an official answer has not been provided, a likely reason for this change was that the new, smaller number reflected the coming strategic rebalance toward Asia initially announced under President Obama and toward focusing on China as part of Trump- and Biden-era strategies of "Great Power Competition" and "strategic competition," respectively. It appears that officials might have simply lumped some smaller Pacific Island states, nations, and territories into larger groups. As far as PACOM strategists were concerned at that time, it seems, smaller governments and territories did not matter as much as big powers and potential adversaries like China. Such a view might be understandable given strategic priorities being set at higher levels in Washington. Other Western powers, including Australia, New Zealand, and Great Britain, also neglected Oceania in revising their strategic maps around this time, as did China's own BRI initially.[52] Yet, Beijing would come to see this "pivot" in US attention away from the Indo-Pacific region's smaller-sized territories as an opportunity for its own strategic outreach. This outreach came via Chinese offers related to investing in Blue Economy-themed projects, among other carrots offered.

Public realization of this strategic miscalculation would come in the form of a surprise leak in March 2022 of a draft agreement between the PRC and the Solomon Islands. With this disclosure, the South Pacific, and the Solomon Islands in particular, suddenly became a focal point once again of geostrategic interest, this time by the United States, its allies, and partners, as well as China. By July 2022, the US vice president, Kamala Harris, would address the Pacific Island Forum (PIF) and acknowledge that "in recent years, the Pacific Islands may not have received the diplomatic attention and support that you deserve. So today I am here to tell you directly: We are going to change that."[53] The vice president also promised to

> significantly deepen our engagement in the Pacific Islands. We will embark on a new chapter in our partnership—a chapter with increased American presence where we commit to work with you in the short and long term to take on the most pressing issues that you face.[54]

Notably, while climate change is mentioned in the address, the notion of a Blue or even Ocean Economy is not.

Once a far-away place—more than 8,000 or 4,000 miles away from Washington or Beijing, respectively—the contest for which global power will be able to forge closer strategic and maritime relations with the Solomons and others in the region once again took center stage in a way that had not occurred since World War II.

China's geostrategic gambit vis-à-vis the Solomon Islands and the subsequent US (and allied) response are the focus of this case study. Importantly, Beijing's entrée into expanding its relationship with and presence in the Solomons was based on leveraging both countries' interest in developing the Blue Economy. The term Blue Economy is well-known among the international community and particularly island states in the Indo-Pacific region, where the term originated. US and allied responses to China's maneuver reflect a growing understanding of the importance of the Blue Economy concept in geostrategic affairs as well, but mainly in response to and *only following* China's secret agreement being made public.

As is the case for many in the region, the contest for power between the United States and the PRC placed the Solomon Islands government in the middle of two behemoths seeking to sway the small island nation-state to their own ideological persuasion (in practice if not also in principle) and offering both tangible carrots and inherent sticks as incentive.

The Solomon Islands is a parliamentary democracy and member of the Commonwealth, having secured its independence in 1978. Its territory includes a site known to most Americans and US allies of a certain age or historical interest: Guadalcanal—the site of a legendary World War II battle that is considered a turning point in the Allies' efforts to secure the Pacific theater. Guadalcanal is located on the SI's main island, where its capital, Honiara, is also located. The US government provides assistance to the Solomon Islands in the form of funding, training, and humanitarian and disaster relief, but mainly as one among other Pacific Island states. The Solomon Islands is a small island of less than 750,000 people and a country smaller geographically than the state of Maryland (see Figure 5.2).

Given their proximity, Australia and New Zealand, both democracies and US allies in WWII and other wars, have interests in and closer ties with the Solomon Islands. Australia, in particular, has contributed aid over many years and helped quell civil unrest there (2003–17) as lead and main sponsor of a 15-nation Regional Assistance Mission to the Solomon Islands (RAMSI). Australia generally has wielded economic and security predominance in the South Pacific.

For all of these reasons, it is possible that a sense of complacency led US and regional officials to believe the Solomon Islands was solidly in the US and allied camp if and when it came to a strategic contest with the PRC. Yet, as the US–China competition has heated up, so too have potential opportunities to play one power off the other. The Philippines is a case in point: its leaders in recent years have deftly leaned toward the PRC and then back, again, toward the United States in an effort to bolster Philippine security and economic opportunities. This approach of playing both sides off one another keeps each major power off balance while gaining economic or security concessions from each as part of a contest for power, influence, and presence in the region. Adopting a similar approach, the Solomon Islands' foreign policy, according to Prime Minister Sogavare in September 2022, is to be "friends to all and enemies to none" and to "not align … with any external power(s)."[55]

Another likely contributing factor in the Solomon Islands case is that one of the flashpoints in SI domestic politics has been over the decision about which government to recognize diplomatically: the PRC or Taiwan?[56] Following its independence, the Solomon Islands established diplomatic relations with Taiwan in 1983.[57] But in 2019, Solomon Islands Prime Minister Sogavare made a still-controversial decision to change diplomatic recognition to the

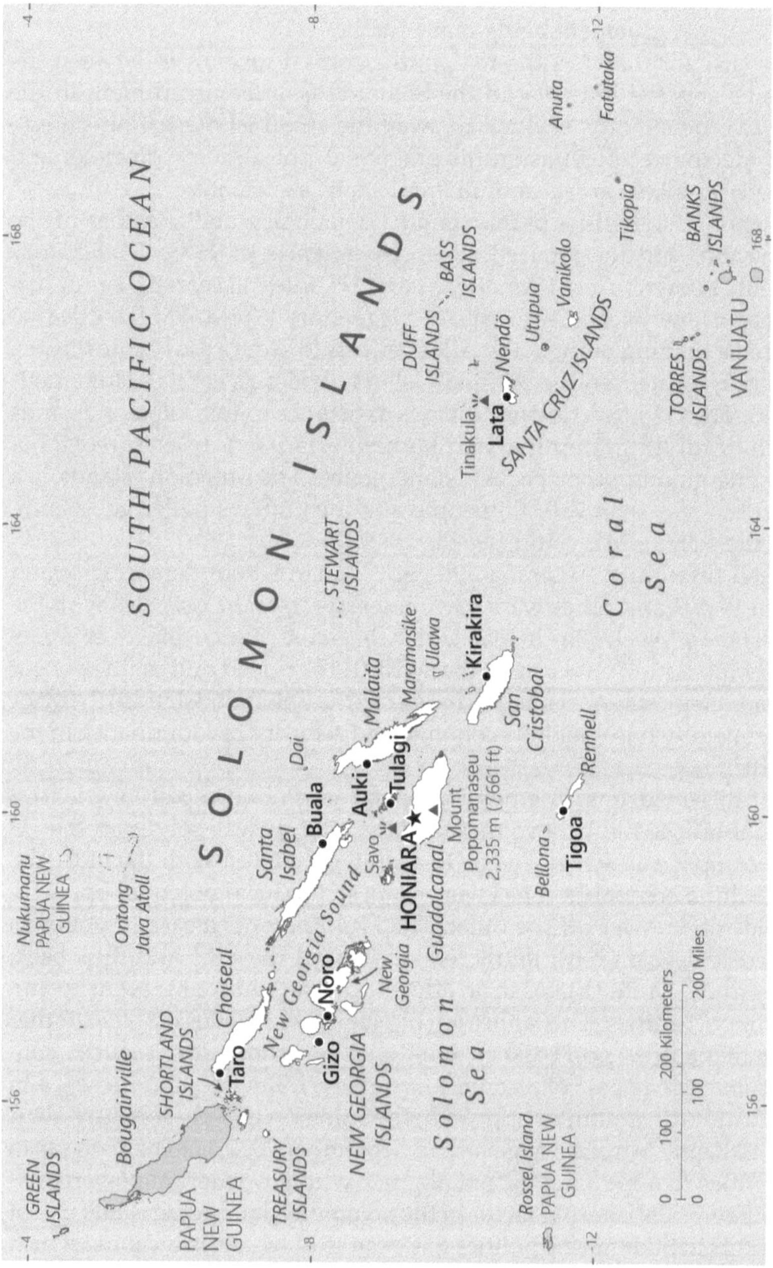

FIGURE 5.2
Map of the Solomon Islands. *Source:* Central Intelligence Agency, n.d.

PRC. While the precise reason(s) for the shift remains unclear, possible rationales mentioned in press accounts include expanded PRC outreach, substantial investment and economic opportunities presented via China's Belt and Road Initiative, and Beijing's promise to match Taiwan's financial aid (an offer estimated at the time to be US$8.5 million).[58]

Before and since announcing the 2019 decision to change diplomatic recognition, press reports indicate a fragile US–Solomon Islands relationship, with officials in both countries claiming to have been snubbed by the other side. Following announcement of the switch, for instance, then-US Vice President Pence reportedly refused to meet with the Solomons prime minister, who had requested a meeting alongside the United Nations General Assembly meeting in New York.[59] Yet, following the civil unrest that damaged the nation's capital in late 2021, US Vice President Pence worked with Solomon Islands Prime Minister Sogavare on a US aid package.[60]

For his part, Prime Minister Sogavare reportedly was annoyed by Secretary of State Anthony Blinken's 2020 announcement of US$25 million direct aid to a Solomon Islands province on the island of Malaita, the country's most-populated, second-largest, but less-developed island. Daniel Suidani, the then-Premier of Malaita Province, is a Sogavare opponent and best known for publicly criticizing "the switch" decision. The riots in the capital were the result of disputes between these two islands, particularly over the growing influx of Chinese interests, which those living on Malaita view as threatening to their economic interests and independence. Malaita's concerns over China's growing influence have led the provincial government to outlaw the use of Chinese firm Huawei's telecommunications technology, among other measures meant to constrain PRC influence, including via maintaining a relationship with Taiwan.[61] Mr. Suidani has since been ousted from his position by Sogavare and is residing in the United States.[62]

The Solomon Islands published its first *National Security Strategy* in 2020, stating clearly that "Climate Change is the number one global security risk facing Solomon Islands."[63] While that document does not explicitly mention the Blue Economy, a *National Ocean Policy* document published in 2018 does.[64] Both documents make clear the Solomon Islands' interest in enhancing maritime security, marine conservation, and making more sustainable use of the country's natural resources. Researchers who have examined SI's views on and implementation of the Blue Economy in detail conclude that "The Blue Economy concept appears to have resonance in the South Pacific region because it embodies the dual need to protect ocean systems for the future and to meet pressing development needs."[65] As such, the Solomon Islands was a clear candidate for outreach on implementing the Blue Economy concept.

It is not surprising, therefore, given an understanding of China's conception of the Blue Economy, that a leaked draft of a recent PRC–Solomon Islands MOU was titled "Memorandum of Understanding on Deepening Blue Economy Cooperation between the People's Republic of China and the Ministry of XXX of Solomon Islands."[66] This MOU apparently was drafted around the same time as another agreement between the Solomon Islands and PRC, this one on security cooperation.[67] The latter received the majority of media attention for its new and expansive forms of cooperation.

Among the terms identified in the unsigned, leaked draft of the security agreement areprovisions for Chinese "police, armed police, military personnel and other law enforcement and armed forces", including that

> China may, according to its own needs and with the consent of the Solomon Islands, make ship visits to, carry out logistical replenishment in, and have stopover and transition in Solomon Islands, and the relevant forces of China can be used to protect the safety of Chinese personnel and major projects in Solomon Islands.[68]

Notably, another provision in the draft precludes its transparency or international consultations, stating that "Without the written consent of the other party, neither party shall disclose the cooperation information to a third party" and that "Any disputes arising from the interpretation shall be resolved by the Parties through consultation."[69]

The Blue Economy MOU draft, also leaked to the media, begins with language likely also written in Beijing declaring the parties as

> actively implementing the Global Development Initiative, and jointly building the 21st Century Maritime Silk Road [both Xi Jinping-initiated programs], to form synergy with the 2050 Strategy for the Blue Pacific Continent (or other development plan of blue economy in SI), and jointly building a maritime community with share[d] future, carrying out China's 14th Five-Year Plan (2021–2025) for National Economic and Social Development and the Long-Range Objectives Through the Year 2035 and National Development Strategy 2016–2035 of Solomon Islands based on the goodwill and needs of businesses of both countries and the practical foundation for strengthening cooperation in the blue economy.[70]

Article 3 of the draft text, given its wide scope, ambitious scale, and dual-use applications, is likely what caused most consternation in Western capitals. It cites

> areas of investment cooperation in the blue economy, including but not limited to the following fields or industries:

- Mariculture, distant water fishing, seafood processing, etc.;
- Marine biopharmaceutical, marine engineering technology, seawater desalination, marine salt industry, etc.;
- Port wharves, submarine optical cable construction, shipbuilding and ship repair, ocean transportation, etc.;

- Marine tourism and leisure services;
- Photovoltaic, wind power, tidal power and other clean energy and transmission networks;
- Exploration and development of offshore oil, gas and mineral resources.[71]

The Security Cooperation and Blue Economy MOUs were two of at least three agreements signed during Foreign Minister Wang Yi's visit to the Solomon Islands in May 2022; another was reportedly an MOU on Health Cooperation, as reportedly was one on "Cooperation between the Ministry of Environment, Climate Change, Disaster Management and Metrology of Solomon Islands and the Ministry of Emergency Management of the People's Republic of China."[72]

The 2022 Blue Economy draft MOU also followed another inked in 2019 between the Solomon Islands and AVIC, a State-Owned Enterprise of the PRC in the aviation sector. The latter agreement included provisions to refurbish airfields, ostensibly for commercial flights (but potentially useful for military purposes), and was updated as part of the 2022 meeting. News broke also in March 2022 of a Solomon Islands–PRC MOU on Policing Cooperation, following a visit to the Solomon Islands by a high-ranking PRC Ministry of Public Security official.[73]

These myriad agreements between the Solomon Islands and the PRC indicate a serious effort by Beijing to reach out to this strategically located nation-state and to employ, among other tools and levers, the Blue Economy as an issue of mutual interest. It was no secret that the Solomon Islands, fellow Small Island Developing States, and South Pacific Islands, among others, had an interest in the Blue Economy. What was lacking was strategic attention from the United States or other major powers who could substantially aid the Solomon Islands and others with their Blue Economy efforts. That is, until China took the lead.

It is possible that the Biden administration and allied governments had planned to do more outreach to the Solomon Islands and other Pacific Island Nations, including specifically on the topic of the Blue Economy and related issues such as climate change, prior to news of the Solomon Islands' move to sign an MOU with the PRC. But it was only after the MOUs leaked in the press that Washington and allied capitals kicked such efforts into high gear and began offering "blue" packages and offers of aid.

As reported in the press, however, the Solomons–PRC deal and draft document were secret and came as a surprise to Western officials. While it is understandable for research, analysis, planning, and policymaking to focus on high-priority concerns and the role of large powers in the region, ignoring other actors and their issues of concern can be hazardous, particularly amid a geostrategic contest for power and influence. In the case of the Solomon Islands, China clearly was able to leverage its Blue Economy soft power to make inroads in this strategic part of the Indo-Pacific region ahead of US efforts to do the same.

Following media reports in March 2022 of a secret PRC–Solomon Islands deal, events moved swiftly. The same month as the draft MOUs leaked, Australia's foreign minister visited, and the White House's National Security Council Coordinator for Indo-Pacific Affairs, Kurt Campbell, conducted a conference call, with fellow Pacific Island of Fiji's leader, among other outreach efforts to the region. The reason for the hastily arranged consultations, according to the *Financial Times*, was to "shore up pacific support," with Western officials clearly concerned that more such secret agreements could be in the works elsewhere in the South Pacific.[74]

Also in March, President Biden signed a new international agreement called the Indo-Pacific Economic Cooperation Framework for Prosperity (IPEF). The IPEF joins a dozen states from Northeast Asia (Japan, South Korea), Southeast Asia (Brunei, Malaysia, Philippines, Singapore, Thailand, and Vietnam), South Asia (India), and the South Pacific (Australian and New Zealand). It is highly likely that this agreement had been in the works for some time prior to its unveiling.

While an important multilateral initiative, particularly following in the wake of the United States' withdrawal from the US-origin Transpacific Partnership (TPP) agreement under the prior administration, the IPEF seemed of limited significance to small island states like the Solomon Islands. The IPEF announcement does commit its members to pursuing what it calls a "Clean Economy" (along with "connected," "resilient," and "fair" economies). This likely compromise term, "Clean Economy," for capturing a wide range of climate-related efforts is short on specifics as they might apply more broadly and to the Pacific Island states.[75]

The IPEF's newest member, Fiji, was announced three days *after* President Biden's initial joint IPEF announcement in Tokyo, yet the announcement notes that Fiji would be joining the new group as a "founding member."[76] It is possible, even likely, that while Beijing was securing secret deals in the Solomons that Washington had been focused on planning the IPEF and its announcement.

By mid-June, however, the United States and key allies were ready to announce another new regional initiative, this one directly responding to China's Blue Economy outreach and offering Pacific Island states an alternative. Joined by Australia, Japan, New Zealand, and the United Kingdom, the United States jointly announced on June 24, 2022, a new "Partners in the Blue Pacific" (PBP) initiative.[77] This new program is described in US Government press releases as an "inclusive, informal mechanism" or "coordination initiative" and one that is intended to be responsive to the needs and interests of South Pacific partners.

While the US PBP statement does not employ the term "Blue Economy," the "Blue" in the name clearly invokes the concept. The inaugural PBP dialogue took place in September 2022, less than three months after the initiative was first announced. The joint statement from this meeting also does not use the term Blue Economy, but the six announced lines of effort encompass its focus. These lines of effort are: (1) climate change resilience, adaptation, and disasters; (2) secure and resilient technology and connectivity; (3) protection of the ocean and environment; (4) people-centered development; (5) resources and economic development; and (6) political leadership and regionalism.[78]

The timing of the PBP announcement is a clear indication of its importance in Washington and in allied capitals. As announced in September 2022, Canada and Germany also reportedly intend to join the PBP.[79]

In addition to the timing and initially small group membership of the PBP initiative, other indicators point to the Pacific Islands and the Blue Economy concept, in particular, as being strategic afterthoughts in Washington and elsewhere. The Biden administration's own "Fact Sheet on a US-Pacific Islands Partnership" following the fall 2022 first-ever summit of Pacific States leaders convened in Washington notes that among the administration's first efforts is a "First-ever National US Strategy for the Pacific Islands."[80] The latter strategy was announced, but as "an addendum to the existing Indo-Pacific Strategy" that the president had announced in September 2021. The strategic addendum would "align with the Pacific Islands Forum's 2050 Strategy for the Blue Pacific Continent," a document that was announced even earlier, in 2019, and formally endorsed and published by the PIF in July 2022.[81]

The White House's Fact Sheet also cited announcements of numerous other new initiatives, including naming the first US envoy to the Pacific Islands Forum, diplomatic recognition of the Cook Islands and Niue ("pending consultations"), and announcement of expanded aid programs, including $810 million more dollars in aid, plus a fellowship program, both of which the administration pledged to request from Congress.[82]

Despite the late date of this effort, however, the initiatives announced by the Biden administration and the details outlined as part of the new strategic addendum are impressive and quite comprehensive in scope. Under the new strategy, US aid to the Pacific Islands will range from "climate adaptation" to "addressing unexploded ordinance," as well as "port and aviation connectivity" aid to the region to assist tourism-bolstering efforts.[83] The United States also re-opened the US Embassy in the Solomon Islands in February 2023, following a 30-year absence.[84] Whether US and allied commitments will be sustained is a key question, as well as the degree to which the United States and others will listen to and consult with the Solomon Islands in the course of providing aid and investments.[85] As important is the absence of a comprehensive US national strategy on developing the Blue Economy as a matter of domestic and international development, which would address similar interests in other parts of the region and beyond.

Other efforts in the region are taking shape, however. In March 2023, the US Department of Commerce announced its intention "to initiate a process to consider designating all US waters around the Pacific Remote Islands as a national marine sanctuary." According to President Biden's statement announcing the initiative, "expanding protections for the Pacific Remote Islands would create the largest protected ocean area on the planet."[86] While clearly advancing US ocean conservation goals, this initiative also is likely to impact any plans China has for operating in these strategic waters.

Ultimately, it is clear that only by courting the PRC did the Solomon Islands and perhaps other South Pacific Island states capture the attention of Washington and other Western capitals, who became suddenly serious about and cognizant of the region's Blue Economy and other regional interests. The Biden administration would go on to sign three more Memoranda of Understanding with the Pacific Island states of Palau, the Marshall Islands, and Federated States of Micronesia (under the Compacts of Free Association with the United States) at the start of 2023.[87] It is not clear at this time what these respective MOUs include beyond general commitments of aid and support. As part of the US Pacific Islands Partnership, the United States also agreed in mid-2022 to recognize as sovereign states the Cook Islands and Niue and committed to provide Blue Economy assistance broadly under the South Pacific Tuna Treaty. These and other recent efforts to re-engage with the Solomon Islands and its South Pacific Island neighbors have re-invigorated a new Great Game between the United States, its allies, partners, and friends, and the PRC, this time based on the Blue Economy (or its precepts) as a linchpin for access, influence, and power.

For its part, the Solomon Islands continues to play its cards on both sides. In what was perceived as a move pushing back against US and allied engagement, the Solomon Islands in the summer of 2022 for the first time denied a US Coast Guard cutter's routine request to make a port call for refueling purposes, following a similar denial issued to a British patrol boat days earlier.[88] The denials made headlines due to new sensitivity in US and allied capitals with regard to relations with the Pacific Islands, and with the Solomon Islands in particular. Later reports appeared to try to dampen the diplomatic fray, with Solomon Island officials claiming the denials were a temporary measure and one that applied to all foreign naval vessels (although the Coast Guard is notably not the same as a Navy vessel, belonging to a different service). Prime Minister Sogavare also welcomed a visit at this time by the US Navy's Hospital Ship *USNS Mercy*.[89]

Will China's Blue Economy gambit in the South Pacific ultimately pay off? Time, and likely money, will tell. In February 2023, *Reuters* reported that China had won a contract to upgrade Honiara's port, the contract going to a State-Owned Enterprise, and that the Solomon Islands had signed onto Xi Jinping's Global Development Initiative. The article also notes that "The Solomon Islands and China have consistently denied that their security pact would allow a naval base." Yet, there are concerns that port "upgrades" and accompanying wharf expansions as part of the contract could serve Chinese naval interests there as well.[90] Coinciding with this announcement was a return visit to the region by the White House National Security Council's Indo-Pacific Coordinator, Kurt Campbell.

What is near certain is that Beijing will continue to open doors across the region by offering its ideas on and assistance in implementing the dynamic and in-demand concept of the Blue Economy. Press reports indicate Beijing has concluded various forms of Blue Economy-themed agreements with other states ranging from Vanuatu to Tanzania and extending to Bangladesh and beyond. Washington and other Western capitals are beginning to catch up in this regard but will be challenged by myriad other interests that could distract over the long term from fulsome development of relations with the strategically important Pacific Islands region and of the Blue Economy concept itself. Moreover, the apparent continued resistance to employing the term Blue Economy, though widely known throughout the Indo Pacific, could cost US diplomacy and efforts at strategic outreach in the region. US officials employ the term at times when speaking abroad to foreign audiences, but usage of the term is otherwise hard to find in official US documents.

For Pacific Island states the issue of climate change is existential, and the Blue Economy a promising solution to some of the challenges climate change and other maritime issues present. For their corner of the globe, the Blue Economy is a tangible pursuit; in Washington, it remains an idea largely on paper and one not yet prioritized in the policymaking or strategic-oriented bureaucracy. Outside of NOAA, part of the US Department of Commerce or the White House, one cannot find a central office or high-level department in the US Government responsible for pursuing "Blue Economy" development and opportunities and addressing related strategic challenges domestically as well as internationally. Until the Blue Economy becomes a regular focus for diplomatic, economic, innovation, environmental, military, and security strategy and policy decision-making, the idea is likely to remain relegated to interagency task forces, lower-level government bureaucracies, and academic, scientific, and local community efforts rather than as the geostrategic leverage that China clearly sees it as and is using it as.

Blue Economy Cooperation and Outreach in an Era of Economic and Strategic Competition

As the Solomon Islands case study makes clear, the United States and China are both actively seeking to use the Blue Economy concept to influence third-party states in the Indo-Pacific region as a means of bolstering each country's maritime power. The Blue Economy is playing a key role in this geostrategic competition and is likely to appear in other contexts, relationships, and strategic maneuvers as well.

A worsening US–China relationship suggests that bilateral cooperation will be limited and collaboration increasingly less likely, especially in areas where national security is deemed a factor. Nevertheless, in pursuit of new, Blue Economy policies, programs, and clusters, the United States and China have substantial opportunities to cooperate and collaborate, both on land and at sea. The opportunity costs of not directly engaging China's Blue Economy development efforts, including in specialized zones and clusters—both those established on the Mainland and by China and others overseas—ought to be part of the United States' economic and national security calculus as new geostrategic opportunities as well as challenges emerge.

There are a number of key issues and dynamics likely to affect future cooperative or competitive development of Blue Economies in the United States, China, the Indo-Pacific region, and beyond as well as implications for US–China relations and the emerging geostrategic Great Blue Game. The nature of the current tensions in US–China relations is based on ideological differences but also long-simmering economic tensions between the PRC and United States that are not easily overcome. Yet, decades of growing economic interdependence between the United States and China show that cooperation and collaboration are possible.

Since China's reform era began under Deng Xiaoping in the late 1970s, US–China economic relations have become increasingly interdependent, though also asymmetric in terms of China's trade surplus with the United States. This asymmetry is due to US imports of goods far exceeding US exports to China, though the United States maintains a *services* trade *surplus* with China.[91] This two-way growth in trade and investment occurred despite periods of high political tension, for example, continuing even in the aftermath of the Tiananmen protests and violent Chinese government crackdown in 1989 and US–China skirmishes since then. Present political tensions appear to be leading US–China economic relations into a new and more substantial trough, however, as the United States and China trade tariff impositions and threaten a widening trade war while strategic concerns grow over issues such as fifth generation (5G) telecommunications technology dependence, competition over contracts to upgrade strategically vital undersea cables, and other mutually perceived security risks affecting the Indo-Pacific region. So long as such fundamental tensions and a primarily strategically competitive approach exist, cooperative development of, and mutual investments in, Blue Economy sectors will be viewed as risky and difficult. Russia's 2022 invasion of Ukraine and the PRC's support of it and Putin's leadership, have served only to exacerbate tensions further.

Despite such political, trade, investment, and security challenges, however, the global maritime industry continues to grow, with many industry analysts anticipating expanding market and growth opportunities. The ocean has become a greater focus among industry, scientists, and environmental advocates around the globe and particularly in the current Ocean Decade (2021–30). New commercial maritime trade opportunities also are opening up due to, among other factors, warming in the Arctic. Consequently, it is likely that the United States, China, and other countries will continue to pursue development of Blue Economies and seek to expand Blue Economy-related competition as well possibly cooperation overseas.

US–China economic competition in "blue" maritime, marine, and sustainable development sectors of the economy could lead to increasing investment opportunities in each country and around the globe also as new, blue sectors (e.g., Bluetech) emerge and expand. Yet, given the current state of US–China economic relations, where both capitals are imposing trade tariffs, threatening a wider trade war, and, in the US case, pursuing a "decoupling" or at least "de-risking" of the two economies in commercial as well as defense sectors, many of these opportunities could evaporate, be regulatorily limited, or be taken up by third parties.

The long-term effects of current trade, technology, and security disputes are not clear: a long-enduring US–China trade war and growing technology restrictions could reshape or even undermine the entire global economy. Alternatively, current disputes could be resolved over a period of time without fundamentally impacting the global economy or US–China trade relations. Time will tell. Nonetheless, the fact that the future shape of economic globalization is an open question is enough to raise the prospect of a new economic order emerging. Depending on its form, a new or novel economic order could leave the United States and China on opposing sides of a new divide, thereby further undermining the potential for cooperation in developing Blue Economies. If so, such a re-ordering would certainly affect the future development of the Blue Economy in both countries and beyond, likely bifurcating its development.

Alternatively, if the current trade frictions ease or other concerns are subordinated to economic expansion, the potential for increased cross-investment and trade in Blue Economy areas grows. As economic opportunity increases, however, so, too, does the potential for Intellectual Property Rights (IPR) infringements and the like, and thus the need for strong export control policies, processes, and expertise in both countries, particularly given the dual-use technology concerns inherent in development of a Blue Economy.

In the United States, federal standards, regulations, and export control policies have not kept up with the fast-growing ocean, maritime, and marine sectors in this regard. Nor have the measures and indicators kept pace that are needed to monitor and understand the increased role that the Blue Economy and related industries play in the US or global economies. This is especially true if including the new "Blue" economy sectors, such as offshore energy and other water-based renewable energy sectors, seabed mining, or Bluetech, and blue carbon business, for example. In order to better estimate the contribution that the Blue Economy and its innovative ecosystem effects provide to the US and other economies, expansion and greater standardization of data collection through revised national and international industrial codes used to track such economic activity is essential.[92] The latter effort will likely require not only cooperation among US allies but also to some degree with China.

For investment in the Blue Economy, whether at home or abroad, to be viewed as an investment opportunity and a strategic advantage, it is essential, too, for investors, entrepreneurs, innovators, and officials to have confidence in such transactions. Trusted indicators of how such activity and investment compare to competitors around the globe is essential, as is transparency in terms of the effects that the Blue Economy is having on the US economy and innovation capabilities, on those of other countries, and whether the Blue Economy is enhancing environmental conservation and sustainable development.

Similarly, transparency in terms of the amount and type of investments being made in maritime- and Blue-Economy oriented innovation clusters around the United States, across China, and elsewhere is critical to understanding the phenomenon. This is especially true given mutual interest in a still-globalized economy where positioning enterprises and research personnel in global innovation clusters such as California's Silicon Valley or China's Blue Silicon Valley matters to both US and PRC economies and beyond. Better data will help reassure officials in both countries that development of and any cooperation on Blue Economy endeavors can be advantageous despite inherent competitive economic and security risks.

Finally, usage (or not) of the term Blue Economy constitutes a form of competition that is likely affecting its development as well as the ability to use the term to advance US interests. A subtle but important part of US–China strategic competition, dating back to the start of diplomatic relations in 1979, is in deciding what terms are used as part of diplomatic communications and outreach. A recent example of this is the Obama administration's experience in first accepting but then rejecting Xi Jinping's use of the phrase "new model of great power relations." This phrase, at first, seemed straightforward and unproblematic from the US side, until it became clear that the ideological meaning on the part of China suggested US–China power parity and inherent agreement on the decline of the US' superpower role. While it is understandable for US and Western officials to resist employing PRC-originated terms of art that are laden with strategically problematic meaning, the term Blue Economy is not of PRC or even US origin. China has adopted it, as have many other states around the globe. If the United States seeks to make terminology the main locus of US–China strategic competition vis-à-vis the Blue Economy concept, such an effort will require considerably more focus and exertion than has been the case to date. Arguably, however, the terminology in this case is not as important as the ways, means, and ends that the Blue Economy offers to achieve a broad range of US strategic interests.

Notes

1. "CNO Delivers Remarks at Trans-Regional Seapower Symposium: Quick Facts," speech by Admiral Mike Gilday delivered in Venice, Italy (October 6, 2022), https://www.navy.mil/DesktopModules/ArticleCS/Print.aspx?PortalId=1&ModuleId=698&Article=3184425.
2. The White House, *National Security Strategy* (Washington, DC: US Government Printing Office, 2022), 22–3.
3. "Remarks on Signing the Oceans Act of 2000 in Martha's Vineyard," The American Presidency Project website (August 7, 2000), https://www.presidency.ucsb.edu/documents/remarks-signing-the-oceans-act-2000-marthas-vineyard.
4. Commission on Ocean Policy, *An Ocean Blueprint for the 21st Century: Final Report* (Washington, DC: Commission on Ocean Policy , 2004), vhttps://govinfo.library.unt.edu/oceancommission/documents/full_color_rpt/000_ocean_full_report.pdf.
5. Bureau of Economic Analysis, "Marine Satellite Account, 2021," Press Release (June 8, 2023), https://www.bea.gov/news/2023/marine-economy-satellite-account-2021.
6. European Commission, *The EU Blue Economy Report 2023* (Luxembourg: European Commission, 2023), 3.
7. European Commission, *EU Blue Economy Report 2023*, 3.
8. James Joliffe, Claire Jolly, and Barrie Stevens, "Science, Technology, and Industry Working Papers: Blueprint for Improved Measurement of the International Ocean Economy: An Exploration of Satellite Accounting for Ocean Economic Activity," Working Paper (Paris: OECD, 2021).
9. OECD, *Experimental Ocean-Based Industry Database, Directorate for Science, Technology and Innovation* (Paris: OECD, 2020).
10. US Congress, *National Defense Authorization Act for Fiscal Year 2023*, Public Law 117-263 (December 23, 2022).
11. US Congress, *National Defense Authorization Act for Fiscal Year 2023.*
12. Conathan et al., Appendices 1 & 2.
13. Executive Office of the President, "Fact Sheet: President Donald J. Trump Is Accelerating Ocean Exploration," The White House website (November 19, 2019).
14. Ocean Policy Committee, "Ocean Policy Committee Meeting Summary," US Archives: Trump White House (September 29, 2020), https://trumpwhitehouse.archives.gov/wp-content/uploads/2020/01/201027-MEETING-SUMMARY-200929-OPC-Meeting-CEQ.pdf.
15. NOAA lists US Pacific territories with EEZs as "American Samoa, the Commonwealth of the Northern Mariana Islands (CNMI), the Federated States of Micronesia (FSM), Guam, the Republic of the Marshall Islands (RMI), the Republic of Palau, as well as the US Minor Outlying Islands of Baker Island, Howland Island, Jarvis Island, Johnston Atoll, Kingman Reef, Midway Atoll, Palmyra Atoll, and Wake Island." NOAA Office of Coast Survey, *Exclusive Economic Zone (EEZs) – US-Affiliated Pacific Islands*, Distributed by Pacific Islands Ocean Observing System (PACIOOS) (2016), https://www.pacioos.hawaii.edu/metadata/pac_ocs_usa_eez.html.

16. Ocean Policy Committee, "Ocean Policy Committee 2022–23 Action Plan Summary," NOAA website (July 1, 2022) https://www.noaa.gov/sites/default/files/2022-06/OPC2022ActionPlanSummary.pdf.
17. Ocean Policy Committee, "Ocean Policy Committee 2022–23 Action Plan Summary."
18. National Oceanographic Partnership Program website, nopp.org.
19. Caitlin Keating-Bitonti and Eva Lipiec, "What Is the Blue Economy?," *In Focus*, IFI2188 (Washington, DC: Congressional Research Service, 2022).
20. US Department of Commerce, "US Department of Commerce National Oceanic Atmospheric Administration Ocean Research Advisory Panel Charter," NOAA website, https://www.noaa.gov/sites/default/files/2022-06/ORAP-CharterEstablishment-5.24.2022.pdf.
21. OECD, *The Ocean Economy in 2030* (Paris, OECD), 2016, 22.
22. See, for instance, Charles S. Cogan, "Ocean Accounts from National Income to Blue Economy." *Journal of Ocean and Coastal Economics: Special Issue: Oceans and National Income*, 2, no. 2 (Monterey, CA: Center for the Blue Economy, Middlebury Institute of International Studies, 2016); and Michael Conathan, Melanie Hart, Blaine Johnson, and Shiva Polefka, *Blue Future: Mapping Opportunities for US-China Ocean Cooperation*. Conference Report, Center for American Progress (Washington, DC: Center for American Progress, 2018).
23. Ocean Policy Committee, *Ocean Climate Action Plan* (Washington, DC: Ocean Policy Committee, The White House, 2023).
24. Walsh, CMSI, 2014.
25. Conathan et al.
26. US Department of State, "Fact Sheet: US Delegation Announced $6 Billion USD in Commitments to Address Threats to Our Ocean, Doubling Last Year's Pledge," State.gov (March 3, 2023).
27. OECD, *The Ocean Economy in 2030* (Paris: OECD Publishing, 2016), 24.
28. OECD, *The Ocean Economy in 2030*, 24.
29. See, for instance, Startup Genome and Global Enterprise Network, *GSER 2022: Blue Economy Edition: Global Blue Economy Trends* (San Francisco, CA: Startup Genome, 2022), https://startupgenome.com/report/gser-blueeconomyedition.
30. Startup Genome and Global Enterprise Network, *GSER 2022*.
31. Startup Genome and Global Enterprise Network, *GSER 2022*.
32. National Ocean Information Center, *2019 China Ocean Economic Development Index* (October 2019), 2.
33. Subcommittee on Ocean Science and Technology, Committee on Environment of the National Science and Technology Council, *Opportunities and Actions for Ocean Science and Technology (2022–2028)* (Washington, DC: Office of Science and Technology Policy, 2022).
34. NOAA, *Building a Climate-Ready Nation: NOAA Strategic Plan FY22–26* (Washington, DC: US Department of Commerce, 2022), https://www.noaa.gov/sites/default/files/2022-06/NOAA_FY2226_Strategic_Plan.pdf.
35. Executive Order 13840 overrode Obama-era policies establishing the National Ocean Policy and replaced the former National Ocean Council with a new Ocean Policy Committee. See Executive Office of the President, "Executive Order 13840" (June 19, 2018), https://www.govinfo.gov/content/pkg/DCPD-201800436/pdf/DCPD-201800436.pdf.

36. The White House, "Remarks by National Security Advisor Jake Sullivan on Biden-Harris Administration's Security Strategy" (October 12, 2022), https://www.whitehouse.gov/briefing-room/speeches-remarks/2022/10/13/remarks-by-national-security-advisor-jake-sullivan-on-the-biden-harris-administrations-national-security-strategy/.
37. Kevin Charles, "Marine Science and Blue Growth: Assessing the Marine Academic Production of 123 Cities and Territories Worldwide." *Marine Policy*, 84 (Amsterdam: Elsvier, 2017): 119–29.
38. Charles, "Marine Science and Blue Growth."
39. Charles, "Marine Science and Blue Growth."
40. Hepeng Jia, "Core Values: Urgent Environmental Problems Center to National Well-Being Jostle for the Attention of China's Scientists as They Strive to Produce Research with Global Prestige," *Nature Index 2018, Earth and Environmental Sciences Supplement* (New York, NY: Springer Nature, June 28, 2018), S14-15, https://media.springer nature.com/original/magazine-assets/d41586-018-05486-2/d41586-018-05486-2.pdf.
41. Jia, "China Digs."
42. Jia, "China Digs."
43. Charles, "Marine Science and Blue Growth."
44. Author interviews and research with US oceanographic experts (2013–19).
45. The author is grateful for insights and information provided on these topics by Dr. Jennifer McCann and Col. Erik Brine of the University of Rhode Island.
46. Sacks, David, "Countries in China's Belt and Road Initiative: Who's in and Who's out." *Asia Unbound*, Council on Foreign Relations Blog, 24 (2021), https://www.cfr.org/blog/countries-chinas-belt-and-road-initiative-whos-and-whos-out.
47. Duchâtel and Duplaix, "Blue China," 5.
48. Alexandra Stevenson, Kate Kelly, and Keith Bradsher, "As Trump's Trade War Mounts, China's Wall Street Allies Lose Clout." *The New York Times (online)* (September 16, 2018).
49. Robert D. Kaplan, "A New Cold War Has Begun." *Foreign Policy* (January 7, 2019), https://foreignpolicy.com/2019/01/07/a-new-cold-war-has-begun/.
50. The 2015 Maritime Strategy includes mention of environmental concerns, climate change, as well as illegal, unreported and unregulated (IUU) fishing, port security, and more—all aspects of what could comprise a broader blue economy strategy. US Navy, US Marine Corps, and US Coast Guard. *A Cooperative Strategy for 21st Century Seapower.* Electronic, US Department of Defense, Washington, DC: Government Printing Office, 2015, 40.
51. Stas Margoronis, "Proposed National Maritime Strategy Will Support US Maritime Growth," *American Journal of Transportation* (May 3, 2023).
52. Kabutaulaka, Tarcisius. "Mapping the Blue Pacific in a Changing Regional Order." *The China Alternative: Changing Regional Order in the Pacific Islands*, Graeme Smith and Terence Wesley-Smith, eds. (Canberra: Australian National University Press, 2021): 41–69, 49, http://doi.org/10.22459/CA.2021.
53. The White House, "Remarks by the Vice President at the Pacific Islands Forum" (July 12, 2022), https://www.whitehouse.gov/briefing-room/speeches-remarks/2022/07/12/remarks-by-vice-president-harris-at-the-pacific-islands-forum.
54. The White House, "Remarks by the Vice President at the Pacific Islands Forum."

55. "Solomon Islands Statement by Honourable Manasseh Damukana Sogavare Prime Minister of Solomon Islands at the Opening Debate of the Seventy Seventh Session of the United Nations General Assembly Theme: 'A Watershed Moment': Transformative Solutions to Interlocking Challenges," Pacific Islands Forum website (September 22, 2022), https://www.forumsec.org/2022/09/23/remarks-solomon-islands-pm-manasseh-d-sogavare-delivers-national-statement-to-unga77/.
56. Yimou Lee and Fabian Hamacher, "Solomon Islands Says Business as Usual with Taiwan as It Mulls Diplomatic Switch to China," *Reuters* (September 9, 2019), https://www.reuters.com/article/us-pacific-china-solomonislands/solomon-islands-says-business-as-usual-with-taiwan-as-it-mulls-diplomatic-switch-to-china-idUSKCN1VU1WH.
57. Lee and Hamacher.
58. David Brunnstrom, "US Reassessing Aid to Solomon Islands after Taiwan Ties Cut," *Reuters* (September 18, 2019), https://www.reuters.com/article/taiwan-diplomacy-usa-solomons/u-s-reassessing-aid-to-solomon-islands-after-taiwan-ties-cut-idINKBN1W32RN.
59. Brunnstrom.
60. Kirsti Needham, "US Ambassador to the Solomons Warns of Aid that Goes to 'One Bank Account'," *Reuters* (December 13, 2021), https://www.reuters.com/world/china/us-ambassador-solomons-warns-aid-that-goes-one-bank-account-2021-12-13/.
61. Michael E. Miller and Frances Vinall, "Solomon Islands Close to Security Deal with China, Alarming Neighbors," *The Washington Post* (March 29, 2022), https://www.washingtonpost.com/world/2022/03/29/solomon-islands-china-security-deal-manasseh-sogavare/.
62. Hoi Man Wu, "Former Solomon Islands Official Ousted from Post 'after Turning Down Chinese Bribes'," *Radio Free Asia* (May 2, 2023), https://www.rfa.org/english/news/pacific/solomon-islands-05022023100229.html.
63. Ministry of Police, National Security and Correctional Service, *National Security Strategy*, Solomon Island Government website (2020), http://macbio-pacific.info/wp-content/uploads/2019/02/SINOP_finalversion_26.11.18-digital-file.pdf.
64. Government of the Solomon Islands, *Solomon Islands National Ocean Policy*, Solomon Islands Government website (2018), http://macbio-pacific.info/wp-content/uploads/2019/02/SINOP_finalversion_26.11.18-digital-file.pdf.
65. Meg R. Keen, Anne-Maree Schwarz, and Lysa Wini-Simeon, "Towards Defining the Blue Economy: Practical Lessons from Pacific Ocean Governance." *Marine Policy*, 88 (2018): 333–41, https://doi.org/10.1016/j.marpol.2017.03.002.
66. "Memorandum of Understanding on Deepening Blue Economy Cooperation between the Ministry of Commerce of the People's Republic of China and the Ministry of XXX of Solomon Islands," *The Australian* (online) (May 6, 2022), https://origin.go.theaustralian.com.au/wp-content/uploads/2022/05/DocScan_05_06_2022.pdf.
67. Dr. Anna Powles (@AnnaPowles), "The draft security cooperation agreement between China and Solomon Islands has been linked on social media and raises a lot of questions (and concerns). (photos of agreement in this and below tweet) 1/6," March 24, 2022, https://twitter.com/AnnaPowles/status/1506845794728837120.

68. "Framework Agreement between the Government of the People's Republic of China and the Government of Solomon Islands on Security Cooperation," draft leaked March 2022. Powles.
69. "Framework Agreement between the Government of the People's Republic of China and the Government of Solomon Islands on Security Cooperation." Powles.
70. "Memorandum of Understanding on Deepening Blue Economy Cooperation."
71. "Memorandum of Understanding on Deepening Blue Economy Cooperation."
72. Solomon Islands Government, "Solomon Islands and People's Republic of China Deepened Relations with the Signing of More Development Cooperation," Solomon Islands Government website (May 27, 2022), http://solomons.gov.sb.
73. "Solomon Islands Sign Police Cooperation Agreement with China," *Solomon Times* (March 24, 2022), https://m.solomontimes.com/news/solomon-islands-signs-police-cooperation-agreement-with-china/11735?.
74. Nic Fildes, Kathrin Hille, and Demetri Sevastopulo, "Australia and US Move to Shore up Pacific Support after China's Overtures," *Financial Times* (May 26, 2022).
75. The White House, "Fact Sheet: In Asia, President Biden and a Dozen Indo-Pacific Partners Launch the Indo-Pacific Economic Framework for Prosperity" (May 23, 2022), https://www.whitehouse.gov/briefing-room/statements-releases/2022/05/23/fact-sheet-in-asia-president-biden-and-a-dozen-indo-pacific-partners-launch-the-indo-pacific-economic-framework-for-prosperity/.
76. The White House, "Statement by National Security Advisor Jake Sullivan on Fiji Joining the Indo-Pacific Economic Framework for Prosperity" (May 26, 2022), https://www.whitehouse.gov/briefing-room/statements-releases/2022/05/26/statement-by-national-security-advisor-jake-sullivan-on-fiji-joining-the-indo-pacific-economic-framework-for-prosperity/.
77. The White House, "Statement by Australia, Japan, New Zealand, the United Kingdom, and the United States on the Establishment of the Partners in the Blue Pacific" (June 24, 2022), https://www.whitehouse.gov/briefing-room/statements-releases/2022/06/24/statement-by-australia-japan-new-zealand-the-united-kingdom-and-the-united-states-on-the-establishment-of-the-partners-in-the-blue-pacific-pbp/.
78. Office of the Spokesperson, "Joint Statement on Partners in the Blue Pacific Foreign Ministers Meeting" (Washington, DC: US Department of State, September 22, 2022), https://www.state.gov/joint-statement-on-partners-in-the-blue-pacific-foreign-ministers-meeting/.
79. Office of the Spokesperson, "Joint Statement on Partners in the Blue Pacific Foreign Ministers Meeting" (September 22, 2022), https://www.state.gov/joint-statement-on-partners-in-the-blue-pacific-foreign-ministers-meeting/.
80. The White House, "Fact Sheet: Roadmap for a 21st Century US-Pacific Island Partnership" (September 29, 2022), https://www.whitehouse.gov/briefing-room/statements-releases/2022/09/29/fact-sheet-roadmap-for-a-21st-century-u-s-pacific-island-partnership/.
81. The White House, "Fact Sheet: Roadmap."
82. The White House, "Fact Sheet: Roadmap."
83. The White House, "Fact Sheet: Roadmap."

84. Gordon Peake and Camilla Pohle, "Six Months in, Where Does the US' Pacific Islands Strategy Stand?," *United States Institute of Peace Analysis & Commentary* (online) (April 12, 2023), https://www.usip.org/publications/2023/04/six-months-where-does-us-pacific-islands-strategy-stand.
85. Peake and Pohle, "Six Months in."
86. Office of Public Affairs, "Following President Biden's Call, US Department of Commerce Announces Plan to Initiate Process to Designate Marine Sanctuary in Pacific Remote Islands," US Department of Commerce website (March 2023), https://www.commerce.gov/news/press-releases/2023/03/following-president-bidens-call-us-department-commerce-announces-plan.
87. "With China Looming, US Signs MOU with Micronesia," *Reuters* (February 10, 2023), https://www.reuters.com/world/asia-pacific/with-china-looming-us-signs-mou-with-another-pacific-island-state-2023-02-10/.
88. Wyatt Olsen, "Solomon Islands Denies Port Call for Guam-Based US Coast Guard Cutter," *Stars and Stripes* (August 25, 2022), https://www.stripes.com/theaters/asia_pacific/2022-08-25/solomon-islands-coast-guard-cutter-china-7106824.html.
89. CNN website, "Solomon Islands to Ban All Foreign Navy Ships from Ports Pending New Approval Process," *Reuters* (August 30, 2022), https://www.cnn.com/2022/08/30/asia/solomon-islands-foreign-ships-moratorium-intl-hnk/index.html.
90. Kirsty Needham, "China Firm Wins Solomon Islands Port Project as Australia Watches on," *Reuters* (March 22, 2023), https://www.reuters.com/world/asia-pacific/chinese-company-wins-tender-redevelop-solomon-islands-port-official-2023-03-22/.
91. Bloomberg News, "The US-China Trade Dispute in Five Charts," *Bloomberg* (July 6, 2018), https://www.bloomberg.com/news/articles/2018-07-06/the-u-s-china-trade-relationship-a-dispute-in-five-charts.
92. Mark J. Spaulding, "The New Blue Economy: The Future of Sustainability." *Journal of Ocean and Coastal Economics*, 2, no. 2 (Monterey, CA: The Center for the Blue Economy, Middlebury Institute): Special Issue: Oceans and National Income Accounts: An International Perspective (February 2016), https://cbe.miis.edu/cgi/viewcontent.cgi?article=1052&content=joce.

References

Author. 2013–19. "Personal Communications with US Oceanographic Experts."

Bloomberg News. 2018. *The US-China Trade Relationship: A Dispute in Five Charts*, July 6. http://www.bloomberg.com/news/articles/2018-07-06/the-u-s-china-trade-relationship-a-dispute-in-five-charts.html.

Brunnstrom, David. 2019. "US Reassessing Aid to Solomon Isalnds After Taiwan Ties Cut." *Reuters*, September 19. https://www.reuters.com/article/taiwan-diplomacy-usa-solomons/u-s-reassessing-aid-to-solomon-islands-after-taiwan-ties-cut-idINKBN1W32RN.

Bureau of Economic Analysis. 2023. *Marine Satellite Account, 2021*. The BEA Wire, June 8. https://www.bea.gov/news/blog/2023-06-08/marine-economy-satellite-account-2021.

Central Intelligence Agency. n.d. World Fact Book, Solomon Islands Map https://www.cia.gov/the-world-factbook/countries/solomon-islands/map.

Charles, Kevin. 2017. "Marine Science and Blue Growth: Assessing the Marine Academic Production of 123 Cities and Territories Worldwide." *Marine Policy* (Elsevier) 84: 119–129.

Cogan, Charles S. 2016. "Ocean Accounts from National Income to Blue Economy." *Journal of Ocean and Coastal Economics: Special Issue: Oceans and National Income* (Center for the Blue Economy, Middlebury Institute of International Studies) 2 (2). https://cbe.miis.edu/joce/vol2/iss2/12.

Commission on Ocean Policy. 2004. *An Ocean Blueprint for the 21st Century*. Washington, DC: Commission on Ocean Policy. https://govinfo.library.unt.edu/oceancommission/documents/full_color_rpt/000_ocean_full_report.pdf.

Conathan, Michael, Melanie Hart, Blaine Johnson, and Shiva Polefka. 2018. *Blue Future: Mapping Opportunities for US-China Ocean Cooperation*. Conference Report, Center for American Progress, Washington, DC: Center for American Progress. https://www.americanprogress.org/issues/green/reports/2018/05/21/451064/blue-future/.

European Commission. 2023. *The EU Blue Economy Report, 2023*. Luxembourg: Publications Office of the European Union. https://op.europa.eu/en/publication-detail/-/publication/9a345396-f9e9-11ed-a05c-01aa75ed71a1.

Executive Office of the President. 2018. *Executive Order 13840: Ocean Policy to Advance the Economic, Security and Environmental Interests of the United States*, June 19. https://www.govinfo.gov/content/pkg/DCPD-201800436/pdf/DCPD-201800436.pdf.

———. 2019. "President Donald J. Trump Is Accelerating Ocean Exploration, Fact Sheet." www.whitehouse.gov. November. Accessed November 19, 2019. www.whitehouse.gov/briefings-statements/president-donald-j-trump-accelerating-ocean-exploration.

Fildes, Nic, Kathrin Hille, and Demetri Sevastopulo. 2022. "Australia and US Move to Shore Up Pacific Support after China's Overtures." *Financial Times*, May 26.

Government of the Solomon Islands. 2018. *Solomon Islands National Ocean Policy*. Solomon Islands Government (website). http://macbio-pacific.info/wp-content/uploads/2019/02/SINOP_finalversion_26.11.18-digital-file.pdf.

———. 2022. "Solomon Islands and People's Republic of China Deepened Relations with the Signing of More Development Cooperation." solomons.gov.sb. May 27. Accessed March 26, 2023. https://solomons.gov.sb/solomon-islands-and-peoples-republic-of-china-deepened-relations-with-the-signing-of-more-development-cooperation/.

Jia, Hepeng. 2018. "Core Values: Urgent Environmental Problems Center to National Well-Being Jostle for the Attention of China's Scientists as They Strive to Produce Research with Global Prestige." *Nature Index*, Earth and Environmental Sciences Supplement(Springer Nature, June 28), S14-15, https://media.nature.com/original/magazine-assets/d41586-018-05486-2/d41586-018-05486-2.pdf.

Joliffe, James, Claire Jolly, and Barrie Stevens. 2021. *Science, Technology, and Industry Working Papers: Blueprint for Improved Measurement of the International Ocean Economy: An Exploration of Satellite Accounting for Ocean Economic Activity*. Working Paper, Paris: OECD. https://doi.org/10.1787/aff5375b-en.

Kaplan, Robert D. 2019. "A New Cold War Has Begun." *Foreign Policy*, https://foreignpolicy.com/2019/01/07/a-new-cold-war-has-begun/.

Kaulaka, Tarcisius. 2021. "Mapping the Blue Pacific in a Changing Regional Order." In *The China Alternative: Changing Regional Order in the Pacific Islands*, 41–69. Canberra: Australian National University Press. http://doi.org/10.22459/CA.2021.

Keating-Bitonti, Caitlin, and Eva Lipiec. 2022. *What Is the Blue Economy?* In Focus: IFI2188, Washington, DC: Congressional Rsearch Service. https://crsreports.congress.gov/product/pdf/IF/IF12188.

Keen, Meg R., Anne-Maree Schwarz, and Lysa Wini-Simeon. 2018. "Towards Defining the Blue Economy: Practical Lessons from Pacific Ocean Governance." *Marine Policy* 88: 333–341. https://doi.org/10.1016/j.marpol.2017.03.002.

Kirsty, Needham. 2023. "China Firm Wins Solomon Islands Port project as Australia Watches On." *Reuters*, March 22. https://www.reuters.com/world/asia-pacific/chinese-company-wins-tender-redevelop-solomon-islands-port-official-2023-03-22/.

Lee, Yimou, and Fabian Harnacher. 2019. "Solomon Islands Says Business as Usual with Taiwan as It Mulls Diplomatic Switch to China." *Reuters*, September 9. https://www.reuters.com/article/us-pacific-china-solomonislands/solomon-islands-says-business-as-usual-.

Margoronis, Stas. 2023. "Proposed National Maritime Strategy Will Support US Maritime Growth." *American Journal of Transportation*. https://www.ajot.com/insights/full/ai-proposed-national-maritime-strategy-will-support-u.s-maritime-growth.

2022. "Memorandum of Understanding on Deepening Blue Economy Cooperation Between the Ministry of Commerce of the People's Republic of China and the Ministry of XXX of Solomon Islands." *The Australian*, May 6. https://origin.go.theaustralian.com.au/wp-content/uploads/2022/05/DocScan_05_06_2022.pdf.

Miller, Michael E., and Frances Vinall. 2022. "Solomon Islands Close to Security Deal with China, Alarming Neighbors." *The Washington Post*, March 29. https://www.washingtonpost.com/world/2022/03/29/solomon-islands-china-security-deal-manasseh-sogavare/.

Ministry of Police, National Security and Correctional Service. 2020. *National Security Strategy*. Solomon Islands Government. https://pacificsecurity.net/wp-content/uploads/2021/03/210201-SOLOMONS-National-Security-Strategy-Final_.pdf.

National Ocean Information Center (2019), *2019 China Ocean Economic Development Index* (October).

National Oceanic and Atmospheric Administration Office of Coast Survey (OCS). 2016. *Exclusive Economic Zone (EEZs) -- US-Affiliated Pacific Islands*. online, Honolulu, HI: Pacific Islands Ocean Observing System (PacIOOS). https://www.pacioos.hawaii.edu/metadata/pac_ocs_usa_eez.html.

National Oceanic and Atmospheric Administration. 2022. *Building a Climate-Ready Nation: NOAA Strategic Plan FY22-26*. https://www.noaa.gov/sites/default/files/2022-06/NOAA_FY2226_Strategic_Plan.pdf, Washington, DC: US Department of Commerce.

———. n.d. a *National Oceanographic Partnership Program*. nopp.org.

———. n.d.b. "Ocean Policy Committee." *Organizational Chart*. https://www.noaa.gov/interagency-ocean-policy.

Needham, Kirsti. 2021. "US Ambassador to the Solomons Warns of Aid That Goes to 'One Bank Account'." *Reuters*, December 13. https://www.reuters.com/world/china/us-ambassador-solomons-warns-aid-that-goes-one-bank-account-2021-12-13/.

Ocean Policy Committee. 2018. "OPC-Summary Initial Meeting." whitehouse.gov. August 1. Accessed January 19, 2019. www.whitehouse.gov/wp-content/2017/11/OPC-Summary-Initial-Meeting-080118.pdf.

———. 2020. "Ocean Policy Committee Meeting Summary." *US Archives: Trump White House*, September 29. Accessed May 7, 2023. chrome-extension://https://trumpwhitehouse.archives.gov/wp-content/uploads/2020/01/201027-MEETING-SUMMARY-200929-OPC-Meeting-CEQ.pdf.

———. 2022. *Ocean Policy Committee 2022–23 Action Plan Summary*. Washington, DC: NOAA.gov. https://www.noaa.gov/sites/default/files/2022-06/OPC2022ActionPlanSummary.pdf.

———. 2023. *Ocean Climate Action Plan*. Washington, DC: The White House. https://www.whitehouse.gov/wp-content/uploads/2023/03/Ocean-Climate-Action-Plan_Final.pdf.

OECD. 2016. *The Ocean Economy in 2030*. Paris: OECD Publishing.

———. 2020. *Experimental Ocean-Based Industry Database, Directorate for Science, Technology and Innovation*. Paris: OECD.

Office of the Spokesperson. 2022. "Joint Statement on Partners in the Blue Pacific Foreign Ministers Meeting." US Department of State, September. https://www.state.gov/joint-statement-on-partners-in-the-blue-pacific-foreign-ministers-meeting/.

Office of Public Affairs. 2023. "Following President Biden's Call, US Department of Commerce Announces Plan to Initiate Process to Designate Marine Sanctuary in Pacific Remote Islands." US Department of Commerce, March. https://www.commerce.gov/news/press-releases/2023/03/following-president-bidens-call-us-department-commerce-announces-plan.

Olsen, Wyatt. 2022. "Solomon Islands Denies Port Call for Guam-Based US Coast Guard Cutter." *Stars and Stripes*, August 26. https://www.stripes.com/theaters/asia_pacific/2022-08-25/solomon-islands-coast-guard-cutter-china-7106824.html.

Peake, Gordon, and Camilla Pohle. 2023. "Six Months In, Where Does the US' Pacific Islands Strategy Stand?" United States Institute of Peace (online), April 12. https://www.usip.org/publications/2023/04/six-months-where-does-us-pacif.

Powles, Anna. 2022. "Dr. Anna Powles (@AnnaPowles), The Draft Security Cooperation Agreement Between China and Solomon Islands Has Been Linked on Social Media and Raises a Lot of Questions (and Concerns). (Photos of Agreement in This and Below Tweet) 1/6." *Twitter (@AnnaPowles)*, March 24. https://twitter.com/AnnaPowles/status/1506845794728837120.

Reuters. 2022. "Solomon Islands to Ban all Foreign Navy Ships from Ports Pending New Approval Process." CNN.com. August 30. Accessed March 26, 2023. https://www.cnn.com/2022/08/30/asia/solomon-islands-foreign-ships-moratorium-intl-hnk/index.html.

———. 2023. *With China Looming, US Signs Assistance Deal with Micronesia*. Washington, DC, February 10. https://www.reuters.com/world/asia-pacific/with-china-looming-us-signs-mou-with-another-pacific-island-state-2023-02-10/.

Sacks, David. 2021. *Countries in China's Belt and Road Initiative: Who's In and Who's Out*. Council on Foreign Relations 24. March 24. https://www.cfr.org/blog/countries-chinas-belt-and-road-initiative-whos-and-whos-out.

Solomon Times. 2022. "Solomon Islands Signs Police Cooperation Agreement with China." March 24. Accessed March 2023. https://m.solomontimes.com/news/solomon-islands-signs-police-cooperation-agreement-with-china/11735?

Spaulding, Mark J. 2016. "The New Blue Economy: The Future of Sustainability." *Journal of Ocean and Coastal Economics* (The Center for the Blue Economy, Middlebury Institute) 2 (2: Special Issue: Oceans and National Income Accounts: An International Perspective): 8.

Startup Genome and Global Enterprise Network. 2022. *GSER 2022: Blue Economy Edition: Global Blue Economy Trends*. San Francisco: Startup Genome. https://startupgenome.com/report/gser-blueeconomyedition.

Stevenson, Alexandra, Kate Kelly, and Keith Bradsher. 2018. "As Trump's Trade War Mounts, China's Wall Street Allies Lose Clout." *The New York Times (online)*, September 16.

Subcommittee on Ocean Science and Technology, Committee on Environment of the National Science and Technology Council. 2022. *Opportunites and Actions for Ocean Science and Technology (2022–2028)*. Washington, DC: Office of Science and Techology Policy. https://www.whitehouse.gov/wp-content/uploads/2022/04/03-2022-SOST-Opportunities-and-Actions-for-Ocean-Science-and-Technology-2022-2028.pdf.

The American Presidency Project. 2000. "Remarks on Signing the Oceans Act of 2000 in Martha's Vineyard." https://www.presidency.ucsb.edu. August 7. Accessed May 7, 2023. https://www.presidency.ucsb.edu/documents/remarks-signing-the-oceans-act-2000-marthas-vineyard.

The White House. 2022. "Fact Sheet: In Asia, President Biden and a Dozen Indo-Pacific Partners Launch the Indo-Pacific Economic Framework for Prosperity." *The White House*, May 23. www.whitehouse.gov; https://www.whitehouse.gov/briefing-room/statements-releases/2022/05/23/fact-sheet-in-asia-president-biden-and-a-dozen-indo-pacific-partners-launch-the-indo-pacific-economic-framework-for-prosperity/.

———. 2022. "Fact Sheet: Roadmap for a 21st-Century US-Pacific Island Partnership." *The White House*, September 29. https://www.whitehouse.gov/briefing-room/statements-releases/2022/09/29/fact-sheet-roadmap-for-a-21st-century-u-s-pacific-island-partnership/.

———. 2022. *National Security Strategy*. Washington, DC: Government Printing Office.

———. 2022. *Remarks by National Security Advisor Jake Sullivan on Biden-Harris Administration's Security Strategy*, October 12. Accessed March 13, 2023. https://www.whitehouse.gov/briefing-room/speeches-remarks/2022/10/13/remarks-by-national-security-advisor-jake-sullivan-on-the-biden-harris-administrations-national-security-strategy/.

———. 2022. *Remarks by the Vice President at the Pacific Islands Forum*, July 12. https://www.whitehouse.gov/briefing-room/speeches-remarks/2022/07/12/remarks-by-vice-president-harris-at-the-pacific-islands-forum.

———. 2022. "Statement by Australia, Japan, New Zealand, the United Kingdom, and the United States on the Establishment of the Partners in the Blue Pacific." www.whitehouse.gov. June 24. https://www.whitehouse.gov/briefing-room/statements-releases/2022/06/24/sta.

———. 2022. "Statement by National Security Advisor Jake Sullivan on Fiji Joining the Indo-Pacific Economic Framework for Prosperity." www.whitehouse.gov. May 26. https://www.whitehouse.gov/briefing-room/statements-releases/2022/05/26/statement-by-national-securi.

United Nations. 2022. *Solomon Islands Statement by Honourable Manasseh Damukana Sogavare Prime Minister of Solomon Islands at the Opening Debate of the Seventy Seventh Session of the United Nations General Assembly Theme: 'A Watershed Moment: Transformative Solutions to Interlocking Challenges.* YouTube. September 23. https://www.forumsec.org/2022/09/23/remarks-solomon-islands-pm-manasseh-d-sogavare-delivers-national-statement-to-unga77/.

US Congress. 2022. *National Defense Authorization Act for Fiscal Year 2023, Public Law 117–263.* Washington, DC: Government Printing Office.

US Department of Commerce. 2022. "US Department of Commerce National Oceanic Atmospheric Administration Ocean Research Advisory Panel Charter." www.noaa.gov. May 24. Accessed May 7, 2023. https://www.noaa.gov/sites/default/files/2022-06/ORAP-CharterEstablishment-5.24.2022.pdf.

US Department of State, Office of the Spokesperson. 2023. "US Delegation Announced $6 billion USD in Commitments to Address Threats to Our Ocean, Doubling Last Year's Pledge: Fact Sheet." State.gov. March 3. Accessed May 3, 2023. https://www.state.gov/u-s-delegation-announced-6-billion-usd-in-commitments-to-address-threats-to-our-ocean-doubling-last-years-pledge/.

US Navy. 2022. *"CNO Delivers Remarks at Trans-Regional Seapower Symposium: Quick Facts," Speech by Admiral Mike Gilday Delivered in Venice, Italy,* October 6. https://www.navy.mil/DesktopModules/ArticleCS/Print.aspx?PortalId=1&ModuleId=698&Article=3184425.

US Navy, US Marine Corps, and US Coast Guard. 2015. *A Cooperative Strategy for 21st Century Seapower.* Electronic, US Department of Defense, Washington, DC: Government Printing Office, 40.

Walsh, Kathleen A. 2015. "CMSI Workshop on US and Chinese Perspectives on the Blue Economy December 11–12, 2014." *CMSI Bulletin No. 2.* Newport: China Maritime Studies Institute, US Naval War College, 14.

Wu, Hoi Man. 2023. "Former Solomon Islands Official Ousted from Post 'After Turning Down Chinese Bribes'." *Radio Free Asia (online),* May 2. https://www.rfa.org/english/news/pacific/solomon-islands-05022023100229.html.

6

Geostrategic Implications of China's Development of the Blue Economy

When news crossed computer screens in 2013 that China had announced something then called the One Belt, One Road (now referred to as the Belt and Road Initiative) along with a map depicting the world-wide scope of China's plan as portrayed by state media (*Xinhua News Agency*), it was the most remarkable thing this author had seen in over three decades studying modern China. The map, in particular, laying out China's plans to connect cities and ports across the Pacific, Indian Ocean, Horn of Africa, Persian Gulf, and the Mediterranean, as well as connecting China to Central Asia through to Eastern and Western Europe, registered as the most remarkable and strategically ambitious document I had ever seen emanating from Beijing, then or since. This map has since expanded to include Latin America, the Arctic, and Antarctica, notably everywhere on the globe except North America.

Why it came as a surprise was because of the time period in which I have been studying China's rise, when Beijing was focused mainly on its domestic economic, technological, and military modernization. In contrast, Xi's Belt and Road concept was, and remains, an imperially bold plan, far from the more cautious approach to foreign policy of Xi's Chinese Communist Party leader predecessors. Although couched in diplomatic rhetoric as a return to the same sort of global economic exchange, trade, and prosperity evoked by stories of the ancient Silk Road, the stunning breadth and scale of Xi's modern conception clearly and immediately marked a new era in modern Chinese history. The latter holds true even if assuming Xi's initiative reflects what China has long wanted to do and was planned, if not disclosed, under previous PRC leadership. It is not entirely clear that that is the case, however. Either way, Xi's willingness to announce to the world and vigorously pursue such a brazen, worldwide plan to project Chinese power via land and sea is new and significant.

When Xi's *Vision for Maritime Cooperation* also came out several years later, it laid a much more detailed blueprint over China's Maritime Silk Road part of the BRI strategy. Taken together, these strategies, plans, and policies are nothing less than an outline for how China plans to become a maritime Great Power. The main question for China analysts and strategists everywhere now is whether or not China can achieve its stated, very bold aims and when.

Many volumes have been written on the Belt and Road Initiative, what it means, what it involves, and whether or not it is succeeding or can succeed.

 DOI: 10.1201/9781003396116-6

The focus of this volume, however, is on China's development of the Blue Economy, which precedes Xi's 2013 announcement of the Belt and Road. Yet, the merging of these two concepts as foundations in Xi's quest for China to become a maritime Great Power and as detailed in his 2017 *Vision for Maritime Cooperation* represents an underappreciated development and one that holds wide-ranging geostrategic implications.

Given that China's Belt and Road Initiative, its Maritime Silk Road component, and Blue Economy development efforts at home and abroad remain ongoing and integrated endeavors, it is still too soon to determine their ultimate success or failure (or mix thereof). Nevertheless, China's announced ambitions to become a maritime Great Power and to develop a Blue Economy date back at least a decade, providing sufficient guideposts to China's future direction, priorities, and likely activities. Consequently, there are important geostrategic questions that arise from what we already know about China's Blue Economy-related strategies, plans, policies, and practices to date (although much more remains to be uncovered). These critical questions are discussed below, followed by a list of policy options and recommendations for US policymakers' consideration.

Critical Geostrategic Questions about China's Blue Economy

There are numerous, strategically important questions that China's development and export of its Blue Economy concept raise for those interested in China's future, in US–China relations, and in the geostrategic contest that is already taking place in the Indo-Pacific region. While a determination of China's ultimate success or failure in its Blue Economy-related endeavors must await further research and study, China's strategies, plans, and activities to date in pursuing its Blue Economy concept indicate several ways in which this development could affect global, regional, and bilateral affairs. As an initial undertaking, seven critical, geostrategic questions stemming from China's development and export of the Blue Economy come to the fore.

Question 1: How Will the Blue Economy Influence Who Will Rule the Seas?

This question might seem at first glance to be too sweeping, even absurd. Yet, as this volume has sought to lay out, China is pursuing the Blue Economy as an industrial development model, as a means to enhance its civil-maritime and naval innovation capabilities, as a more effective means of sustainable development, and as a tool, lever, and export in its efforts to influence countries across the Indo-Pacific region, many of whom have indicated interest in all that the Blue Economy concept has to offer. As such, the Blue Economy approach to development aids China's quest to become a maritime Great Power in *all* dimensions and relative to the United States.

At the same time, the United States' lack of comprehensive national security and maritime strategies that include both foreign and domestic elements of developing and leveraging the Blue Economy (or, if preferred, using an alternative term) provides China with essentially a lead in the ongoing strategic competition between our two states. As the case study on the Solomon Islands demonstrates, China has taken the first mover advantage in engaging on the Blue Economy and in a strategically vital part of the region. The United States (and others) felt the need to respond, and at the highest levels of government, to what was viewed as a regional security concern and potential strategic loss of influence and possibly also access in the region. What happened in this case is likely not the last such action-reaction dynamic over competing interests in the Blue Economy or efforts to otherwise leverage the Blue Economy to enhance strategic influence that we are likely to witness in the US–China strategic competition centered on the Indo-Pacific region.

Introduction of the Blue Economy concept into the geostrategic contest in the Indo Pacific also changes the nature of the game. In order to understand how and how fast China will be able to develop its maritime power, attention to the Blue Economy as it supports China's domestic development and its foreign affairs is key.

The Blue Economy is a now-essential indicator of China's growing maritime power, as it is for the United States, whether widely recognized as such yet or not. Will the United States catch up to China in terms of both developing the Blue Economy at home and leveraging it overseas? This is still to be determined, although the United States tends to move swiftly and forcefully once it has recognized a security or technology challenge. The first step to ensure the United States maintains its stature as the world's leading maritime power overall, however, is to recognize the Blue Economy as a new and significant factor in maritime development, power, and influence.

As modern China grows from being primarily a land power to also a sea power, strategists will need to look anew at what constitutes the Mainland's sources of power. The Blue Economy is one such indicator and could help to accelerate Beijing's efforts to make China a maritime Great Power in all dimensions and more quickly than might be presumed. The PRC already possesses large-scale naval assets and other traditional forms of maritime power. What it lacks—and the Blue Economy offers—is the softer side of maritime power and a form of power that will be more attractive to other countries in the region than hard power demonstrations alone.

Question 2: How Will the Blue Economy Influence Ocean Governance and Who Will Write the Rules?

"International ocean governance" as defined by the European Commission "is about managing the world's oceans and their resources together so that they are healthy and productive, for the benefit of current and future generations."[1] In addition to altruistic goals, this basic definition captures a key consideration: who manages the world's oceans and their resources? The definition suggests this will be done "together," but the current, troubled status of US–China relations (and little reason to think this will reverse any time soon), suggests that ocean governance will be complicated to accomplish, at best.

As in other areas of world affairs, China seeks a leading role in ocean governance based on its rising economic status and related power. Where China's leaders have not felt its interests are being sufficiently met, Beijing has established new bilateral and multilateral organizations, where China plays the lead role. Examples include the Shanghai Cooperation Organization (SCO) and the Asian Infrastructure Investment Bank (AIIB), the latter established in 2015 to support China's BRI. In the United Nations Security Council, where China is one of five Permanent Members along with the United States, Russia, the United Kingdom, and France, China has moved to re-interpret long-standing laws, rules, and norms to serve its own strategic intent. Many of the clashes taking place in the South China Sea and elsewhere, for instance, are based on Beijing's re-interpretations of existing law and maritime norms. Based on this record, it is unlikely that Beijing will change course where applied to ocean governance. In terms of the Blue Economy, China has already led efforts to re-interpret the term's meaning (as in the Xiamen Declaration announced at the APEC meeting chaired by China) and is likely to do the same in related matters.

How might the Blue Economy, and China's development thereof, affect ocean governance internationally? China's 14th Five-Year Plan spells out Beijing's intentions clearly. Section 3 (under Article XXXIII) of the document, entitled "Deeply Participate in Global Ocean Governance," outlines China's plan as follows:

> We will actively develop blue partnerships, deeply participate in the formulation and implementation of international ocean governance mechanisms and related rules, promote the construction of a fair and reasonable international maritime order, and promote the construction of a maritime community of common destiny (海洋命运共同 体). We will deepen practical cooperation with coastal nations in the fields of marine environmental monitoring and protection, scientific research, and maritime search and rescue and strengthen the survey and evaluation of deep-sea strategic resources and biodiversity. We will participate in pragmatic cooperation in the Arctic and build the "Ice Silk Road" ("冰上丝绸之路"). We will improve our ability to participate in the protection and utilization of Antarctica. We will strengthen situational research and judgment, risk prevention, and legal theory struggles (法理斗争), strengthen judicial construction for maritime affairs, and resolutely safeguard national maritime rights and interests. We will advance legislation concerning basic maritime law in an orderly manner.[2]

Xi Jinping's approach to ocean governance expands the BRI into the polar regions as well as the deep sea. The plan asserts Beijing's intention to build what is presumably meant to be an alternative "international maritime order" to the existing one, which is dominated at present by the United States and its allies and partners. This revisionist approach fits with past efforts to take the lead and to attract other countries to follow China's lead. The latter efforts can be expected of a rising power and conceivably even be welcome where change is needed or additional resources, support, and expertise add value. In the case of China, however, current tensions, long-standing security concerns, and lack of transparency and data sharing raise serious concerns. Two examples in the ocean space explain how and why China's ocean governance leadership could prove problematic.

Beijing seeks to take the lead and enhance cooperation in several maritime endeavors. For instance, like the United States and other maritime centers, China cooperates in international ocean observation programs (such as the international Argos float program). Yet, in 2018, Beijing made clear that China's participation in such collaborative ocean observation programs will be *in addition to* an ocean observation network Beijing is developing separately for the Chinese-designed *Beidou* satellite network. China claims that the *Beidou* project will "alter the dominance in satellite float technology by several Western countries and allow China to build a more independent ocean observation network along the Maritime Silk Road as well as provide more maritime public goods."[3] This parallel approach, while perhaps understandable from China's own security perspective, raises science, technology, and security dilemmas for others in the region and beyond who share ocean science interests in the strategically vital Indo-Pacific region.

Similarly, China's plan to establish a new tsunami warning center in the South China Sea (SCS) sparked concerns over its rationale, focus, and location given the existence of, and ongoing regional cooperation with, the Pacific Tsunami Warning Center (PTWC) based in Hawaii. The PTWC shares its data and warnings worldwide. In 2015, the United States and China agreed that Beijing's proposed South China Sea Tsunami Advisory Center (SCSTAC) would "share sensing, forecasting, and modeling data with all relevant member states in the Asia-Pacific and the Pacific-Tsunami Warning and Mitigation System Member States, including the United States and coastal states of the SCS."[4] Despite the US withdrawal from the United Nations Educational, Scientific and Cultural Organization (UNESCO) in October 2017, it appears the PTWC is still engaging as part of the international Tsunami Warning System (although the US National Tsunami Warning Center's data "are outside the framework of the IOC-coordinated tsunami warning systems").[5] However, China's reluctance to engage and share data with PTWC prior to announcing the SCSTAC center leaves doubt as to how effective data sharing with China will be with regard to the SCS Tsunami Advisory Center. The SCSTAC became fully operational in early November 2019, joining ten other such centers around the globe.[6]

As recounted above, the record thus far of China's ocean governance and even participation in existing international cooperative ventures has been perceived by some as being problematic. Clearly, Beijing seeks autonomy from any US-dominated system. The same can be said in reverse, however, as China's maritime power grows and in ways that appear hostile to US and allied interests. The Blue Economy, as an attractive form of international development and diplomacy, could enhance China's prospects of leading or dominating more international ocean programs.

Question 3: How Will the Blue Economy Influence Who Dominates Key Maritime and Blue Sectors?

While the first question looks at the geostrategic contest for maritime power and the second at ocean governance, this question seeks to get at the maritime industrial implications of the Blue Economy as part of PRC and US development efforts. As Chapters 2 through 5 lay out, the United States and China are already in a maritime contest and in terms of developing a Blue Economy, whether it is called such or not. The notions of Blue Economy industry clusters or development zones are essentially the same, if pursued by different means. The United States already has maritime industry clusters that are becoming more "blue"; in China, the challenge is to, in the first place, develop maritime industry clusters (or development zones) and to make them blue at the same time. One is an upgrade of sorts, the other establishing something almost entirely new. Which approach will prove easier and faster to accomplish is unknown, and a developing state's typical "fast follower" advantage might not apply in this instance. But the country that does exploit their country's Blue Economy potential most effectively will win out and have advantage in developing as well as exporting their maritime concepts, processes, products, and technologies to third parties.

In order to understand the shift to the Blue Economy in both countries, more data and more standardized data and metrics are needed, as well as transparency in both regards. Which development model or mix of top-down or bottom-up dynamics works best can only be known if there is sufficient data to track Blue Economy activity, with confidence in the numbers, and as tracked over time.

In addition, as the Blue Economy evolves, not only will standards in data collection, research, and analysis be essential, but so will be development of policy and technical standards in terms of new "blue" technologies and innovations. Technology policy and technical standards guide entrepreneurs, engineers, and innovators toward certain quality considerations and, in the case of the Blue Economy, can be used to determine what innovative technology is truly "blue" (e.g., sustainably developed or contributing) or not. China has indicated it values the importance of technology standards in competing in global markets, and is sure to establish its own standards in this respect in an effort to dominate the marine, maritime, and naval marketplaces, as Beijing has attempted to do in other strategic industry sectors.

Given China's surge in maritime industrial capacity and capabilities over the past two decades, the United States (and its allies and partners) are being challenged in ways like never before. China's now world-largest navy, coast guard, and fishing fleet plus sizeable paramilitary maritime forces represent a strategic challenge in sheer quantity alone, as well as in terms of maritime security and marine conservation and sustainability efforts in the region. Domestically, China's Blue Economy concept, in theory, promises more sustainable development over time on the Mainland as well as greater dual-use innovative capability. If effectively implemented, China's maritime ascendence could be bolstered even further, and in a qualitative way by Blue Economy-oriented development. The Blue Economy concept also raises the potential of greater access for China to overseas maritime locales and possibly also a naval presence or base. Of course, the same holds true of the United States in terms of choosing to strategically pursue development of a Blue Economy at home and abroad.

Question 4: Will China's Blue Economy Clusters Lead to Significant Naval and Maritime Inventions and Innovations?

China's current, 14th Five-Year Plan makes clear the leadership's continued focus on developing what constitutes a Blue Economy and connecting these efforts elsewhere in the region:

> We will build a number of high quality maritime economic development demonstration zones and specialized maritime industry clusters and comprehensively improve the development levels of the three major maritime economic circles in the north, east, and south [referring to the Bohai Sea, Yangtze River, and Pearl River Delta regions]. With the support provided by the coastal economic belt, we will deepen maritime cooperation with neighboring countries.[7]

The question of innovation in China is a complicated one, due in part to China's political, societal, cultural, and economic environment. Having explored this question for nearly three decades, the answer as to whether China can innovate or not has been answered: as China's technological advances demonstrate, of course, innovation is possible in China, even under Communist Party leadership.

What explains China's fast-paced economic and technological advances over the past 30–40 years is the degree to which Beijing has allowed innovation to occur and for Chinese people (and foreign partners) to take risks. Chinese leader Deng Xiaoping and his next three successors repeatedly made clear to the Chinese population that taking some risks, when it came to economic development and, later, technology innovation, was acceptable as part of China's efforts to modernize. This clear and repeated message from top leadership over decades accompanied by substantial state funding, foreign investment, and technology transfers, SEZ development and similar zones for prioritized and clustered development of strategic industries, as well as state planning that over time became less rigid and more strategically oriented guidance, all contributed to China's ability to rapidly develop and ascend the technology development and innovation ladder. Xi Jinping, however, has upended this approach and re-emphasized the importance of the CCP and its ideology as drivers of Chinese modernization. Because of this seismic shift in emphasis, the likelihood of entrepreneurial-level innovation in China is reduced, although state-level science programs are likely to continue apace or even be accelerated.

What does this forecast for China's Blue Economy development zones and industry clusters? If the above reflects an accurate assessment of the main constraint on innovation occurring in China today, then one can expect not terribly much from Blue Economy development efforts in commercially reliant zones and clusters in China nor much that is truly inventive or more than marginally innovative for some time to come. That said, if China's leadership were to tack in a different direction or the leadership, itself, were to change, the prior assessment, expecting more advanced innovation, could again take hold. Nevertheless, despite the ideological obstacles in place, it is still possible for China to continue to progress in terms of its industrial, technological, and especially scientific capabilities, all of which will be used in service of China's military and particularly naval modernization.

Another factor in this equation is also the role played by US–China relations as a bellwether of what is possible in terms of foreign investment and technology transfer. At present, the serious downturn in bilateral relations bodes ill for expanded innovation opportunities in China, whether by US investors or those allied with the United States. This lack of engagement, however, comes at a cost to overall development of the Blue Economy and particularly to the extent that development of the Blue Economy is considered a key aspect of fighting climate change and other environmental concerns. It is likely that some level of foreign investment and technology transfer will occur, however, even amid declining US–China relations, and as other markets seek to fill the vacuum.

Question 5: Will China's Blue Economy Development Lead to Improvements in China's and the Region's Marine Environment?

China's marine environmental efforts continue, but it appears that in a practical sense these efforts are largely conducted on a separate track, as in the past. This situation bodes ill for China's overall efforts to clean up its own waters and to establish more sustainable methods of development elsewhere. Though on a separate track, there remains potential for improvement, at least in some areas, if China's marine environmental efforts continue in a serious way and as a priority over many years. But China's past record suggests that these improvements will not be of large-scale, given priority over other interests, or fundamentally change the country's environmental situation in the near-term.

If this assessment holds true, the effects will not be felt in China alone. Water pollution and unsustainable development practices do not know borders and can impact populations, both human and marine life, far away from the source. If China's economic development, both at home and as tied to overseas investments, does not become more sustainable overall, the impacts on climate change, fisheries, and human populations are also likely to be detrimental. Notably, the same can be said of the United States and others.

Similarly, Chinese resource exploitation practices on land have wrought enormous destruction on PRC territory. Taking a similar approach to water, ocean, and undersea resources elsewhere would have just as destructive an effect, although others might not know of it until long after the activity has taken place, particularly if conducted in the deep sea.

Alternatively, if China's Blue Economy concept represents a fundamental shift in the country's mode of development toward more sustainable and environmentally friendly approaches, this could have positive impacts both domestically and in marine areas surrounding the PRC and beyond. Moreover, such advances could serve PRC foreign policy endeavors vis-à-vis the Blue Economy by providing much more positive messaging about China's maritime and marine activities, capabilities, and intentions. The latter does not appear to be the case as yet, however, meaning that the earlier-described risks seem most likely, at least in the near-term future.

Question 6: How Much Will Pursuit of the Blue Economy Enhance What We Learn about the Ocean and Where (or Where Not)?

As noted in Chapter 1, in September 2021, the United Nations announced the start of the UN Decade of the Ocean.[8] This ten-year endeavor is meant to accelerate the UN's Sustainable Development Goal 14, whose focus is the oceans. The ocean remains a largely unexplored frontier for science. Only a quarter of the world's oceans have been mapped to date, an accomplishment reached only recently.[9] If humanity is to understand the oceans, their depths, and their import for climate change and other natural phenomena, ocean science is the starting point. Given the vast expanse of the oceans, covering over three-quarters of our planet, this endeavor is likely to require a global effort. The United States and China, as major world powers, UN Security Council members, and maritime powers, are expected to be in the forefront of such efforts.

But this is where it gets complicated. As discussed elsewhere in this volume, US–PRC scientific cooperation (in the form of co-authored studies, joint research, and academic or government exchanges on a wide range of ocean science-related issues) has continued to some degree over decades despite occasionally downward-turning US–China relations. This might not remain the case, however, as lawmakers and policymakers in Washington look at China anew as a 21st-century strategic competitor.

Coinciding with the US Secretary of State's first official visit to China more than two years into the Biden administration, reports in the press indicate that the long-standing US–China science and technology (S&T) cooperation agreement could come to an end soon if not renewed. This oldest cooperation agreement between the United States and the PRC, signed at the start of US–PRC diplomatic relations in 1979, is potentially at risk, according to press reports.[10] The US–China Science and Technology Agreement (STA) has been renewed regularly every five years and was due to expire in August 2023 unless once again officially renewed.[11] An ongoing (as of this writing) review by the Biden administration is reportedly continuing, likely due to many months of bilateral tensions between the United States and China.[12] Despite past concerns over Chinese technology transfer and other troubling policies, the STA has remained in place, in part to ensure basic scientific exchange continues. Advocates for changing or cancelling the current STA cite China's continuously problematic technology transfers, copyright and intellectual property rights infringements, as well as espionage activities as causes to at least re-negotiate, update, or outright cancel the more than 40-year-old agreement.[13]

Yet, China's cooperation on ocean science and data sharing is important, particularly if Beijing is establishing alternative networks or organizations that might or might not share data with Western or US-based researchers. Ocean science and international maritime scientific and technical cooperation are essential to understanding what many see as a new scientific frontier: humans know less about the deep ocean than we do about outer space. Operating in the deep sea is at least as challenging, if not more so, than operating in outer space, which is likely to spur on scientific discoveries, technological leaps, and military operational advantages.

China is becoming an important actor in international ocean science but to date has not shared its ocean data and research much beyond joint authorship of publications, many of which are co-published with US authors. If global powers are to lead the effort against cascading climate change effects and other global challenges, some degree of ocean science collaboration and data-sharing is likely needed as well. Of course, this requires China's willingness to share its data with global ocean scientists, which appears to not yet have been fully the case. Will China eventually freely share its collected data with the world, as does NOAA in the United States and in a way that users can be confident in the data itself? The answer to this question will go a long way toward determining how much in-depth (if any) cooperation will exist between the United States and China on matters of ocean science and research.

The prospects, too, for China's own strategic plans for ocean science cooperation and expanded joint research and development on ocean science at home and abroad will be challenged by growing security concerns in the region as well as by long-standing irritants surrounding intellectual property rights, copyright, patenting, and academic publishing practices in China, as noted in the STA context. A joint research cooperation program, for instance, between Woods Hole Oceanographic Institution (WHOI) in the United States and Ocean University in Qingdao, China, was scaled back dramatically after concerns arose in the United States as to how the agreement was being implemented.[14]

China's track record to date of protecting foreign intellectual property combined with a relative lack of sharing or making transparent its own ocean science and data is concerning. This is why China's development of separate, potentially proprietary technology, and independent ocean observation systems, as China has been establishing in recent years, will increase existing concerns about China's maritime intentions and naval capabilities in the region.

Finally, as mentioned earlier in the text, China's intent and ability to deter or coerce other countries involved in ocean science exploration in or near areas that the PRC claims to be its sovereign territory (whether on land or sea) remain a significant barrier to advancement of ocean science, to human understanding, and to international relations.

Question 7: Will China's Blue Economy Remain an Underappreciated Element of the PRC's Pursuit of Becoming a Maritime Great Power?

As this volume has sought to outline in detail, China's development of the Blue Economy is an end but also an important means of enhancing its maritime power, both at home and abroad. This dimension of Chinese maritime power is a neglected component in almost every strategic analysis on China published by the US government, whether by the Department of Defense or the Intelligence Community, as well as by US think tanks, academics, and consultancies. As laid out in this volume's initial chapters, this lack of serious strategic attention to the Blue Economy as an issue is likely due to the fact that few even know of the Blue Economy, whatever name it goes by, much less appreciate its strategic significance, unless involved in maritime, environment, or climate activities.

But as highlighted in the Director of National Intelligence's *Global Trends 2040* report, the environment, economics, and technology constitute what the report terms "structural forces" over the next 15–20 years that will "shape the contours of our future world."[15] The Blue Economy, including as conceived in China, represents the nexus of these three critical domains.

China's Blue Economy pursuits as part of its Maritime Silk Road and *Vision for Maritime Cooperation*, furthermore, are likely to impact regional development and security considerations in the Indo-Pacific region, particularly to the extent that China's Blue Economy development efforts at home and abroad succeed in aiding the PRC's quest to become a maritime Great Power.

Will the Blue Economy serve as the needed soft power and welcome carrot in Chinese diplomacy, as it has in the Solomon Islands? The answer is likely so, especially given the region's interest in this topic. There also are considerations beyond the Indo Pacific about the wider ocean environment, climate change effects, our understanding of the large underwater parts of the planet that serve to connect all of the continents, and the role that the Blue Economy, as developed in China and elsewhere, will play.

These and more geostrategic implications of China's Blue Economy development efforts will determine the future maritime environment, literally and figuratively, in the Indo-Pacific region. In the meantime, what is the United States to do about such considerations? The following section lays out a range of policy options available to US policymakers charged with advancing US national interests.

Winning the Great Blue Game: Policy and Strategy Recommendations

"Victory though Sea Power." That is the US Naval War College's motto. The college's former president, Captain Alfred Thayer Mahan, a naval historian, is remembered for his seminal work, *The Influence of Sea Power upon History, 1660–1783*. This volume is considered a classic for its insights into the role that naval power played in Great Britain's rise to empire and, later, would play in the United States' ascendence to global power. The economy plays a central role in this story, as it does still today. But today's maritime economy is turning blue, all around the globe. If the United States is to remain the preeminent maritime power in the Indo Pacific and beyond, greater strategic attention to the Blue Economy in US policy, strategy, and practices is essential.

As the United States and China remain entangled in a competition for global dominance and military modernization while at the same time heavily interdependent in economic, financial, and environmental terms, the balancing act between economic and security interests makes for a complex relationship. These shifting sands will affect the degree to which the United States and China can or will find common areas of interest in developing the Blue Economy at home and abroad despite inherent risks, or whether this contest will become more competitive and even hostile.

The implications of an emerging "Great Blue Game" for US national security and foreign policy, strategy, and interests are potentially extensive, indicating a need for US strategists and policymakers to take action, lest the game be lost for not having played. There is risk and uncertainty in all of the potential options and recommendations outlined below but also opportunities to chart a new, more prosperous, and sustainable course vis-à-vis US–China relations and the growing geostrategic contest of the Great Blue Game.

Fundamentally, two options exist: to do something or to do nothing about what appears to be a growing competition in development of the Blue Economy as an element of being a 21st-century maritime power. Doing nothing, to include a wait and see approach, is not advised, although it appears to largely constitute the general US approach to the Indo Pacific writ large when it comes to the Blue Economy and its broader geostrategic implications. Though more research, data, and analysis are needed to make fully informed decisions about exactly how best to address the new, "blue" challenges and opportunities that are arising across the Indo Pacific and particularly in and by China, some decisions and actions can be taken in the near term.[16]

Wait and See How the Blue Economy Concept Develops in China and Elsewhere?

A common, if often unwise, de facto policy option is to simply do (or actively decide to do) nothing about a strategic and policy challenge. This is particularly true of complex challenges, which make for hard decisions and play to one's natural inclination to want more information before making a decision. A version of the risk-averse, do-nothing approach to tackling new ideas and challenges is to wait and see what develops, how, where, and how fast, waiting to decide what, if anything, to do until a later, more certain time.

With regard to development of the Blue Economy and the Great Blue Game, however, doing nothing would be disadvantageous to US interests across diplomatic, economic, scientific and technological, environmental, and military-security dimensions. The Blue Economy, as generally conceived to be a sustainable development-oriented maritime economic development and innovation dynamic, is an idea that serves all aspects of US national interests and could help to strengthen allies', partners', and friends' economies, environments, and (if perhaps to a lesser degree) maritime and naval innovation capabilities. Moreover, doing nothing would cede the game and its rules to others, including, most prominently, China. As such, doing nothing would be the worst possible option. As the saying goes, one has to play to win.

There are some activities related to the Blue Economy on which the US government is already engaged, including the State Department's hosting of the annual "Our Ocean" conference, the Commerce Department's NOAA-led (but mainly "NOAA-wide") Blue Economy Initiative, conferences sponsored by the Energy Department that have included a focus on the Blue Economy, and more. Searches of the State Department website prior to the Biden administration for the terms "Ocean Economy" or "Blue Economy," however, yielded only a few official statements related to diplomatic visits overseas (e.g., India, the Seychelles, Mauritius), suggesting the concept was not a top priority for the Department of State, at least not under prior administrations or State Department leadership. Similarly, former National Security Advisor John Bolton's December 2018 speech on US strategy toward Africa made several critical mentions of China but made no mention of opportunities related to the Ocean or Blue Economy, despite China's existing outreach there on Blue Economy matters. These are some recent examples, but one remains hard-pressed to find US government pronouncements on the Blue Economy outside of a few, select initiatives and remarks. None of these engagements, policies, press releases, or programs equates to a national strategic vision, cohesive strategy, or plan to explore Blue Economy-related opportunities and challenges in a comprehensive and strategic manner and in ways meant to enhance US maritime power for geostrategic intent.

The Biden White House has been comparably more actively engaged on matters of the Blue Economy than the prior administration, both in terms of domestic issues and foreign policy. Yet these efforts remain focused largely on the development and measuring of US *domestic* Blue Economy activities (or as related to climate initiatives) and only in limited respects in terms of foreign policy, such as aid and outreach to select locales like the Solomon Islands. These still-nascent and piecemeal efforts, while essential, also do not constitute a holistic and comprehensive strategy that takes into account the Blue Economy's role in our geostrategic contest with China. This contest will continue in some fashion even if US–China relations improve substantially but will matter even more so if they worsen.

In short, the US government should do more to develop a coherent strategy and national as well as government-wide policies that ensure the United States can engage effectively on development of the Blue Economy at home and abroad and be an active participant in any Blue Economy developments and opportunities that arise around the globe but especially in the Indo-Pacific region. Time is of the essence. Not only is the planet rapidly heating up, which development of the Blue Economy could help to address, but there exists a new period of opportunity in the post-COVID era. Blue Economy efforts around the globe were affected by the scourge of the global pandemic, with these activities only slowly getting back under way at the time of this writing. Where the United States had fallen behind China's Blue Economy strategic efforts initially, there is opportunity again now to move quickly and to lead global efforts in this regard.

If the United States is going to act or react in some fashion to the opportunities and challenges posed by the Blue Economy concept and China's development thereof, several policy options exist. Some combination of the below is likely necessary to ensure that the United States and our allies, partners, and friends can compete across all dimensions of the emerging Great Blue Game.

Draft a Comprehensive US Strategy for Developing the Blue Economy and to Address China's Development via the Maritime Silk Road

One strategic option that US officials could consider is to develop an explicit *counter*-strategy approach (paralleling China's MSR and Blue Economy plans). This approach could be tempting to policymakers as it would provide an alternative vision not only for the United States but also for US allies, partners, and friends. It is unlikely, however, that the United States can or ought to copy or mirror China's expansive Maritime Silk Road initiative and related plans; it is more important for the United States to be present and active in these same areas than necessarily to devise and fund a separate, parallel, competing strategic vision to China's MSR. Neither the discretionary federal budget nor political will appears present to support such a grand, new undertaking at this time.

While an updated and more comprehensive maritime strategy is clearly needed to advance US broad maritime interests with regard to development of the Blue Economy, a tit-for-tat strategic approach to counter China's MSR is unlikely to lead to a constructive outcome, nor attract US allies into such an either-or, zero-sum dynamic between the United States and China. This approach also could hasten the prospects for a US–China conflict.

Rather, an expansion of existing US national and maritime strategies to encompass the Blue Economy in all its dimensions—with the Blue Economy incorporated specifically into and coordinated with diplomatic, regional, and theater security combatant commands, and other plans and assets—would provide a more implementable approach. Alternatively, a separate strategy that lays out both domestic and international ends, ways, and means would provide the sort of comprehensive strategic intent and blueprint that could be implemented across the US government and in tandem with US allies, partners, and friends. Such a comprehensive approach would ensure a multidimensional and, where possible, multilateral approach is adopted such that all elements of US power and maritime interests are enhanced.

As a first step in this direction, the Biden administration could update the US national, defense, and maritime strategies to incorporate all dimensions of the Blue Economy—diplomatic, economic, informational, scientific, technological, environmental, and military-security interests—to ensure that the US develops a healthy Blue Economy and is able to export these ideas and practices abroad. Over time, US officials should develop a separate and comprehensive Blue Economy strategy addressing both domestic and international concerns. Aiding implementation would be the establishment of an independent agency of some sort operating outside of the White House, which would ensure the implementation and permanency of US Blue Economy strategic efforts.

Create New Opportunities for US International Engagement on Blue Economy Matters, in Particular, in the Indo-Pacific Region

The emerging Great Blue Game contest between the United States and China over development of the Blue Economy is still in the early stages, where opportunity exists to design the rules of the game, to identify key players and partners, and to develop standards by which the game is going to be played. China's plans to develop "Blue Economy" development zones across the MSR appear to be an effort to do just that and to cement first-mover advantages that such an approach could afford in terms of China and other countries cooperating in developing "blue" development policies and practices, standards and regulations, technologies, and infrastructure, as well as determinations on the locations where these developments take place (or not). Such plans could have long-term implications for US naval capabilities, presence, and access, particularly in the Indo-Pacific region, given US forward-basing of forces, supplies, and services. Examples include regional ports developed as part of, or connected to, new, Blue Economy zones potentially dominated by Chinese hardware, software, technology, services, funding, and perhaps workers. To the extent (if at all) the MSR map suggests the United States, US allies, partners, and friends might be excluded from or limited in our ability to engage in PRC-led Blue Economy-oriented opportunities across the region, this should concern the United States and others involved in the region.

In order to thwart any such exclusionary intentions, the United States can expand US international engagement on—and leadership of—Blue Economy matters, especially in the Indo Pacific. The aim would be to ensure the United States has a seat at the table and a presence in any overseas Blue Economy clusters as well as being a leading voice when and where decisions about the Blue Economy concept, development efforts, investment practices, and policies are made.

The United States, again, need not develop a separate playing board, but must be regularly and intimately engaged in ensuring the rules of this new game are fair, transparent, and represent best business, investment, environmental, intellectual property rights practices, and so on. Doing so will require extended multilateral engagement—with China and others in the region, with international governmental organizations, non-governmental and private-sector actors, and particularly with US allies, partners, and friends—to ensure the development of the Blue Economy at least does not undermine or exclude US interests and those of others in the region. Establishing the new rules and standards for Blue Economy-themed development would ensure US, Western, and allied interests are not excluded but are, in fact, enhanced. This approach does not exclude China, but would be open to any country meeting certain standards of practice.

Moreover, advice recommended in a 2015 Council on Foreign Relations study on conceiving a new US grand strategy vis-à-vis China still holds true:

> The administration should construct a geoeconomic policy to deal with China over the long term, using the strength and positive power of the US economy, innovation, and networks to attract Asian nations; and deal with the PRC's coercive pressure on its neighbors, in ways that are always consistent with an international rules-based system that is so obviously in the national interest of the United States and its friends and allies.[17]

Developing the Blue Economy—and strategic consideration of how to enhance US and allied innovative capabilities in the maritime realm and naval domain in a sustainable way—is an essential and critically important part of being a 21st-century maritime power and, thus, of US grand strategy.

As the emergence of the Blue Economy concept and its implications for both countries' commercial, scientific, and naval advancement become more apparent, US interests will be best served by informed policymaking rather than through policy decisions made out of ignorance, fear, or uncertainty due to a lack of good data and analysis of what the evolving Blue Economy concept means for US interests and those of our allies, partners, and friends. Establishing such confidence includes illuminating areas of concern such as the lack of, or limitations to, undersea research in contested maritime areas that are nonetheless important to our understanding of climate change and other global scientific concerns.

A still-promising area of potential economic and scientific cooperation and impact related to Blue Economy development is in the field of environmental studies. Improving environmental conditions—on land, in the air, water, and climate overall—is a common concern for China and the United States, as elsewhere. This is true even when Washington (as under the Trump administration) is not as engaged or supportive of such foreign policy initiatives. When faced with such lack of interest from Washington, US states and municipalities have continued to engage on these issues overseas. Moreover, US–China cooperation and collaboration in terms of addressing energy and climate change issues, for example, is considered a positive example of how the two major powers can work constructively together toward common goals (as during the Obama administration).[18] Similarly, a recent Track II study group of US and Chinese experts found that although

> the ocean space does not yet provide good platforms for nongovernmental US-China engagement and cooperation ... each country's stated interests in developing "blue" or maritime economies in environmentally sustainable ways suggest that there is value in promoting further US-China ocean-expert exchanges to ensure that opportunities for cooperation and progress are not lost.[19]

Further Promote Domestic Blue Economy Development

The US government could provide greater support, assistance, and transparency to US businesses, entrepreneurs, and others than has been available to date. By collecting data and publicly providing such information, making more clear to the broader public existing policy efforts and legal considerations, as well as promoting greater insight into regional Blue Economy developments around the world all would be helpful to current and potential future stakeholders in marine, maritime, and naval development. For such a fast-moving and increasingly global phenomenon, it is difficult for individuals or small groups to gather the information needed to understand how, where, and why the Blue Economy has taken root and is developing around the country and across the globe. The US business and innovation model is primarily a bottom-up approach, but local and regional enterprises can benefit from understanding the bigger picture and myriad domestic and international approaches to Blue Economy development. Government is better equipped to provide such information and analysis in the aggregate given its resources, breadth, and reach. An expansion of public-private ventures aimed at funding studies, and developing strategies and policies related to the Blue Economy and the MSR, particularly in science, research, and technology areas, would add to our understanding and yield additional opportunities.

The Trump administration's Ocean Policy Committee, for instance, tasked its Ocean Resource Management subcommittee

> to conduct outreach to stakeholders ... to identify local and regional data needs, and to develop recommendations to streamline the release of unclassified Federal data that addresses key regional data needs ... [via] a common information management system that facilitates the sharing of ocean data and serves as a platform to expand public access to ocean-related data.[20]

This is certainly a start, as was the tasking for the Ocean Science and Technology subcommittee "to facilitate the collection, development, dissemination and exchange of information between agencies on ocean-related matters."[21] Congress is also pressing for better data and more collaboration in these areas. Given different terminologies, definitions, and data collection methods when it comes to understanding the Blue Economy, however, vigilance is needed to ensure business leaders and policymakers have a systemic understanding of Blue Economy development data and development trends such that they can compete and take full advantage of US government assistance.

For US-based innovative Blue Economy clusters to thrive requires public- and private-sector collaboration, even when originating in an entrepreneurial, free-market environment. In order to survive what is known as the innovative "Valley of Death" that lies between the spark of a new idea and the ability to bring that idea to market often entails receiving support from government or some larger entity that has the financial and other resources necessary to bridge the idea-reality gap that innovators and entrepreneurs face. This public-private relationship can be mutually advantageous for both government and private-sector enterprises, especially in new or complex engineering-based or emerging innovation-oriented industries. It is the prospect of private-sector innovation, for instance, that drives the Department of Defense's and US Navy's interest in supporting Blue Economy-oriented developments from San Diego, California, to Newport, Rhode Island, and locations in between. Blue Economy innovation clusters serve the US Navy's interests and hold the promise of enriching the municipal areas in which they are located. But more can be done to publicly recognize the importance of the Blue Economy as a strategic approach to maritime development both nationally and internationally.

In order to ensure that trade and investment in the Blue Economy serve rather than undermine US national security interests, it is incumbent also on federal and local officials to facilitate understanding by US business and others of the technology transfer opportunities and risks as well as legal constraints involved, especially transactions with investors or partners from China and elsewhere overseas. As development of the Blue Economy advances, new industry and technology sectors are emerging at home and abroad, creating new technology and export control challenges. Getting ahead of these challenges rather than responding to them once violations become apparent is advisable for both business and government interests.

Lastly, capitalism and innovation both fare best when there is perceived to be a fair playing field, which only government can enforce. The trust factor with regard to there being equal opportunity via enforcement of the rule of law plays an important role in how innovation and spillover effects happen at the local level (as in the United States) or not (as has been a persistent challenge for China).

In order to achieve the objectives laid out above, it is advisable to expand efforts by relevant US government departments (e.g., White House Ocean Policy Committee and Departments of State, Commerce, Energy, and Defense) to provide information, data, and studies on developments in the Blue Economy at home, abroad, and particularly across the MSR in order to better serve the public need for timely, transparent, and reliable information. Moving such efforts as they relate to the Blue Economy to an independent agency or office is, again, likely to ensure such efforts survive partisan shifts.

An additional approach would be to commission in-depth case studies on China's Blue Economy development efforts, both domestic and overseas, to better understand China's progress (or lack thereof) domestically and in terms of international outreach, investments, and collaborations (in determining efforts that prove successful or not). Case studies, for instance, contrasting Blue Economy plans and actions on the Shandong Peninsula centered around the northern port city of Qingdao and site of China's first Blue Economy zone and those being planned and implemented in some fashion in Shenzhen or on Hainan Island, China's southern-most province, would be a useful next step for scholars, officials, and others to better understand how Beijing's Blue Economy efforts are succeeding (or not), how quickly or not, and what impact they are having on industry, innovation, and conservation objectives.

Similarly, case studies detailing China's overseas Blue Economy plans, investments, and activities in two or more locations would help to further illuminate—even if in preliminary stages of development or implementation—what Beijing both aspires to and is likely capable of doing to project its Blue Economy concept across the region as part of Xi's *Vision for Maritime Cooperation*. In particular, the latter case studies would add substance to the many studies ongoing related to China's Belt and Road Initiative, but which have tended to focus on identifying and evaluating separate incidents of investment, aid, and infrastructure developments but that often do not take into account the more holistic approach reflected in China's Blue Economy concept. Establishing a literature of such research over time would provide a much fuller picture of how the Blue Economy is impacting the Indo-Pacific region and China's role in it.

Promote US Ocean Science, Technology, and Education to Advance the Blue Economy

The 21st-century's focus on the oceans as a frontier for scientific exploration is reason for increased federal government support for ocean science research, technology development, and education so that the United States can continue to lead the world in ocean and marine science. The ocean is a critical factor in the climate, in climate change, and as the main transportation route underpinning economic globalization. Maritime power requires mastery of the ocean domain. As China endeavors to enhance its maritime power, the United States must ensure US ocean science, technology, innovation, and education continue to be resourced and vibrant so as to remain competitive, preferably dominant.

The need to explore and better understand the oceans is a global concern. The United States and its allies, partners, friends, and others in the international community should ensure that scientific research is conducted in a way that is open, fair, transparent, and according to established international law and scientific protocols. This includes ocean scientific research in disputed waters such as in the South China Sea. The United States is leading the effort to challenge China's revised interpretations of maritime law, its gray-zone activities, and dangerous, coercive encounters at sea; the United States also needs to lead the way on the Blue Economy. One way of doing so is through the power of science, technology, and innovation—arguably one of the most significant forms of US power in the modern age.

In order to fulfill these aims, increased US federal funding for ocean science research and related educational programs at the elementary, secondary, through university levels is needed in terms of promoting the Blue Economy concept and the myriad disciplines that feed into it. Also essential is supporting and protecting the United States' and others' ability to access and conduct ocean science research across the globe. An ocean science, technology engineering, and math or "O-STEM" educational approach could aid these efforts and tie them also to US and international Blue Economy and other maritime clusters, zones, or centers.

Support Allied and Partner Blue Economy Efforts in the Indo-Pacific Region and Beyond

Information is difficult to obtain with regard to details about what the United States government has done and is already doing to support Blue Economy development efforts abroad. This suggests that more could be done, if only with regard to the publicity and transparency of any such efforts.

In the meantime, it is clear that local governments have taken the initiative and are working with foreign counterparts in terms of developing ideas for and lessons learned in establishing Blue Economy clusters. While the US federal government would not be wise to interfere in such organic engagements arising from entrepreneurial or innovative outreach, there is likely more that US government officials could do to support the efforts of allies, partners, and friends in developing their Blue Economy strategies and plans and in ways that also aid US interests and entities seeking to engage overseas while making the United States the partner of choice. Hosting more Blue Economy-themed international conferences, workshops, courses, and other forms of international engagement would serve these purposes and more.

US officials should also solicit ideas from the private sector and allies, partners, and friends on how the US government might better support the development of Blue Economies around the globe and in ways that engage US partners at the national, regional, and local levels. In these ways, the lessons learned afar can be used in US development of our own Blue Economy.

Finally, US leadership in the area of international maritime law and in developing new rules, norms, and practices in the "Blue" arena is needed. To bolster US strategic interests as well as to counter reinterpretations of existing international law, the United States Senate ought to ratify the United Nations Convention on the Law of the Sea (UNCLOS). There is no strategic reason not to do so, with US military leaders advocating ratification, and every reason to add this tool to our maritime powers. Absent that, the United States ought then to work on developing a new maritime regime that will address US and allied interests as well as issues related to ocean science, technology, resources, and sustainability. Being outside the current international maritime legal regime (even if adhering to its principles) is simply insufficient in the face of China's quest to become a rival maritime Great Power. The Blue Economy offers both opportunities and challenges to US leadership in international maritime affairs and ocean governance.

Continue to Engage China on the Blue Economy

The United States and China are already engaged on matters of the Blue Economy, as outlined in Chapter 5 on US–China relations, if in limited ways. As Blue Economy clusters and maritime development zones emerge and expand across the United States, in China, across the Indo-Pacific region, and beyond, Americans and Chinese are likely to continue to interact and engage, both cooperatively and in competition.

Even if US–China relations were to improve substantially in the near-term (which seems unlikely), the competition between the world's two most ideologically distant but largest economies will continue in terms of maritime and naval technology, industry, and innovation. The looming question is what degree of cooperation, or not, will there be between the United States and China on issues like the Blue Economy, in all its dimensions? The latter should include at the very least matters related to conservation and sustainability, lest the contest to develop Blue Economies lead to greater exploitation—and environmental degradation—of the oceans and other bodies of water, thereby exacerbating rather than alleviating the challenges from pollution and climate change. Any cooperation or collaboration should also ensure transparency and reciprocity in terms of sharing data, access, and findings in accord with oceanographic exploration and scientific research and data-sharing protocols. The need for more and new agreements will arise as the Blue Economy expands and evolves. US–China cooperation in these new areas is possible, if both sides are willing.

Earlier administrations found a way to cooperate with China in a comprehensive manner while ensuring US interests were being served. Along the lines of the US–China strategic dialogue framework implemented by the George W. Bush and Obama administrations, the Trump administration announced in 2017 "a new and cabinet-level framework for negotiations": the then-newly named United States-China Comprehensive Dialogue.[22] Similar to earlier Bush- and Obama-era incarnations of high-level, bilateral economic and security dialogues, the Trump administration initially continued to engage Beijing through this framework on a range of diplomatic, cyber, economic, technology, and security interests, challenges, and opportunities. These efforts were broken down into four separate dialogues. These dialogue "pillars" included "the Diplomatic and Security Dialogue; the Comprehensive Economic Dialogue; the Law Enforcement and Cybersecurity Dialogue; and the Social and Cultural Issues Dialogue."[23]

Yet unlike earlier-era dialogues, which regularly involved detailed, cross-disciplinary discussions of ocean, environmental, climate, and even Blue Economy concerns and interests, during the Trump-era dialogues only the Social and Cultural Issues Dialogue appears to have included any such discussions, beyond concerns related to legal and security disputes over activities in the South China Sea taken up in the Diplomatic and Security Dialogue.[24] The Social and Cultural Issues Dialogue, however, did "recognize the importance of the EcoPartnerships program" and

> cooperative action to protect the ocean, ensure sustainable fisheries, combat wildlife trafficking of marine and terrestrial species, promote environment and energy technologies with full intellectual property protection, address climate change issues, improve environmental law enforcement and compliance, and help protect and improve the ambient environmental (air, water, and soil ecosystems) from pollution for generations to come.[25]

Based on past such US–China dialogues, there is clearly greater potential and arguably a need for a more detailed and comprehensive dialogue on Blue Economy-related issues with China, if the political will exists in both Washington and Beijing to do so. It does not appear as of this writing (summer 2023), however, that any of these formal dialogues continue or are likely to in the Biden–Xi era.

Yet, as stated on the US Embassy website in 2019 (during the latter part of the Trump administration),

> The United States seeks to build a positive, cooperative, and comprehensive relationship with China by expanding areas of cooperation and addressing areas of disagreements, such as human rights and cybersecurity. The United States welcomes a strong, peaceful, and prosperous China playing a greater role in world affairs and seeks to advance practical cooperation with China.[26]

Fundamentally, US policy toward China has not changed, even under a new administration led by the opposite political party, which also seeks to cooperate, as well as compete, with China, if hedging even more to the side of competition. As such, there remains opportunity to continue to engage China on maritime and Blue Economy matters in a strategically comprehensive way, even with the downturn in US–China relations. Communication will remain important, if only aimed at understanding what the Blue Economy means to each country's strategic aims. Dialogue on how the Blue Economy also factors into each state's foreign and domestic development efforts (to include infrastructure, technology, impact on environmental and climate concerns, and more) from an official and strategic perspective would also be useful.

If US–China relations continue along the present downward trajectory, cooperation of any sort—but particularly with regard to any militarily useful, blue-oriented science, technology, innovation, or business—is likely to be restricted, in part or in full. The United States and China have balanced economic and security concerns since the start of China's reform era four decades ago, suggesting there is reason to think the present course of hedging, though complex and often difficult to manage, will continue for some time. If so, cooperative engagements on the Blue Economy wherever they take place must be undertaken with as much information as possible to ensure both the risks and the opportunities involved are fully considered by US stakeholders.

Given the potential for some degree of continued US–China engagement on Blue Economy matters, the United States—perhaps in coordination with allies and others—should develop dedicated information monitoring capabilities with regard to tracking China's progress and international outreach, investments, and collaboration on the Blue Economy so as to inform US decision making by both public- and private-sector leaders. Too much of the discussion of China's strategic intent and actual activities around the globe is based on anecdotal, questionable, piecemeal, or headline-grabbing stories that do not always reflect the ground truth or else is likely classified or proprietary information; Chinese propaganda exacerbates this challenge. All interests, including those of our allies, partners, and friends, would be served by having a reliable, transparent, and more accurate and official documentation of China's efforts in developing the Blue Economy both domestically and overseas. As an already powerful state that aspires to be a maritime Great Power, the United States and others should also press China to be more forthcoming in the practices it implements and applies in regional Blue Economy zones and clusters in order to help assuage US and regional concerns about the prospects of these places surreptitiously becoming de facto naval assets or bases ringing the Indo Pacific.

Based on the above policy considerations, some combination of the "do something" options would be most pragmatic as a means of both leveraging Blue Economy opportunities and minimizing the risks involved in cooperating with China while ensuring the United States continues to expand and enhance all elements of maritime power, including naval and "blue" elements thereof. Deciding to do all of the above—and perhaps even more—is also possible. Notably, all of the above would prove useful to US interests even if it turns out that China Blue Economy efforts do not succeed as planned.

Policymakers will need to gauge how best to implement any or all of the above options but with an informed understanding of the Blue Economy's strategic importance. The Blue Economy will change our understanding of maritime power as comprising more than traditional naval and maritime capabilities and involving also whole new industries, new discoveries, and forms of innovation as well as stewardship of the oceans and waters as a way of ensuring prosperity, security, *and* sustainability. Doing nothing and simply waiting to see how China advances its Blue Economy plans and strategies would prove shortsighted and is not recommended given an evolving understanding of the importance of the oceans, the increasingly competitive nature of US–China relations, and the role the Blue Economy will play in the strategic maritime realm.

Notes

1. European Commission, "International Ocean Governance," https://oceans-and-fisheries.ec.europa.eu/ocean/international-ocean-governance_en.
2. Xinhua News Agency, *Outline of the People's Republic of China 14th Five-Year Plan for National Economic and Social Development and Long Range Objectives for 2035*, trans. Etcetera Language Group, Inc. for Center for Security and Emerging Technology, Georgetown University (March 12, 2021), https://cset.georgetown.edu/wp-content/uploads/t0284_14th_Five_Year_Plan_EN.pdf.

3. Xinhua News Agency, *China's Real-Time Global Ocean Observation Network Established* (February 6, 2018), https://www.xinhuanet.com/english/2018-02/06/c_136953672.html.
4. US Department of State, *US-China Strategic & Economic Dialogue Outcomes of the Strategic Track*, Washington, DC: Office of the Spokesperson (June 24, 2015).
5. Intergovernmental Oceanographic Commission (IOC) of UNESCO, *Existing Services of the Global Tsunami Warning System*. UNESCO (February 2018), https://itic.ioc-unesco/images/stories/ptws/TsunamiWarningMap_20180218.pdf.
6. United Nations Educational, Scientific and Cultural Organization (UNESCO), "Tsunami Center for South China Sea Becomes Fully Operational on World Tsunami Awareness Day," press release (November 6, 2019), https://en.unesco.org/news/tsunami-center-south-china-sea-becomes-fully-operational-world-tsunami-awareness-day.
7. Xinhua News Agency, *Outline of the People's Republic of China 14th Five-Year Plan*.
8. The full title of this effort is the United Nations Decade of Ocean Science for Sustainable Development 2021–2030, known also by the shorthand, the "Ocean Decade." See https://en.unesco.org/ocean-decade.
9. UNESCO, "HSH Prince Albert II of Monaco Announces a Quarter of the Ocean Is Now Mapped," UNESCO website (May 3, 2023), https://www.unesco.org/en/articles/hsh-prince-albert-ii-monaco-announces-quarter-ocean-now-mapped.
10. Michael Martina, "Amid US-China Rivalry, A Landmark Science Deal Faces New Scrutiny," *Reuters* (June 18, 2023).
11. Michael Martina, "Amid US-China Rivalry."
12. Michael Martina, "Amid US-China Rivalry."
13. Michael Martina, "Amid US-China Rivalry."
14. Personal communications to the author, 2013–18.
15. Director of National Intelligence, *Global Trends 2040: A More Contested World* (Washington, DC: National Intelligence Council, March 2021), 5.
16. Part of the section on policy recommendations is adapted from testimony in 2019 to Congress. See Walsh, Katheen, Congressional Testimony on "China's Maritime Silk Road Initiative: Implications for the Global Maritime Supply Chain" before the House Subcommittee on Coast Guard and Maritime Transportation (October 2019) https://transportation.house.gov/committee-activity/hearings/chinas-maritime-silk-road-initiative-implications-for-the-global-maritime-supply-chain.
17. Robert D. Blakwill and Ashley J. Tellis, *Revising US Grand Strategy toward China*, Council Special Report No. 72 (New York, NY: Council on Foreign Relations, 2015), 24, https://cfrd8-files.cfr.org/sites/default/files/pdf/2015/04/China_CSR72.pdf.
18. Melanie Hart, *Charting a New Course for the US-China Relationship* (Washington, DC: Center for American Progress, 2016).
19. Hart, *Charting a New Course*, 12.
20. Ocean Policy Committee (2018).
21. Ocean Policy Committee (2018).
22. The White House, *Statement from the Press Secretary on the United States-China Visit*, Washington, DC (April 7, 2017), https://www.whitehouse.gov/briefings-statements/statement-press-secretary-united-states-china-visit/.

23. The White House, *Statement from the Press Secretary on the United States-China Visit*. Two annual Diplomatic and Security Dialogues occurred during the Trump administration, one in June 2017 and another in November 2018, the latter being delayed due to US–China diplomatic and security tensions. Only one Comprehensive Economic Dialogue took place, in July 2017; the meeting failed to result in any agreements, and the dialogue has since fallen afoul of the ongoing US–China trade war. CNBC, "US, China Fail to Agree on Trade, Casting Doubt on Other Issues" (July 19, 2017), https://www.cnbc.com/2017/07/19/us-china-comprehensiv-economic-dialogue-disagreement-over-how-to-reduce-trade-deficit-offical-says.html. It appears there was only one Social and Cultural Issues Dialogue, held in September 2017, and one Law Enforcement and Cybersecurity Dialogue, in October 2017.
24. US Department of State, *US-China Social and Cultural Dialogue*, Washington, DC (September 29, 2017), https://www.state.gov/r/pa/prs.ps/2017/09/274520.html.
25. US Department of State, *US-China Social and Cultural Dialogue*.
26. United States Embassy, *US Embassy Beijing, China* (January 11, 2019), https://www.state.gov/discoverdiplomacy/explorer/170172.htm.

References

Blakwill, Robert D., and Ashley J. Tellis. 2015. *Revising US Grand Strategy Toward China*. Council Special Report No. 72, Council on Foreign Relations, New York: Council on Foreign Relations, 72.

CNBC. 2017. *US, China Fail to Agree on Trade, Casting Doubt on Other Issues*, September 19.

European Commission. n.d. *International Ocean Governance*. https://oceans-and-fisheries.ec.europa.eu/ocean/international-ocean-governance_en.

Hart, Melanie. 2016. *Charting a New Course for the US-China Relationship*. Electronie, Center for American Progress, Washington, DC: Center for American Progress, 28.

Intergovernmental Oceanographic Commission (IOC) of UNESCO. 2018. *Existing Services of the Global Tsunami Warning System*, February. UNESCO.

Martina, Michael. 2023. "Amid US-China Rivalry, A Landmark Science Deal Faces New Scrutiny." *Reuters*, June 18.

Ocean Policy Committee. 2018. "OPC-Summary Initial Meeting." whitehouse.gov. August 1. Accessed January 19, 2019. www.whitehouse.gov/wp-content/2017/11/OPC-Summary-Initial-Meeting-080118.pdf.

Office of the Director of National Intelligence. 2021. *Global Trends 2040: A More Contested World*. Washington, DC: National Intelligence Council.

Office of the Spokesperson. 2015. "US-China Strategic & Economic Dialogue Outcomes of the Strategic Track." *US Department of State*, June 24.

2013–18. "Personal communications to the author."

The White House. 2017. *Statement from the Press Secretary on the United States-China Visit*, April 7. Washington, DC.

United Nations Educational, Scientific and Cultural Organization (UNESCO) Press Release. 2019. "Tsunami Center for South China Sea Becomes Fully Operational on World Tsunami Awareness Day." unesco.org. November 6. https://en.unesco.org/news/tsunami-center-south-china-sea-becomes-fully-operational-world-tsunami-awareness-day.

United Nations Educational, Scientific, and Cultural Organization (UNESCO). 2023. *HSH Prince Albert II of Monaco Announces a Quarter of the Ocean is Now Mapped.* May 3. https://www.unesco.org/en/articles/hsh-prince-albert-ii-monaco-announces-quarter-ocean-now-mapped.

United States Embassy. 2019. *US Embassy Beijing*, January 11. Beijing.

US Department of State. 2017. www.state.gov. September 29. https://www.state.gov/r/pa/prs.ps/2017/09/274520.html.

Walsh, Kathleen A. 2019. "Testimony." *House Subcommittee on Coast Guard and Maritime Transportation Hearing on "China's Maritime Silk Road Initiative: Implications for the Global Maritime Supply Chain"*, October 19.Washington, DC,

Xinhua News Agency. 2018. *China's Real-Time Global Ocean Observation Network Established*, February 6. Beijing.

———. 2021. "Outline of the People's Republic of China 14th Five-Year Plan for National Economic and Social Development and Long-Range Objectives for 2035." *Center for Security and Emerging Technology, Georgetown University*, March 12. Edited by Inc Trans. Etcetera Language Group. Accessed June 2023. https://cset.georgetown.edu/wp-content/uploads/t0284_14th_Five_Year_Plan_EN.pdf.

7

Conclusion

Comparing the strategy games of chess and Go is a too-often-used way of explaining fundamental differences in strategic thinking among Western- and Eastern-oriented strategists, respectively, and one prone to exaggerations. Yet, there are also few better ways of depicting competition for power than through the imagery of game play.[1] Here, the metaphor illuminates an important question regarding the Great Blue Game: which game is each side playing? [2]

The Blue Economy concept is a central part of China's strategy to advance maritime power at home and abroad, though a broadly overlooked concept among US China or Asia scholars and naval strategists. This suggests that, indeed, the United States and China are playing different geostrategic games in the contest for influence, access, and leverage across the Indo Pacific.

As the United States faces a rising power in China, Washington is focused on maritime game play in the Indo Pacific in a way that accords with the norms, patterns, and expected game play common among Western powers—in the way a chess player, for instance, might be: focused on defeating the other player's leader (king) and counting pieces on the board, in this case Chinese naval vessels and maritime assets, in the event their defeat becomes necessary to win the game, as is expected of the game itself.

China under Xi Jinping's leadership, meanwhile, envisions employing the Blue Economy concept across the region as a means of influence, access, and leverage in the way a player in the game of Go would do: developing new maritime capabilities (influence, access, and leverage) around the corners or edges of the board (i.e., along the conceptual Maritime Silk Road and beyond, such as in the South Pacific's Solomon Islands), and countering the US Navy presence and alliance network in the region with China's own "blue" places, bases, and development zones, from which to exploit as well as contest, and potentially control, the land and adjoining seas if necessary. Among the problems with these two perspectives on the game being played is that while a stalemate is a possible, even common, outcome in the game of chess (as, for instance, exists at the Demilitarized Zone on the Korean peninsula) and focusing on the center of the board is advantageous, the same cannot be said of the game of Go, in which case the corners of the board matter more and draws are very rare, with one side usually winning and the other losing, decisively.

DOI: 10.1201/9781003396116-7

If the United States is, at a minimum, to not lose the emerging Great Blue Game, attention to the Blue Economy concept and its implications for US and allied diplomatic, economic, industrial, scientific, technological, environmental, and military-security capabilities is needed from Washington and beyond. Local officials, business communities, innovators, environmentalists, and others are already engaging on this front. What has been lacking is strategic direction, information, and support from the federal government on a comprehensive approach that is needed to spur these efforts on continuously and to provide greater strategic insight, information, and guidance with regard to regional and global Blue Economy developments. The United States' free-market, bottom-up innovation model is ideal and necessary for innovation to flourish, but insufficient to effectively compete in a geostrategic contest such as the emerging Great Blue Game.

A bureaucracy's typical response to slow-developing phenomena—even those that could threaten national security—is to wait until the threat is readily apparent. Not acting prematurely is admirable in many respects but hinders strategic foresight if it means the United States is unprepared to play the Great Blue Game, a contest that is already underway. As this study has endeavored to convey, China is pursuing development of the Blue Economy in a geostrategic manner; the United States ought to at the very least understand that a new strategic game is afoot and factor this more clearly into our own strategic plans, policies, and programs.

A first step toward understanding the Blue Economy as a geostrategic concept is to ensure that more Americans understand the term and what it means to them. Much like the American public has become more environmentally aware since the 1970s, when public- and private-sector campaigns began to convey to the US masses the importance and benefits of land conservation, recycling, and (later) other "green" programs, a broader "blue" effort is needed today.

Development of a Blue Economy is something that select local and regional officials, experts, and businesses in the United States already are engaged in doing. Meanwhile, many more are in the dark as to what the Blue Economy is, much less what it means to them, to the economy, to the environment, and to our national security. Once the term Blue Economy is understood more widely in City Halls, schools, and universities, in corporate executive board rooms, and throughout the Pentagon as well as where it is already understood (in the maritime industries, ocean and marine scientific and environmental groups, climate and aid officials, Commerce's NOAA, and key offices in the White House), only then will the United States be well prepared for a new, Blue future and what it means for our relationship vis-à-vis China and the rest of the globe, most of which is blue.

Notes

1. In Medcalf's astute strategic overview, for instance, he also employs the game metaphor, concluding that "The emerging power contest in the Indo-Pacific combines all three – the Great Game, chess, and Go." See Medcalf, Rory, "Games and Giants," Chapter 5 in *Indo-Pacific Empire: China, America, and the Contest for the World's Pivotal Region* (Manchester: Manchester University Press, 2020), 119–50.
2. This section relies on expert players' comparison of the two games of chess and Go. See British Go Association, *A Comparison of Chess and Go* (Oct 25, 2017), https://www.britgo.org/learners/chessgo.

References

British Go Association. 2017. *A Comparison of Chess and Go*. October 25. Accessed June 29, 2018. https://www.britgo.org/learners/chessgo.

Medcalf, Rory. 2020. "Games and Giants." In *Indo-Pacific Empire: China, America, and the Contest for the World's Pivotal Region*, 119–150. Manchester: Manchester University Press.

Index